W0227730

Women in Indian
Borderlands

Thank you for choosing a SAGE product! If you have any comment, observation or feedback, I would like to personally hear from you. Please write to me at <u>contactceo@sagepub.in</u>

—Vivek Mehra, Managing Director and CEO, SAGE Publications India Pvt Ltd, New Delhi

Bulk Sales

SAGE India offers special discounts for purchase of books in bulk. We also make available special imprints and excerpts from our books on demand.

For orders and enquiries, write to us at

Marketing Department
SAGE Publications India Pvt Ltd
B1/I-1, Mohan Cooperative Industrial Area
Mathura Road, Post Bag 7
New Delhi 110044, India
E-mail us at <u>marketing@sagepub.in</u>

Get to know more about SAGE, be invited to SAGE events, get on our mailing list. Write today to <u>marketing@sagepub.in</u>

This book is also available as an e-book.

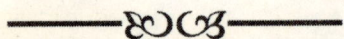

Women in Indian Borderlands

Edited by

Paula Banerjee
Anasua Basu Ray Chaudhury

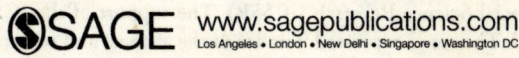
www.sagepublications.com
Los Angeles • London • New Delhi • Singapore • Washington DC

Copyright © Mahanirban Calcutta Research Group, 2011

All rights reserved. No part of this book may be reproduced or utilised in any form or by any means, electronic or mechanical, including photocopying, recording or by any information storage or retrieval system, without permission in writing from the publisher.

First published in 2011 by

SAGE Publications India Pvt Ltd
B1/I-1 Mohan Cooperative Industrial Area
Mathura Road, New Delhi 110 044, India
www.sagepub.in

SAGE Publications Inc
2455 Teller Road
Thousand Oaks, California 91320, USA

SAGE Publications Ltd
1 Oliver's Yard, 55 City Road
London EC1Y 1SP, United Kingdom

SAGE Publications Asia-Pacific Pte Ltd
33 Pekin Street
#02-01 Far East Square
Singapore 048763

Published by Vivek Mehra for SAGE Publications India Pvt Ltd, typeset in 10/13 pt Adobe Garamond by Star Compugraphics Private Limited, Delhi and printed at Chaman Enterprises, New Delhi.

Library of Congress Cataloging-in-Publication Data

Women in Indian borderlands/edited by Paula Banerjee, Anasua Basu Ray Chaudhury.

    p. cm.
   Includes bibliographical references and index.
   1. Women—India—Social conditions. 2. Women immigrants—India—Social conditions. 3. Borderlands—Social aspects—India. I. Banerjee, Paula.
II. Basu Ray Chaudhury, Anasua

HQ1742.W66566   305.40954'1—dc23   2011   2011018816

ISBN: 978-81-321-0650-0 (HB)

The SAGE Team: Elina Majumdar, Sonalika Rellan, Mathew P. J. and Deepti Saxena

This volume is an outcome of a research programme supported by the Indian Council of Social Science Research (ICSSR). The support of the ICSSR is kindly acknowledged. The views expressed here are of the authors and editors.

Contents

Part 3 Northeast

Part 4 Voices

List of Tables

List of Photographs

List of Maps

Acknowledgements

This volume is an outcome of a two-year-long research programme on 'Globalization, Democracy, Citizenship, Gender and Peace Studies' conducted by the Calcutta Research Group. This broad research programme has two segments namely, 'Globalization and Sustainability of Rights' and 'Women and Borders in South Asia'. As a research collective that works on issues of women and borders in South Asia in general and women and Indian borderlands in particular, the CRG undertook this particular segment dealing into women and borders in order to take a hard look at the interface of gender and democracy.

We have accumulated numerous debts in preparing this volume. We are really thankful to Bhaskar Chakraborty, Bharati Ray, Rekha Chowdhary, Sanjukta Bhattacharya, N.Vijaylakshmi Brara, Gina Sangkham, Kheseli Chishi, Ritu Menon, Asha Hans, Bodhisattva Kar, Subhoranjan Dasgupta, Pradip Kumar Bose, T.C.A Anant, Pradeep Bhargava, Sharit Bhowmik, Bhupinder Brar, Partha Chatterjee, Sanjay Chaturvedi, Kalpana Kannabiran, Dipankar Sinha and Virginius Xaxa. Their valuable suggestions have helped the authors and editors of this volume to shape their ideas in finer ways. We have no words to express our gratitude to Ranabir Samaddar, who has taken the pain to go through each of the articles. His constant support, encouragement and criticism have enriched our research. We express our sincere gratitude to him. This volume may not have appeared without the editorial assistance of Purna Banerjee and we thank her for that.

We also thank our colleagues, Samir Kumar Das, Sabyasachi Basu Ray Chaudhury, Ishita Dey, Supurna Banerjee, Sutirtha Bedajna, Rajat Kanti Sur, Geetisha Dasgupta and Sucharita Sengupta, for helping us in various ways in preparing this volume. We would also like to thank Samaresh Guchhait for designing the web segment of the research programme. Without the assistance of our administrative staff, we would not have been able to finish this study in time.

This work has been possible due to the generous support of the Indian Council of Social Science Research (ICSSR). We are thankful to the then chairperson of the ICSSR, Javeed Alam, and other members of the ICSSR. We would also like to put on record our thanks to the ICSSR office, in particular G.S. Saun, for his constant advice and support that facilitated the research programme. We also thank the members of the mid-term appraisal team, R.S. Deshpande, Vasanthi Raman and Chairman of the Appraisal Team, Apurba Kumar Baruah, in particular, whose suggestions and recommendations helped us in improving the papers. We also thank all the contributors of this volume. Our happiness in associating with the SAGE Publications increases with every venture.

We hope that this volume will help those who work on feminism, partition, displacement and also those who strive to put an end to racist, sexist and militarist domination in the borderlands of this region and elsewhere.

Kolkata   **Paula Banerjee**
August 2010   **Anasua Basu Ray Chaudhury**

Introduction: Resistance in the Borderlands

Paula Banerjee and Anasua Basu Ray Chaudhury

This is an ethnographic collection on the complex correlation between gender and border. There is hardly any literature, other than one recently published volume by SAGE Publications entitled *Borders, Histories, Existences: Gender and Beyond*, on women's role in the borderlands of India and this collection is meant to address that lacunae. The present state system in South Asia, in particular the state system of the subcontinent, is a result largely of the partitions in the eastern and western parts of the erstwhile united India, giving birth to three states—India, Pakistan and Bangladesh. The borders dividing these countries are markers of past bitter history, current separate, distinct and independent existence, and the sign of the territorial integrity/disintegration of these states. The bitterness of the past, the lack of mutual confidence at present, the security concerns of all these states, at the same time the existence of thousand and one linkages make the South Asian borders unique, both spatially and metaphorically, and it also makes this space or borderlands more complex. These spaces bear within lines of hatred, disunity, informal connections and voluminous informal trade, securitized and militarized lines, heavy para-military presence, communal discord, humanitarian crisis, human rights abuses and enormous suspicion that makes it particularly problematic for women. Recently, a few studies have appeared on the borderlands, but hardly any on the myriad roles that women play here. This collection of essays concentrate on every aspect of the borderlands on India. Paula Banerjee's volume *Borders*,

Histories, Existences: Gender and Beyond deals with the border and women's presence in it from a designated historical perspective and gives us a theoretical scaffolding of the subject. However, the present volume contains a host of ethnographic studies that at times supports Banerjee's thesis and at other times problematizes it through actual narratives and its analysis. Perhaps it will be correct to say that this book takes up from where the other volume leaves off; thereby it takes the narrative of women and borders further by foregrounding the element of justice in it.

The only borderland where a strong and separate discourse on women exists is the US–Mexico borderland. No one more than Gloria Anzaldua is responsible for the discourse to take such a trajectory. Anzaldua rebels against the cultural tyranny faced by women in this borderland, where anything that she desired for her improving her life was marked as her 'selfishness'. She creates the 'New Mestiza' who dramatically reclaims the ground for female historical presence. She is also the woman who lacks an official history but creates her own legacy. Anzaldua finds many followers, not least among them Vicki Ruiz. Ruiz studies women's border journeys not in terms of travel, but in terms of accommodating, resisting and transforming through migration. Their journeys are those of survival and resilience. But what about those that did not survive so well, did they not have histories? There is little discussion on such a history. A little later when Debbie Nathan writes about *Women and Other Aliens: Essays from the US–Mexico Border* (1991) she also speaks of how women in the borders transform not just their dress but also their stance towards parents, husbands, children, boyfriends and birth control. Nathan, however, is much less celebratory as she discusses on the one hand how immigration is transformative for both family and gender roles, but on the other hand also talks about a plethora of other challenges women on the border face, such as abortion of illegal and unplanned child, jail sentences for petty crimes and lack of jobs for illegal existences. Interest on gender and women's lives in the region has continued. Today there are a number of works such as Mattingly and Hansen's (2006) volume that discusses socio-economic conditions on the border as they shape and are shaped by both daily life at the local level and the global economy. They discuss the change in the maquiladora workforce, the political activism of women in the borders and role of women's non-governmental organizations. Perhaps no other borderland can claim such a rich feminist discourse. Our effort is certainly not to replicate it. Our geographical location have some similarities but also many differences that create different histories.

The borderlands within the purview of our discussion are marked by similar violence that plagues the US–Mexico borderland. In this site of violence a few get included but many more are left out, excluded as aliens, and most of those who are left out have feminine forms. They embody the difference that marks the borders. The border as the site where this contest over inclusion and exclusion is played out every day becomes a zone of endemic violence where masculinity is privileged. The states views them as territories that needs to be possessed by blood, if required, as they are thought to demarcate the inside from the outside, sovereignty from anarchy and the singular/pure from pluralistic/contaminated spaces. They construct the space of agency, the mode of participation in which we act as citizens in the multilayered polities to which we belong. Hence, borders to the state or its leaders are not merely lines. They are zones that situate the grey areas where the jurisdiction of the state ends and the other state takes over. They are the common ground of two or more states that share them and also interpret its meanings in very different ways to its citizens in their national narratives, history writing and collective spatialized memories. In the case of India, just like that of the USA, security concerns overwhelm all other equally legitimate concerns and values. Military security dominates over human security in the border region.

However, unlike the US–Mexico borderlands, none of India's borderlands have any industrial development. There are no common economic planning and no health services. Does one hear a sigh of relief? We can say with clear conscience that after all India does not treat its borders as vestiges of colonialism to be used and abused at will. But this does not preclude the fact that these borderlands remain as regions of endemic poverty and violence. Women living in Indian borderlands are not as fortunate as their mestiza counterpart, as they neither have a celebratory history nor have developed a celebratory discourse such as the Chicana women. Yet they survive the ordeal of violence and resist in their small ways the massive structure of state power, while some of their Western counterparts and governments are often more caught up in spending resources in trying to save them from fate worse than death or from being trafficked particularly to their respective countries and squander fortunes on anti-trafficking programmes without considering how they can save themselves and their families from hunger deaths because such deaths are a reality in the world of our borderlands. So we feel the need to tell the story of these women who, albeit ordinary live in the borders, are its markers and resist everyday violence in all its multiplicities. These essays then concern themselves with women living in Indian borderlands and discuss how they negotiate their differences with a state, though democratic, but denies space to difference based on either ethnicity, religion, class or gender. Women living in the borders are the subject of this series of articles not only because they belong to these perilous territories or the borders but also because in many ways they form them.

The universalistic nature of citizenship that emanates from traditional liberal and social democratic discourses is extremely deceptive as it conceals the exclusion of women from national identities of citizenship. The nation and the state are both premised in particular gender identities. Thus the ideological constructions of the state are weighted against women who remain in the borders of democracy. Yet in moments of conflict at times women assume centrality. This is because in areas of civil conflict men withdraw from civic life for compulsions of war and self-defence, and borderlands of India are often spaces of conflict. In such a situation, the public sphere retreats into the private and women form the civil societies. They assume roles that are completely new to them and confront and negotiate with the massive power of the state machinery in their everyday lives. Further, as transmitters of cultural value, women construct differences that shape the future of the nation and the border. Yet in borderlands the feminization of civil space seldom happens, and when it happens, it seldom stays that way for long, as the recent history of Manipur suggests, which we have written elsewhere. Conflict here leads to further masculinization of the space as this is the space that demarcates the citizens from the aliens, and only men can be pristine or model citizens who can draw blood for the state, albeit the blood that is drawn can be and often is women's blood. Therefore, in fact most of our traditional efforts to make geopolitical regions such as borderlands more secure are nothing but attempts to privilege a masculine definition of security that result in only feminine insecurities. In addressing questions of security, the insecurities of women always remain in the back of beyond. In this volume we deal with insecurities of women posited on the borderlands and analyse how they deal with them. This volume is a collection of micro-narratives discussing different aspects of women's lives on the borders. We ask how women deal with the multiple hazards that these borders present. We do not question whether women's negotiations with the borders as bordered existences are merely an act of coping or of agency. We assume all forms of coping contain within it some form of agency. We question how women deal with perennial conflicts that are found in Indian borderlands. Whether their acts of resistance mark them as feminists or not is something that does not perturb us. We wish to recover all acts of resistance feminist or otherwise. In our essays we ask whether the effects of the border are restricted only to the borderland. We also look at bordered people, especially refugee women and analyse how the act of migration affects women's abilities to negotiate complex social, political and economic relationships? A further question that we pose is how globalization impacts on all of this. Does it in any way help us to move beyond cyclical patterns of violence? This collection of articles try to interpret these issues from new angles and locations if not answer these questions in proper social science terms. The essays throw up many issues that should interest social scientists such as how the paradigm of trafficking homogenizes offences against women, how the border becomes both a reality and a metaphor, how migration is transformative for women, how violence percolates borders, how the urge to control resources pushes matrilineal tribes to margins, etc. Spatially also this collection of essays is varied and interesting as it includes two articles that are located on the Bengal–Bangladesh border, two on Kashmir–Pakistan border and two others on Northeast–Myanmar–Bangladesh border. The last section is entitled voices. The volume gives us glimpses of the 'real' women living in the border dealing with complexities much larger than themselves creating, resisting and transforming their realities in their own terms. The kaleidoscopic images disturb, excite, confuse but always push us to know about these women a little more.

The first chapter is entitled 'Bengal–Bangladesh Boderland: Chronicles from Nadia, Murshidabad and Malda' by Paula Banerjee. Banerjee refers to three major works on borderland, including her own book entitled *Borders, Histories, Existences: Gender and Beyond*. Besides which the other two publications include *The Marginal Nation: Transborder Migration from Bangladesh to West Bengal* written by Ranabir Samaddar, and *The Bengal Borderland: Beyond State and Nation in South Asia* by Willem Van Schendel. Banerjee states that she wanted to move away from meta-narratives and look at borders from the perspective of capillaries of political and historical spaces.

In this chapter she addresses a vexed issue that she has not previously dealt with. She looks at the notions of flows, and how that impacts on notions of security. With every election and every census, borders become an issue. The concern remains over undocumented migrants and whether their arrival threatens the nation. She also addresses notions of increasing violence in the borders as tool of managing and the paradigm shift in what is considered crime as a result of these flows. She looks at fencing as a marker of such violence and discusses women in this border and the evolution of their relationship to the border. She argues that violence in the borders privileges certain forms of crime. She discusses how stopping trafficking became part of the international agenda whereas all other crimes become negligible. She returns to an intensive demographic study of the Bengal–Bangladesh borderlands in the three districts of Nadia, Murshidabad and Malda. Instead of meta-narratives she comes back to the question of micro politics and questions whether present-day flows have any relation to past histories or not. Her argument is that borders have historically evolved as gendered entity and thereby these have become spaces of extraordinary control and violence against women. Concentration on trafficking does not give justice to women but rather creates more unjust border regimes for them. All other offences are forgotten while trafficking assumes the centre stage.

Are borders real or metaphors is the question addressed in the next chapter. This chapter is entitled 'Narrated Time and Constructed Space: Remembering the Communal Violence of 1950 in Hooghly' and in it Anasua Basu Ray Chaudhury argues that borders are not just lines in the landscape, they actively shape the societies and cultures that they enclose. Borders denote a spatial dimension of social relationships that are continually being configured and, in this process, the meaning of borders is produced, reconstructed, strengthened or weakened. The notion of borders in today's world is a testimony to the importance of territoriality with the creation of the 'other'. The imagery of borders has become a popular metaphor in the study of socio-spatial development in post-partition societies. In this study, Basu Ray Chaudhury unravels the stories of three Muslim women of Hooghly, an otherwise calm and quiet place, during the turbulent years of partition. Anasua's study captures the lives and experiences of the people who live through the 'partitioned time', of the way in which the events accompanying the partition constructs in their minds, and the identities or uncertainties that partition creates or re-enforces. The main purpose of the study is to enquire on how women negotiate borders—borders of sect, community, patriarchy, and of conflicts not only in their own land but also in an alien land away from their homeland. She analyses the self-representation of the Muslims once displaced. She focuses on their narratives of victimhood, which tends to be framed in rhetoric of Hindu–Muslim differences. She argues that their memories may be subjective in nature, but their selective memories help us to understand how the displaced women negotiate. In this article she attempts to deal with the inner process of 'line making' and 'line negotiating' based on the narratives of those women, which shapes their memories of displacements with the gender-specific experiences as 're-turnees'.

Much has already been written on Kashmir and its women but very little is known about the women saddling the India–Pakistan border. In the next section there are two narratives from Kashmir. The two chapters are namely 'Women's Voices: From Jammu and Kashmir' by Anuradha Bhasin Jamwal and Suchismita and 'Renegotiating Internal Boundaries by Women of Jammu and Kashmir' by Sumona DasGupta. Anuradha in her chapter highlights women as the major victims of warfare. One of the most obvious examples of specific victimhood of women in armed conflict, she argues, is their vulnerability to sexual assault and rape. Rape and sexual abuse is nothing new in the history of warfare. Marauding armies have through different periods of history, around the globe, taken advantage of women in the course of military conquests. What is new is the role of media. Instant reporting from the field results in rapid sensitization of public opinion. It greatly reduces the time lapse between the perpetration of such tragedies and their responses to them and thereby generating responses from the people very quickly. However, in the case of borders, lack of access and no reportage make the consequent sensitization elusive. She argues that the victimization started when the borders were carved out in 1947–1948, when people living in fairly peaceful areas suddenly found themselves on the fringes of nowhere, close to places that had become simply lines drawn on a map for everybody else in South Asia. The brunt was borne not only by women living on the borders; the prolonged trauma was also shared by women living away from the borders but affected in many ways by the sudden carving of new boundaries, dislocation and its multiple consequences. For the majority population of India and Pakistan, the traumatic memories of partition have become historical narratives, but in Jammu and Kashmir because of the disputed nature of its borders, these memories are a festering sore, which continues to bleed and makes people suffer in the form of displacements and dispossession on account of border skirmishes between the hostile neighbours. She claims that weird border contours on the maps of J&K intensify the militarization of borders on both sides, thus adding to the insecurity among the border population in general and women in particular. A continuum of tragedy and victimization has followed till date due to constant hostility and wars that have adversely affected the border people in many ways. In her chapter she gives examples of great onslaughts that these border people witnessed in 1965, 1971 and in the post-insurgency period of 1989 and beyond. Through narratives she argues in her chapter that violence and victimhood at the borders does not stop at the borders but percolates deep inside the nation form adding to the gendered dimension of the Indian nation.

At the very outset Sumona DasGupta identifies the term 'border' not just as physical boundaries represented by *de facto* and *de jure* cartographic lines that separate the sovereign writ of one state from another, but also as other fault lines generated or accentuated by a conflict. Acknowledging borders as lines that separate and delimit spaces, she goes beyond 'cartographic anxieties' and physical landscapes to 'non-cartographic anxieties'—borders that are etched on mindscapes—lines that separate 'us' from 'them'. In doing so she recognizes that there can be an overlap between these two sets of anxieties, and that where they intersect, fault lines come into even sharper relief. In her research she portrays how these borderlines are mediated by gender. Gender is used not just as a descriptive category but as an analytical tool that is as much about men and masculinity as it is about women and femininity. A gender perspective consequently explores how men and women's roles are constructed in society and gender sensitive conflict analysis looks at ways in which gender roles, gender identities, gender ideologies and gendered power structures may be altered in the course of a protracted conflict. Informed by this, the chapter explores some of the fault lines/borderlines in the iconography of the contemporary conflict in Jammu and Kashmir, using gender as a cross-cutting variable rather than as a separate, add-on issue.

The next section is composed of two articles from the Northeast India–Myanmar and Northeast India–Bangladesh borders. The Indo-Myanmar border is considered a fairly safe and friendly unlike the previous two borders that we discussed. Sanitized or not, even this border has its own compulsions. Sahana Basavapatna in her chapter entitled 'Sanitized Society and Dangerous Interlopers: Law and the Chins in Mizoram' analyses from a legal perspective the experiences of Burmese women who in migrating across international borders problematize democracy, identity and citizenship. She explores the theme from two perspectives—first, how the legal frame and, second, how cultural and political ties of Mizoram themselves affect the Burmese migrants in India. A host of factors lead to the migration of the people from the Chin state to Mizoram. The Indo-Burma border thus becomes extremely significant for continuing migration and cross-border terrorism. Sahana focuses on the experiences of women crossing these borders and the responses of both the state and the central governments. It is through the legal frame that she seeks to analyse how women who have been forced to migrate negotiate the complex social, political and economic web of relationships of being branded as foreigner and in many cases illegal. She argues that the law being rooted in the patriarchal mindset is inadequate in perceiving and responding to women's needs. She concludes how Mizoram through its restrictions of foreigners become another example of how a state seeks to sanitize society. At the focal point of Sahana's research are the Chin refugees. By considering the issue at a more transitive level where it is more than purely a struggle for ethnic and cultural rights, Sahana argues that the case represents a control over circuits of legal and paralegal trade and other transactions. Within the problematic, gender is not yet another site of difference but it is an inseparable constitutive element of the conflict itself. And here, trade and other transactions figure as processes where the element of gender plays a role.

Anjuman Ara Begum in her chapter entitled 'Engendered Lives: Women in the West Garo Hills' argues that partition is conceptually distinct from population transfer, though in most cases, it is accompanied by substantial sorting of populations. Partition is a political outcome that impacts social life tremendously. With partition, the border creeps in, creating lines that divides people, society and nation. The border becomes physically visible when it is fenced. Fences along the border lines make the border a concrete and fixed structure representing control of land and people. Border gives birth to the extremities of particular forms of violence that are enacted in the name of security and well-being checkpoints, walls, fences, technologies of surveillance and governance. Physical borders create metaphorical borders between people living in the area of West Garo Hill. Here the border is between the tribal Garos and the non-tribal Muslims. Each community looks upon each other with extreme suspicion, thereby always making violence a possibility. Other than that paradigms of control over borders create regimes of violence. With newer forms of border protection, women face new inequalities. For example, Border Security Force (BSF) put a stop to historical flows across borders and fencing put a stop to women's economic activities through bartering of goods across borders leading to their further pauperization. Any violence lead to backlash against women and tribal women, who are matrilineal, and are forced so that they give up their symbolic control over land and non-tribal women are forcefully pushed out of it. The author says that women's lives in the borderlines of West Garo hills reflect their sheer resilience, silent tears and a burning desire to put a step outside the line called 'border'. It also reflects their sheer energy and will to overcome all inequity and injustice.

In the section on 'Voices' we have brought together interviews of women from the Bengal–Bangladesh and the Northeast–Myanmar borders. This is a project of recovery. We hope to recover the feminine voices of resistance in the borderlands. In formalistic, institutional and militarized spaces that privilege the masculine what gets primarily lost is the feminine voice. By speaking about their lives, the women regain some of the agency that had been lost. Through this process of auto-ethnography we hope to recover the lost voices of women in this highly masculine and militarized space called the 'borders'. These interviews are brought to us by Aditi Bhaduri and Chitra Ahanthem. Aditi conducted her interviews in villages of Jayantipur, Hatkhola, Petrapole, Shutiya and correctional facilities in Kolkata. By the act of speaking, women invoke justice and resist injustices that they face in their everyday lives as marginal beings. Chitra focuses exclusively in the plight of women in the border town of Moreh. The everyday life stories of these women reflect not only their identity as women but how these realities are shaped by their location near a porous international border town where the border not only divides the lives of 'women' but plays a crucial role in joining them in their labouring lives as women. The border that Moreh women traverses is supposedly as safe but does it lead to feminine securities? We leave it as a question for the readers to address.

The chapters are exceptional in many ways. They deal with an issue that is seldom dealt within Indian social science. As stated earlier, there is currently only one book on the gendered dimension of borderlands in South Asia. Therefore, this in many ways is an exceptional topic. Yet borderlands are an extremely vexed issue in this day of securitization and cross-border flows of all kinds. And the role that women play in these flows is extremely pertinent. Apart from that the chapters also confirm that violence is a constitutive element of borderlands when analysed from a gender perspective. All the chapters deal with violence in their own respective ways. Violence foregrounds women's experiences in all the borders, even the ones considered as benign. But with violence there is also the story of resistance, perhaps not glorious, grandiose or heroic resistance but in women's narratives those stories are few and far between. Here we speak of resistance often seemingly insignificant but transformative in its entirerity. Apart from that the chapters go beyond the trope of 'coping' and 'agents'. They make the theoretical claim that all coping mechanisms are agentive. So in terms of feminist theory they mark a departure. They also deal with a number of contentious issues such as AIDS and its effects on women in the borderlands; they also feminize subjects of migrant trade and migrant labour, and grapple with the effects of globalization on bordered entities such as women. Above all they celebrate what it means to be a woman in the border and a survivor, notwithstanding whether the state recognizes her efforts as that of an agent or someone merely coping for survival. Our project is to recover her from erasure and foreground her resistance, and in this can be sought the seeds of the future project of transformation.

Part 1

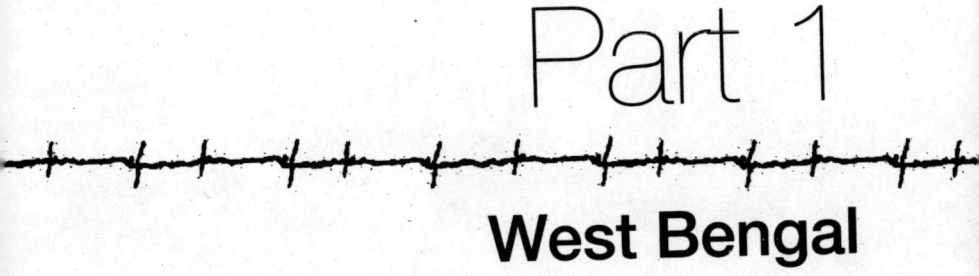

West Bengal

1

Bengal–Bangladesh Borderland: Chronicles from Nadia, Murshidabad and Malda*

Paula Banerjee

INTRODUCTION

Borderland studies, particularly in the context of South Asia, are a fairly recent phenomenon. I can think of three works that have made border-lands, particularly the Bengal–Bangladesh borderland as the focal area of their study in the last decade. Ranabir Samaddar's *The Marginal Nation: Transborder Migration from Bangladesh to West Bengal* started a trend that was continued by Willem Van Schendel in his *The Bengal Borderland: Beyond State and Nation in South Asia*. Both these books argue that the border is part of a larger zone or the borderland that at once constructs and subverts the nation. Samaddar goes beyond the security and immutable border discourses and problematizes the borderland by speaking of flows across the border. He argues that such flows are prompted by historical and social affinities, geographical contiguities and economic imperatives.

*I am grateful to Shri Rajat Kanti Sur for helping me with the research for this chapter. I am also grateful to Shri Ramen Moitro of Shikarpur and Dr Anandolal Bhattacharya of the West Bengal State Archives for advising me on complex aspects of demography, border and archival research.

People move when their survival is threatened and rigid borders mean little to
the desperate. They question the nation form that challenges their existence.
If need be they find illegal ways to tackle any obstacle that stands in their
path of moving, particularly when that makes the difference between life and
death. Thereby, Samaddar questions ideas of the nation state and national
security in present day South Asia when and if it privileges land over the
people, who inhabit that land. Van Schendel also takes the argument along
similar lines by stating that without understanding the borderland it is
impossible to understand the nation form that develops in South Asia, the
economy that emerges or the ways in which national identities are internal-
ized. Van Schendel challenges the glib assumption that globalization has
done away with borders and also questions the penchant of analysing soci
eties, identities and nations as fixed.

Joya Chatterji in *Bengal Divided* (Chatterji, 2002) argues that to understand the boundary formed by partition one needs to dig beyond received
histories. She is of the opinion that one needs to look at Hindu communalism for the act of partition rather than at Muslim communalism. The
Radcliffe Line, she says, was not surgically crafted but evolved through other
forms of practices. Accepting Joya's arguments about essentials of historical
analysis, I have tried to push Samaddar's and Van Schendel's arguments further in my book on *Borders, Histories, Existences: Gender and Beyond* where
I have suggested that borderlands are often sites of exclusion/inclusion in
the context of South Asia. This is because there the national will to exclude
and include is played out. I analyse how state constructs borders and tries to
make them static. This stasis is disturbed by bordered existences, of which
women, migrant workers, trafficked bodies and victims of HIV/AIDS are
all parts whose survival is carried out within a milieu of endemic violence.
The tussle in the borderlands is often on the question of who controls. In
this chapter I want to address an issue that I have not addressed previously.
I want to look at this notion of flows and how that impacts notions of
security. With every election and every census, borders become an issue.
I will address the notion of how borders have a penchant of becoming a
marker of security. The moment borders become securitized, the question
of flows across it acquires particular importance. In the colonial period it is
marked by dacoits, thugs and hooligans who cross the district border at will.
In the post-colonial period concern remains over undocumented migrants

and whether their arrival threatens the nation form. In this chapter I will address the notion of flows and increasing violence in the borders, fencing as the most recent marker of such violence and how women and the evolution of their relationship to the border is shaped through the discourses of violence. I hope to portray that from the beginning violence makes the borders exceptional, albeit this violence may be a continuation from the colonial times, but the processes of state formation have changed the nature of this violence. One of the impacts of this recent form of violence is to reduce the entire question of gender to women's trafficking and obliterating all other forms of violence in the process. I return then to the study of the Bengal–Bangladesh borderlands in the three districts of Nadia, Murshidabad and Malda and look at the nature of the population movement, violence and its effects on women. Instead of meta-narratives, I come back to the question of micro-politics and see whether present-day flows and concomitant violence have any relation to past histories or not and how it impacts the present histories of women.

THE FORMATION OF THE THREE DISTRICTS IN THE COLONIAL TIMES

The district of Nadia was and still is situated in the heart of the Bengal Delta held within the arms of Ganges and Bhagirathi in the west and Padma running into the Meghna estuary in the east. Nadia was acquired by the British Company under the Diwani grant of 1765. The Nadia Raj, 3,151 sq. mi., corresponding with Nadia Sadar and Ranaghat subdivisions with a very small portion of southern Meherpur, at the time of the Permanent Settlement also included Satsikka and the riparian strip east of the Saraswati. In the post Permanent Settlement period the boundary was changed a number of times. I have taken in consideration only the changes with Jessore and Pabna, as they pertain to the final boundary settlement. In 1796, the boundary between Jessore and Nadia was demarcated by the Administrative Convenience Order of 1796. For reasons sited as 'thefts and decoities' and by the Administrative Orders dated 17 October 1812 thanas Taki and Suksagar were given from Jessore to Nadia and thana Kotchandpur was transferred to Jessore. From police sources it is well known that a number of gangs were operating in Nadia, including the Banke Muchi gang, the Dedar Biswas gang, the Janakinagar gang, the Latif Sardar gang, the Brojo Bagdi gang, etc.[1] In 1816, Sunderbans were placed under a Commissioner. In 1854, the Karimpur subdivision was created including Dewanganj, Hurdi and Meherpur thanas and Jalangi and Newada thanas of Murshidabad. Even today it is one of the most problematic border areas and includes Nasirerpara, which a few years back was the most crime-prone of all the subdivisions. Beyond it lies Shikarpur today, which is the poorest subdivision in Nadia. In 1863, Kushtia was transferred from Pabna to Nadia. In 1883, Bongaon subdivision was transferred to Jessore. By 1911, Nadia had a population of 1,617,846 and a land area of 2,790 sq. mi.[2]

Murshidabad was the capital of Bengal under the nawabs. The company acquired it by the Diwani of 1765. Murshidabad included the *zamindaris* of Fatehsing and Chunakhali with a part of Rajshahi and a small portion of Nadia Raj. According to Hunter's *A Statistical Account of Bengal* (Hunter, 1876), the British built barracks there incurring the enormous cost of £302,270 by 1767. By an administrative order dated 11 January 1793 the portion of Rajsahi *zamindari* lying west of the Padma River was transferred to the Murshidabad collectorate. In 1824, Murshidabad acquired the Calcapore village from the Dutch. By the Administrative Convenience Order of 5 March 1839 thana Palsa was transferred to Birbhum. In 1848 and 1855, the thanas Calcapore and Farakabad were transferred from Bhagalpur. In 1875, district boundaries were rearranged and 39 villages were transferred to Birbhum and 7 to the Santhal Parganas. In 1879, thanas Ramporhat, Nalhatui and Palsa were transferred to Birbhum. By 1911, the population of Murshidabad was 1,372,274 and the area in 1916 was 2,143 sq. mi.[3]

The 1765 Diwani of Bengal handed over Malda to the British company. At the time of the Permanent Settlement it included the three districts of Rajsahi, Dinajpur and Purnea. By the Administrative Convenience Order dated 25 August 1825, the thanas Rahanpur and Chappae were judicially transferred from Rajsahi. In 1859 Malda got its own magistrate and collector. In 1875, Malda was drastically reorganized with 65 villages joining it from Murshidabad and 237 villages being transferred from Dinajpur. In 1879 Malda was transferred from the judgeship of Dinajpur to that of Rajsahi. By 1911 Malda had a population of 1,004,159 and by 1916 Malda had 1,899 sq. mi.[4]

From the beginning then it was obvious that the boundaries of these three districts were never fixed but kept evolving. In fact, in this period major changes were planned and implemented for a short time. These changes were in nationalist discourses termed as the partition of Bengal. The lieutenant governor of Bengal proposed a scheme for the amalgamation of Assam with the Chittagong and Dacca divisions and the districts of Pabna, Bogra and Rangpur. But compared to Bengal, this new province was still extremely small and so it was decided to transfer the districts of Rajsahi, Dinajpur, Jalpaiguri, Malda and the state of Cooch Behar:

> These additions were thought by the Government of India to be justified on the grounds that they would constitute a new province with a population of over 31 millions, while leaving Bengal with a little more than 54 millions; that they would provide a clearly defined western boundary corresponding with well recognised characteristics, both geographical, ethnological, social and linguistics, that they would concentrate in a single province the typical Muhammadan population of Bengal ....[5]

Although the scheme was cordially accepted by the Governments of Bengal and Assam, it was not popular among the Indian leadership. They inspired the common people to revolt partly by sentiment and partly by fear. The zamindars often inspired their tenants to revolt particularly in Jessore, Khulna, Nadia, Hooghly, Rajsahi, Mymensingh and Pabna.[6] Soon there was widespread protest against the decision to partition Bengal. In a report on the agitations, the government noted that although agitations were not very severe in Malda, there was discontent in the region for having been included in the new province. As for Murshidabad, it was said that the agitation was confined to the babu classes though it was agreed that many people took the vow of swadeshi. In Nadia, however, the anti-partition agitations took serious proportions. In a report it was said that the principal towns and villages of Nadia took up the agitations against the use of foreign goods in earnest:

> Pleaders and schoolmasters busied themselves lecturing on the subject. The teachers and boys of several schools raised funds out of which they purchased cigarettes and made bonfires of them. The usual processions of schoolboys and others, bareheaded and barefooted, marched through the principal towns, mourning for the partition of Bengal.[7]

The Goswamis of Santipur and Nawadwip lent weight to these agitations. They used their religious authorities to convince the people to give up the use of foreign sugar, salt and other goods. Soon family priests took up the issue and carried the matter into every home. Even Muslims in Nadia responded to the call against partition. Both Hindus and Muslims tried to supply the people with indigenous dhotis but found it difficult to compete with Manchester cotton. It was from Nadia that the report reached the Special Branch that there are plans afoot to organize anti-partition protests when the Prince and Princess of Wales came down for their visit. This could be stopped but the partition could not be made viable and was revoked in 1911. Thus, experimentation with the borders continued. It would now be essential to look at the flows across the border and to analyse whether the rate of migration to and from these border areas can be termed as a historical trend that was definitive of these borderlands.

In the colonial period, higher decadal growth rate was not considered as a threat. In fact, lower decadal growth was considered as a marker of the ill health of the population. The decade of 1911 to 1921 was the only time Bengal registered a negative decadal rate because of the influenza and malaria epidemics as is shown in Table 1.1. Arthur Geddes, a famous geographer, concerned by this trend comments in 1931 that Bengal's population was an unhealthy population and so there is not a steady rise in this population. However, even in this situation it was said that one-third of Calcutta (now Kolkata) consisted of people from outside of the province. Therefore, migrants were a common presence in this part of the country. Between 1911 and 1931, there is one decade of decrease from the national levels and one decade of increase:

> The statistics for 1911–1921 showed terrible mortality, and, as was foreseen, those of 1921–1931 have compared favourably with them and even with those for the decade before the war. The decade to 1931 may therefore seem to show improvement in health and vitality and hold out promise for the future. Unfortunately we cannot call this a true advance, since unless 'reconstruction' is undertaken the coming census of 1941 may belie the apparent recovery shown in 1931. Since the calamities of the war and post-war period of 1914–1921 were so great, with their combined economic hardship and epidemics, they carried off many who would normally have lived longer, and whose deaths would only have occurred in 1921–1931. Their premature decease before 1921 does not therefore

Table 1.1 Decadal Variation of Population (1901–1961) (in percentage)

REGION		1901–1911	1911–1921	1921–1931	1931–1941	1941–1951	1951–1961
West Bengal	Total	6.25	-2.91	8.14	22.90	13.20	32.80
	Rural	5.21	-4.43	6.98	15.50	8.27	31.80
	Urban	13.70	7.16	15.00	63.60	32.50	35.90
Nadia	T	0.36	-8.26	1.48	16.40	36.10	49.80
	R	0.34	-9.80	0.71	13.80	29.20	49.40
	U	0.52	-0.29	7.51	35.40	78.90	51.50
Murshidabad	T	1.71	-8.99	11.90	19.60	4.61	33.40
	R	1.20	-9.93	12.50	18.80	4.02	32.40
	U	9.98	5.27	4.46	31.20	12.00	44.80
Malda	T	15.72	-1.77	4.99	17.10	11.00	30.30
	R	16.07	-1.69	4.75	16.60	10.40	29.70
	U	3.80	-4.81	14.4	38.00	29.30	44.40

Source: Government of India, 2001.

prove the last decade to be more healthy than other periods of peace, but is simply to be accounted for by the fact that the war years and those immediately following them were so mortal in their effects; the same is even truer for India as a whole in these two decades. In other words, when the province was suddenly forced to spend itself in deaths in one decade, it paid its debt to Nature ahead of time and was liable for less at the normal time when it came. Yet, unless assets of vitality are being built up meantime, its people are no better off, and the apparent improvement, judged from a fall in the death-rate, is in part illusory.[8]

However, what is even more important for our purposes is that according to Geddes the density of population and population growth rate is traditionally higher in eastern part of undivided Bengal.[9] After looking at how these districts are administratively constructed it becomes essential to look at the decadal growth rate, percentage variations in population and density of population to understand population movements in these areas. It becomes apparent that the flow of population in Bengal is traditionally from east to west or from areas of excess to areas of lower density.

POPULATION MOVEMENT PRIOR TO 1947

There is no data on the decadal growth rate of the population of West Bengal in 1901. However, from 1911 we have the complete data. In 1921 the decadal growth rate was in the negative but from 1931 it is continuously increasing. The decadal growth rate had reduced in 1921, as has already been said because of the famous influenza epidemic. It is clear that for the whole of West Bengal the decadal rate is higher after 1947 than before it. Now let us turn towards the three districts under review.

In Nadia the decadal growth has increased steadily from 1921 onwards. In terms of percentage variation in population, the Sadar Subdivision jumps from −9.7 in 1921 to +5.7 in 1931. Perhaps even more outstanding is the increase to +18.1 by 1941. If on the basis of Geddes' argument we believe that because many of the people who were meant to die between 1921 and 1931, died in the decade between 1911 and 1921, nothing similar happened between 1931 and 1941 as Table 1.3 clearly shows. Yet the percentage of population increased by leaps and bounds. In the decade between 1931 and 1941, both Krishnanagar and Nawadwip registered a growth of +20.9 and

+35.6 respectively. In Nadia the decadal variation of population remained less than that of Bengal as a whole until 1941, after which it became more than that of Bengal, as Table 1.1 suggests. Percentage variation of population in Nadia was at its highest by 1961 and after that year it steadily declined. Although Krishnanagar and Nawadwip registered the highest growth rate in the decade between 1941 and 1951. Karimpur and the other police stations areas registered highest growth rate in the decade between 1951 and 1961. From 1921 until 1947 one sees a steady increase in population of Nadia district although the more dramatic increases happen later. Between 1951 and 1961 the areas of Nakasipara, Kaliganj, Tehatta and Karimpur register dramatic increases in growth as Tables 1.1 and 1.2 suggest. But there is another side to this story. While Tehatta and Karimpur are border areas, Nakasipara and Kaliganj are not and yet here the increases are equally dramatic which portrays that in-migration from other parts of Bengal and Bihar might also result in increase of the population of Nadia district. Also, Karimpur and Tehatta registered a much lower growth rate between 1941 and 1951. Yet the growth rate of Nadia did not decrease. This shows that not only Bangladesh border, but other borders might have been active as well. However, it goes without saying that the years between 1951 and 1961 were years of huge increase in flows into West Bengal.

In the case of Murshidabad the decadal growth rate of 1921–1931 was more than that of Bengal as a whole, as Table 1.1 shows. What is even more magnificent is that in the decade between 1921 and 1931 the decadal

Table 1.2 Population of Administrative Division of Nadia (Sadar Subdivisions) 1911–1961

REGION	1961	1951	1941	1931	1921	1911
Nadia	1,713,324	1,144,924	840,303	721,907	711,706	775,986
Sadar Subdivision	1,011,808	706,616	580,657	549,684	473,728	525,692
Krishnanagar	219,381	161,726	97,997	85,451	84,805	93,005
Nawadwip	125,142	91,380	54,208	39,962	34,120	36,914
Chapra	110,754	77,675	70,321	62,990	59,263	64,116
Krishnaganj	52,034	38,696	34,102	28,846	28,492	35,752
Nakasipara	119,176	81,747	66,827	56,749	52,898	56,163
Kaliganj	112,325	77,305	63,391	53,247	47,414	53,122
Tehatta	133,803	90,402	92,539	80,083	83,441	92,270
Karimpur	139,193	87,685	101,272	88,717	83,295	94,350

Source: Government of India (1965: 103).

Table 1.3 Percentage Variation in Population in Nadia (Sadar Subdivision)

REGION	1951–1961	1941–1951	1931–1941	1921–1931	1911–1921	1901–1911
Nadia	+49.65	+36.30	+16.40	+1.40	−8.30	+0.40
Sadar Subdivision	+43.20	+22.40	+18.10	+5.60	−9.70	−0.60
Krishnanagar	+35.60	+72.50	+20.90	+5.70	−7.60	+4.20
Nawadwip	+36.95	+68.60	+35.60	+17.10	−7.60	+4.20
Chapra	+42.59	+10.50	+11.60	+6.30	−7.60	+4.20
Krishnaganj	+34.47	+13.50	+18.20	+1.20	−20.30	−5.10
Nakasipara	+45.79	+22.30	+17.80	+7.30	−5.80	−1.00
Kaliganj	+45.30	+21.90	+19.00	+12.30	−10.70	+0.60
Tehatta	+48.01	+2.30	+15.60	−4.00	−9.60	−1.70
Karimpur	+58.74	+13.40	+14.20	+6.50	−11.70	−6.50

Source: Government of India (1965: 104).

growth rate of the rural areas of Murshidabad grew more than that of the urban areas. Murshidabad is one such place where the percentage of rural population is much higher than the urban population. In 1901, the rural population numbered 1,246,578 to an urban population of 75,908 only and until 1951 the rural population formed majority of the total population. This is particularly interesting because regions facing sudden migrational onslaughts often have a larger growth rate of urban population, as migrants often prefer to live in the cities because jobs are easily available there. In the last few decades that percentage reduced to 87.51 per cent of the total population in Murshidabad. There are evidences that there was population movement prior to 1947 but these trends sharpened after 1947. The sex ratio also slowly declined in the colonial period and that trend continued in the post-colonial period as Table 1.4 shows. But does migration to rural areas in Murshidabad suggests that migrants were following traditional migrational routes? This is a question of some significance for our study. It should be noted here that as Table 1.1 suggests, immediately in the aftermath of partition, both in Nadia and Murshidabad, the urban population growth rate increased dramatically. This increase was matched by the increase of urban growth rate between 1991 and 2001.

In Malda, as Table 1.5 suggests, in some regions the highest percentage variations in population occurred between 1872 and 1921. In regions such as

Table 1.4 Growth of Population by Sex in Murshidabad in Census Years 1901–2001

YEAR	TOTAL	INDEX WITH 1901 BASE	NO. OF MALES	NO. OF FEMALES	SEX RATIO PER 100 MEN
1901	1,322,486	100	648,343	674,143	104
1911	1,345,073	102	665,227	679,846	102
1921	1,224,181	93	610,162	614,019	101
1931	1,370,677	104	683,483	687,194	101
1941	1,640,530	124	824,483	816,047	99
1951	1,715,759	130	869,458	846,301	97
1961	2,290,010	173	1,160,283	1,129,727	97
1971	2,940,204	222	1,503,427	1,436,777	96
1981	3,697,552	280	1,887,426	1,810,126	96
1991	4,740,149	358	2,439,342	2,300,807	94
2001	5,866,569	444	3,005,000	2,861,569	95

Source: Government of West Bengal (2007b: 7).

Table 1.5 Percentage Variations in Population of Malda District from Decade to Decade, 1901–1951

	1901–1951	1921–1951	1872–1921	1941–1951	1931–1941	1921–1931	1911–1921	1901–1911
Malda district	+55.30	+36.30	+52.70	+11.00	+17.20	+5.00	−1.80	+15.70
Sadar subdivision	+55.30	+36.60	+52.70	+11.00	+17.20	+5.00	−1.80	+15.70
English Bazar	+33.40	+49.20	−5.60	+12.40	+19.90	+10.70	−14.50	+4.60
Kaliachak	+52.60	+43.30	+32.20	+16.40	+18.10	+4.30	−4.20	+11.20
Malda	+26.70	+14.40	+58.50	+10.10	+11.10	−6.50	−4.90	+16.40
Habibpur	+68.60	+52.30	+58.50	+38.00	+6.80	+3.30	−4.90	+16.40
Patna	+67.10	+42.90	+109.20	+12.50	+20.00	+5.80	−4.20	+22.20
Manikchak	+64.30	+40.50	+106.20	+19.80	+14.70	+2.30	−4.20	+22.20
Kharba	+41.90	+24.80	+53.00	−2.50	+23.30	+3.80	−2.30	+16.40
Harishchandrapur	+112.50	+40.80	+82.50	+1.20	+21.00	+15.00	+25.90	+19.90
Gajol	+38.10	+11.20	+74.70	−0.30	+9.50	+1.90	+2.70	+20.90
Bamongola	+59.50	+28.50	+74.70	+10.30	+15.40	+1.00	+2.70	+20.90

Source: Government of West Bengal (1951: xvi).

Patna and Manikchak, the population variations were as high as +109.2 and +106.2 respectively. It was as high as +74.7 in Gajol and Bamongola also. In Harishchandrapur, although it was as high as +82.5 between 1872 and 1921, it was +112.5 between 1901 and 1951. For the whole of Malda district percentage variations in population between 1872 and 1921 were almost the same as that of 1901 and 1951. For the former it was +52.7 and for the latter it was +55.3. This portrays that migration was always a reality in this region.

Table 1.6 Balance of Migration from Murshidabad to Malda, 1891–1921 and 1951

	1891	1901	1921	1951
Balance of migration from Murshidabad to Malda	–9,318	–7,162	–20,232	+7,597

Source: Samaddar (1999: 172).
Notes: +shows excess of immigration over emigration.
       –shows excess of emigration over immigration.

As for Malda there is a long tradition of both in- and out-migration as Table 1.7 suggests. The decadal growth from 1931 to 1941 was greater than that between 1941 and 1951 as Table 1.1 shows. In the case of Malda both in-migration and out-migration are more from contiguous districts. From other districts it is much lesser in the pre-1947 period as can be seen from Table 1.7. The migration of large groups of women may perhaps be due to reasons of marriage. There is no evidence that this might be due to trafficking. Immigration and emigration between Malda and Murshidabad was a common phenomenon, as is clear from Table 1.6. By 1951 in Malda, English Bazar and Habibpur became the primary entry points. They had been the entry points from 1921 onwards showing linkages between pre- and post-1947 migration pattern.

Demographic statistics from the three states suggest that population movement in all these three states is a historical reality. Trends also suggest that migrants came not just from the eastern part of Bengal but from other parts as well. In the colonial times there remained some popular destinations that remained popular even in the post-colonial period. Also, is it surprising that migrants from a region of very high density of population should come to a region of lower density of population? Particularly, when historically they

Table 1.7 Migration between Malda and Other Districts of Bengal during 1891–1921 and West Bengal in 1951

YEAR	FROM CONTIGUOUS DISTRICTS		IMMIGRATION FROM OTHER DISTRICTS		TO CONTIGUOUS DISTRICTS		TO OTHER DISTRICTS	
	M	F	M	F	M	F	M	F
1891	28,247	23,164	3,616	3,204	18,060	15,091	1,478	613
1901	33,995	33,093	14,927	7,428	11,887	12,779	1,224	688
1911	17,000	18,000	3,000	1,000	11,000	10,000	1,000	1,000
1921	18,000	17,000	2,000	1,000	11,000	9,000	1,000	1,000
1951	6,626	3,489	3,810	1,363	15,639	7,818	5,207	2,320

Source: Government of West Bengal (1951: xiv).

have been following similar routes because the region of lower density of population also had higher rate of economic development.

THE BORDER AREAS POST-1947

The Radcliffe Line divided Bengal into two distinct parts. Map 1.1 shows the border from the western part. The Nadia border was one of those troubled borders where a tribunal had to be appointed. It was the Bagge Tribunal in 1949 that solved the Nadia border problem. Migration continued and increased in the post-colonial period into Nadia. From the Nadia *Gazetteer* we come to know that immigrants:

> [...] form a sizable population of the district. The number of emigrants is also considerable. To avail of the opportunities for economic gain rural people have flocked to the recently grown towns of the district; besides, a good number of migrants have come over from East Pakistan (now Bangladesh) following the partition and have settled in urbanized colonies and urban areas. There are also immigrants from other districts of West Bengal and from other states of India.[10]

According to the Census of India 1961, 70,122 persons born in other districts of West Bengal migrated into Nadia of whom 26,077 were males and 44,045 were females. The contiguous Murshidabad and 24 Parganas sent 18,300 persons and 16,640 persons respectively forming 26.10 per cent and 23.73 per cent of the total number of immigrants. Bardhaman, Calcutta and Hooghly sent respectively 9,664, 7,531 and 4,498 respectively forming 13.78, 10.74 and 7.85 per cent of the total number of immigrants into the district.

There were also 27,252 immigrants from other states of India in the district. The immigrants from East Pakistan numbered as many as 5,02,645 persons. The Census of 1961 recorded 1,17,269 emigrants from the districts to the other districts of the state. Of these 33,107, 23,572, 17,495, 15,553, 11,008 and 6,565 migrated to 24 Parganas, Calcutta, Bardhaman, Murshidabad, Hooghly and Howrah districts. The districts that attracted the immigrants were largely industrialized and urbanized. The Census of 1951 enumerated 424,656 persons of whom 218,712 were males and 205,944 were females belonging to the minority community in East Pakistan. They had come to the district between 1946 and 1951.[11]

Map 1.1 Map of West Bengal

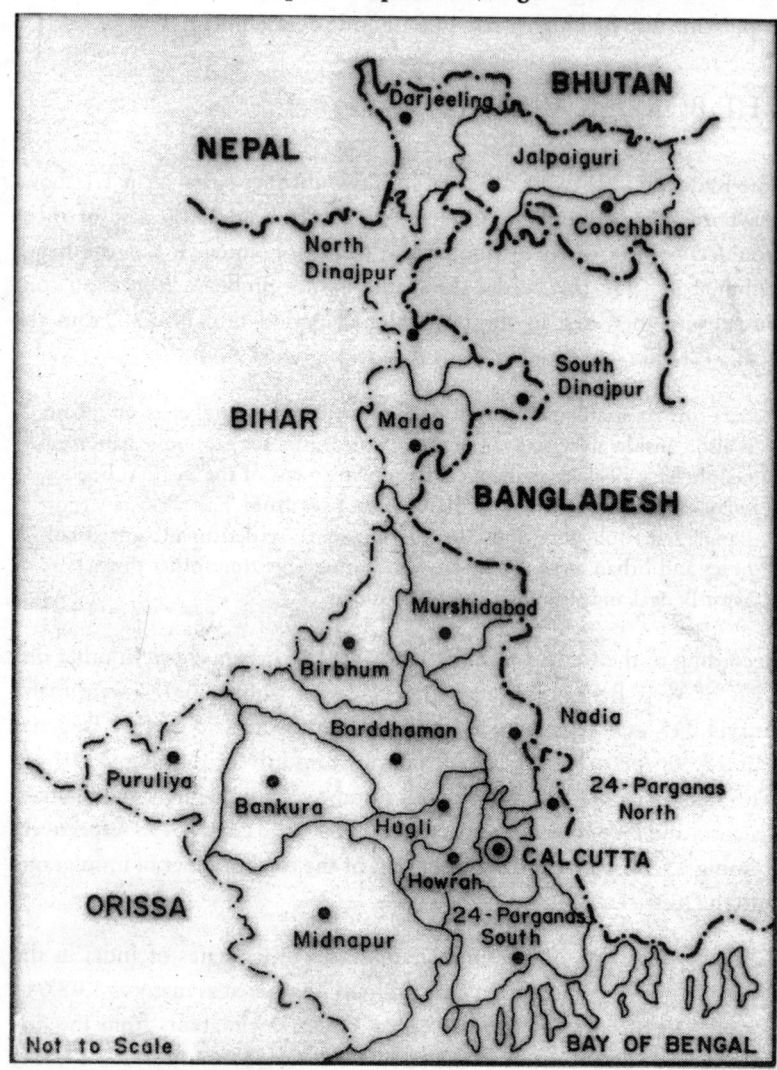

Source: Map drawn by Falguni Biswas.

In Map 1.2, the Bengal–Bangladesh border is clearly demarcated through the Nadia district. In another report presented in the *District Handbook Nadia*, it was stated that 4, 03,804 migrated to the district between 1947 and 1951. Of these 16.76 per cent, numbering 67,696 settled

Map 1.2 Map of Nadia and the Bangladesh Border

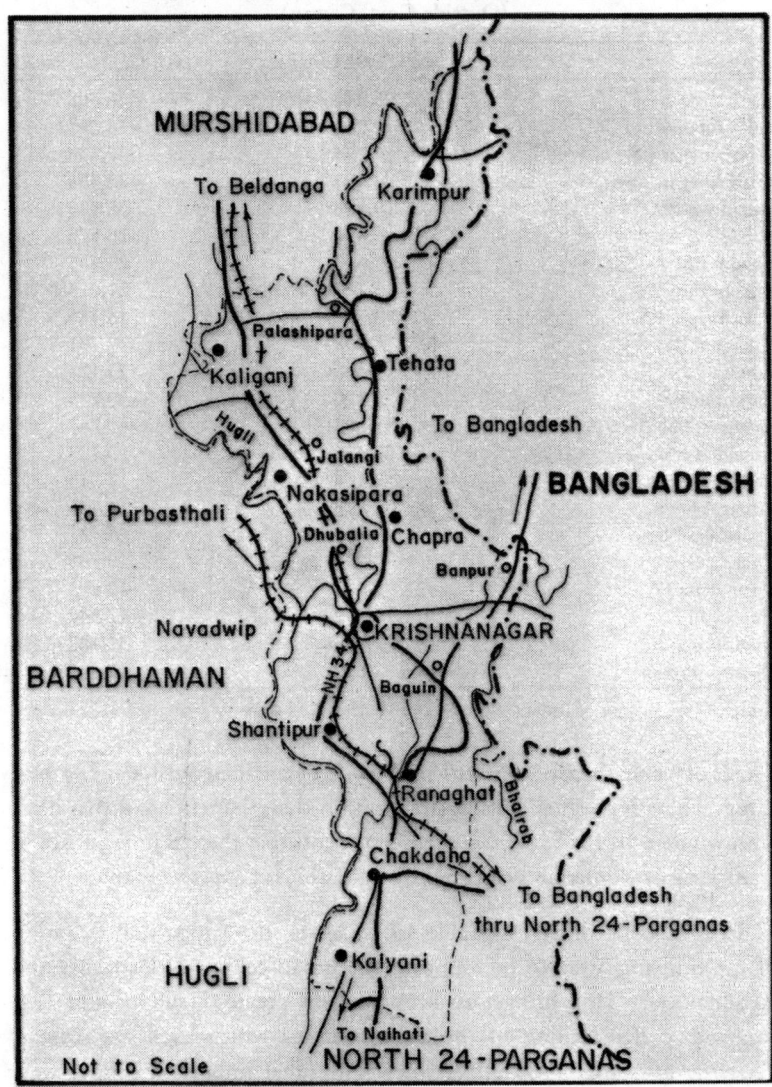

Source: Map drawn by Falguni Biswas.

in urban areas. The migrants mostly came from the ceded portion of Nadia district and other contiguous areas such as Jessore, Faridpur, etc. Some also came from Dacca.[12] Again people coming from East Pakistan followed their predecessors and often settled in areas just across the border. Table 1.8 gives

Table 1.8 Distribution of Displaced Persons in Nadia District, 1955
(Outside Govt. Camps)

	NO. OF FAMILIES	NO. OF MEMBERS
Nadia district	105,841	466,608
Sadar subdivision	50,238	216,861
Krishnanagar P.S.	10,794	47,838
Krishnanagar town	4,454	22,364
Nabadwip P.S.	9,165	38,927
Nabadwip town	6,096	26,575
Chapra P.S.	5,642	23,445
Krishnagunj P.S.	5,117	21,015
Nakashipara P.S.	3,386	15,485
Kaliagunj P.S.	1,668	7,781
Tehatta P.S.	5,646	23,115
Karimpur P.S.	8,820	39,225
Ranaghat Subdivision	55,603	249,747
Ranaghat P.S.	20,426	93,123
Ranaghat town	2,154	11,015
Birnagar town	928	4,426
Chakdaha P.S.	14,681	65,437
Chakdaha town	4,052	18,735
Haringhata P.S.	2,641	12,473
Hanskhali P.S.	10,799	47,532
Shantipur P.S.	7,056	31,182
Shantipur town	2,670	12,346

Source: Government of India (1965: 80).

details of where these people settled when they remained outside the refugee camp. There is another sinister story within these statistics and that deals with women. In 1965, the *Gazetteer* comments that there is no evidence of trafficking of women in Nadia but by 2001 this becomes rampant.

In the Nadia district as Table 1.8 suggests, the largest concentration of the migrants were to be found in the urban centres of Ranaghat and Krishnanagar. This brings us back to our previous supposition that migrants prefer settling in the urban centres which even the *District Gazetteer of Nadia*, 1965 underscores. The other important centres were Chakdah, Nawadwip and Karimpur. In Nadia the decadal growth rate kept increasing until 1981, when it was 33.29. This was larger than the decadal growth rate of Bengal that was 23.1. Inter-district migrations also contin-ued just as migration from Bangladesh also continued. In the 1971 Census, 17,328 males and 36,160 females from rural areas and 12,421 males and

18,139 females born in urban areas reported that they were from other districts of West Bengal. Most of these people came from Murshidabad and 24 Parganas. Also, a sizeable number also came from Calcutta and Burdwan.[13]

As for Murshidabad the decadal growth was at its highest in 1961 as is portrayed by Table 1.9. This was because repression of Bengali speaking people was also severe in that decade in East Pakistan. This is true of all the districts. However, there is evidence to suggest that many who came at that time have eventually gone back. Also, this was a time of high inter-district migration as people were barely getting used to the partition. Also, the decadal growth rate of Murshidabad was never as high as Nadia in the post-1947 period. The decadal growth in fact kept declining from time to time. From 28.75 in 1971, the decadal growth rate declined to 25.4 in 1981. From the 1991 figure of 28.2, the decadal growth rate again declined in 2001 to 23.7. It is still higher than the decadal growth rate of the state of West Bengal. Between 1991 and 2001 the Muslim population of Murshidabad increased. But it did not increase alarmingly as Table 1.10 suggests. In fact in the same period the Christian population more than doubled. Yet often this 2 per cent increase in Muslim population is perceived of as a threat. Although the percentage of Hindus declined between 1991 and 2001, in real terms their numbers increased by 287,881.[14] One also has to remember that Murshidabad is a Muslim stronghold from before 1947.

Table 1.9 Decadal Variation of Population, 1961–2001

REGION		1961–1971	1971–1981	1981–1991	1991–2001
West Bengal	Total	26.87	23.10	24.70	17.70
	Rural	26.38	20.30	23.00	16.90
	Urban	28.41	31.70	29.40	19.80
Nadia	T	30.14	33.20	29.90	19.50
	R	29.77	28.20	28.20	21.60
	U	32.57	53.00	36.20	12.30
Murshidabad	T	28.57	25.40	28.20	23.70
	R	28.40	24.50	26.60	20.90
	U	27.10	39.20	42.80	48.20
Malda	T	31.98	26.00	29.70	24.70
	R	31.89	25.20	26.60	24.40
	U	33.95	42.80	91.90	29.10

Source: Government of India (2001).

Table 1.10 Population by Religion, Murshidabad, 1991–2001

RELIGIOUS COMMUNITIES	1991 POPULATION	1991 (%)	2001 POPULATION	2001 (%)
Hindus	1,819,588	38.39	2,107,469	35.92
Muslims	2,910,220	61.40	3,735,380	63.67
Christians	6,832	0.14	13,723	0.23
Religion not stated	–	–	4,638	0.08
Others	3,409	0.07	5,359	0.10
Total	4,740,149	100	5,866,569	100

Source: Government of West Bengal (2007b).

In Malda the decadal growth rate has declined from 31.98 in 1971 to 24.7 in 2001. The total population of Malda district was 937,580 in 1951 and increased to 1,612,657 in 1971, and has become 3,290,468 in 2001. Malda is still predominantly a rural centre with 92.68 per cent of its population still living in villages. The density of population increased from 706 to 881 from 1991 to 2001. The scheduled caste population of Malda numbered 554,165 in 2001. In 1951 the population of scheduled caste people was over 11 per cent and today it is over 15 per cent portraying that a large number of lower caste Hindus might have come across the border. The population of Muslims increased from 47.49 per cent in 1991 to 49.72 per cent in 2001. Around the same time the Christian population almost doubled from 5,118 in 1991 to 8,388 in 2001.[15] The highest number of in-migrants in 1951 came from Rajsahi as Table 1.11 suggests, not for any sinister reason but because people from Rajsahi and Malda speak the same dialect.

From the migration pattern portrayed above it is my contention that migration between Bangladesh and West Bengal continued on the basis of historical routes established in the colonial period. Also this is not the only form of migration. Inter-district migration also exists from within West Bengal and from other parts of India. So there is little reason to treat migrants from Bangladesh as an aberration. Neither are they solely responsible for the increase in density of population of West Bengal. In this respect it is necessary to pay heed to the *Human Development Report of West Bengal,* 2004. This report suggests:

Contrary to some popular perceptions, it is not very likely that recent increases in population density have resulted dominantly from in-migration from neighbouring countries. Out of the nineteen districts (Medinipur

**Table 1.11 Displaced Persons Arriving in Malda by
District of Origin, 1946–1951**

DISTRICT OF ORIGIN	NUMBER
Kusthia	36
Jessore	322
Khulna	802
Rajsahi	42,532
Dinajpur	2,609
Rangpur	430
Bogura	580
Pabna	3,056
Dhaka	1,344
Mymensingh	864
Bakhargunj	4,309
Tipperah	2,343
Noakhali	310
Chittagong	301
Sylhet	167
Total	60,026

Source: Government of India (1951: 79).

has recently been bifurcated) of the State, nine have international borders with Bangladesh. Two such districts—Jalpaiguri and Koch Bihar—show uniformly a declining rate of growth over the decades from 1961–1971 to 1991–2001. Nadia, another border district, also experienced a sharp decline in growth rate from 3.3 per cent in 1971–1981 to only 2.0 per cent in 1991–2001. In the cases of 24 Parganas and Dinajpurs, the increase in growth rates from 1971–1981 to 1981–1991 was followed by a sharp decline in 1991–2001. The other two border districts Malda and Murshidabad contributed a little over 12 per cent to the decadal (1981–1991) growth of population of West Bengal.

All the border districts together account for 44.5 per cent of the 13.4 million population that were added to 1981 census aggregate to make the State population size stands at 68 million in 1991. On consideration of the contribution of natural growth (that is, excess of births and deaths), which is not insignificant, a major concentration of recent migrants in the border districts does not seem to have occurred. Non-border districts accounted for 55.5 per cent of the total population growth of West Bengal in 1981–1991. Given the moderate levels of vital rates, this implies that the reported increase in immigration over the decade was not confined to a few border districts, but has possibly undergone a spatial diffusion to other parts of the state.[16]

Perhaps of greater concern to students of security should be the fact that reportedly there were no trafficking routes through Nadia in 1961; today trafficking is seen as rampant in this area. Also from the Active Criminal List of December 2009 of Hogalbaria P.S. another phenomenon becomes clear, that is, more than 50 per cent of the cases are for violation of Arms Act, and that there are daily sacrifices of Indian citizens to bullets, portraying the ever increasing violence of the border areas. Or even the situation of Indian nationals living in the *char* (enclave) beyond fenced areas as in Char Meghna might be a subject of grave concern. Compared to this, migration from Bangladesh or increase in density of population seems like a lesser concern.

CHANGING PATTERNS OF VIOLENCE IN THE BORDERLAND

Population flows itself does not become a security concern unless they are perceived of as affecting law and order. In the colonial period in the region under review the major law and order preoccupation was with gangs that were responsible for dacoity, burglary and theft. Each district had its list of gangs that operated in that area. In Nadia, a famous gang in the early 20th century was the Latif Sardar's gang. This gang, as we know from police records, consisted of 24 Muslims and 1 Hindu, all from the Ranakhari police station of Mirpur. The field of operation of the gang was not restricted to Mirpur and extended to the jurisdiction of police stations of Krishnanagar, Kushtia and Damurhuda. The gang also worked in Faridpur, Rajshahi and Rangpur. The existence of the gang came to be noticed in 1895 in course of the investigations into the outbreak of dacoities in the Mirpur area. Eleven members of the gang including one called Madan Mandal became suspects in seven other dacoities in Rangpur, Faridpur and Rajshahi. Again in the beginning of 1914 there was an outbreak of dacoities in the Kushtia district and the gang members were suspected. One of the members became the Crown's witness and four of the gang members including Latif Sardar were sentenced to seven years' rigorous imprisonment. The gang was booked under the Criminal Tribes Act in May 1916. Then again in 1918 Jubbar Mandal, the son in law of Madan Mandal was caught after a series of dacoities and confessed to the guilt, thereby implicating 30 other gang members. Twenty-one members of the gang were convicted under Section 110 of Criminal Procedure Code (CrPC) in 1919 and several others were convicted under Section 395 of IPC. There were a few years of lull after which new members joined the gang and the gang resurfaced in 1922. A few of these new members were booked under the Criminal Tribes Act in 1923. By 1929 most of the gang were either behind bars or forced to live honestly. However, by then there were other gangs which were by and large active in the Nadia district including Broja Bagdi's gang, Tamil Shaikh's gang and others.[17]

In Murshidabad district among the gangs the more famous was the Bholla gang composed of Bagdis, Haris and Muchis. Initially the gang had 45 members under the leadership of Bara Suchand Bholla of Saora, police station Burwan and district Murshidabad. The gang's activities were not restricted to Murshidabad but also spread to Birbhum. Nine cases of dacoity were traced to the gang between 1887 and 1903. In three of these cases, four members were sentenced to five to seven years of rigorous imprisonment. In December 1903, 15 members of the gang were convicted and sentenced and this stymied much of the gang's activities. Until 1916 not much was heard about this gang. In 1918 the gang was said to have reorganized itself under the leadership of new and younger members after the original leader died. The new gang was composed of over 147 members. Ten cases of dacoity in Burwan, Mayureswar, Labhpur and Nanoor were traced to this gang and some of the members were convicted. In 1921, 29 members of the gang were booked under the Criminal Tribes Act. Some of the members were booked in 1924 for a dacoity in Mayureswar under Section 395 of IPC. By 1926 many more of the gang members were booked under the Criminal Tribes Act and sentenced to rigorous imprisonment. By the end of 1929 only seven members were booked under the Criminal Tribes Act and the rest were removed. Although in 1930 none of the gang members were convicted of any crimes and no one was heard to have changed their residence but the police record indicated that the gang was still partially active.[18] This was not the only gang in Murshidabad. There were many others such as the Popara–Jugar gang, Mayam Shaikh's gang, Hiru Ghosh's gang, Bhugi Shaikh's gang, etc., who were all active.

In Malda by 1930 there were 16 known gangs. Among these gangs there were some like Samir Shaikh's gang, whose membership was mixed in character and about 50 in number. They largely operated in the English Bazar area of Malda. Members of this gang were either suspected or convicted in 16 dacoity cases and 17 theft and burglary cases. Some members were convicted under Section 110 of the CrPC. This gang was an inter-district gang with connections in Dinajpur. The gang did not have a designated *adda* (place where they hung out and planned their heists) and met in local *haat*s and bazaars. Their modus operandi varied from crime to crime and the structure of this gang was fairly fluid. There were other gangs such as Kabatulla Shaikh's gang that had by 1930 expunged much of its membership because of inactivity. Three of its active members were convicted and imprisoned by April 1924 after which the gang became almost defunct. But there were some gangs that were more active than the others such as the Jangli Bind's gang. This gang operated in the Kaliachak area of Malda. Jangli Bind was originally a member of the Pearpur gang. He came out of his organization and organized a group of criminals into an independent gang. The gang assumed a formidable character in 1924 and started committing crimes in Malda and Rajmahal areas. The members were either suspected or convicted in 27 theft and burglary cases and five dacoity cases up until 1930.[19] This was one among many of the active gangs in the district of Malda.

Apart from concern over gangs there were concerns with the erstwhile seditionists, who are now known as freedom fighters. But law and order concerns changed drastically after partition during the decade of 1951–1960 with increase in population flows. If one looks at IB files during these years one notices the difference. For one thing in the aftermath of partition the police was expected to make fortnightly reports about the border areas. These reports reveal the changing pattern of violence in the borderlands. In one such report from 1950, it was stated:

It is reported by a D.I.O. that one Samuel Haque s/o Late Mabesuddin Mandal of Kusumpur, P.S. Mahespur, Dist. Jessore (Pakistan) and some Muslims of Pakistan have formed an unholy alliance with Sri Jai Gopal Ray PUB Bhajanghat, P.S. Krishnaganj and his brother Hajari Lal Ray for smuggling jute from Pakistan to Indian Union. These Muslim Jute smugglers are suspected of collecting information of this side taking the advantage of their movements to our area over smuggling affair. Samuel

Haque was an employee of Ordinance Factory, Cownpur before partition. There is a Pak BOP in Kushumpur. On 27.11.50, Samuel Haque passed his night in the house of PUB Jai Gopal Ray and Hajari Lal Ray of Bhajanghat, P.S. Krishanganj and contacted them for smuggling jute from Pakistan. On 28.11.50 Hajari Lal Ray met Sri Badri Narayan Chetlangiak a zamindar and a Crongressite at Krishnanagar and talked with him over this matter. Jai Gopal Ray is said to be anti police.

(The movements of Jai Gopal Ray and others are being watched. We have got one BOP at Bhajanghat.)

O/C Krishnaganj P.S. reports that on 19.11.50 at about 9:30 hrs. Pak Muslims supported by Pak police took away about 100 heads of cattle from Joynagar field, Krishnaganj after assaulting the cow heards who were tending the cattle.[20]

In post-partition days dacoity was no longer an internal problem. It usually meant dacoity by the Pakistani miscreant. A new category of crime appeared on the horizon and that was smuggling. Something that was legitimate even a few years back became illegitimate. The administration responsible for looking after the border constantly strove to control the flow, failing which they had to observe it closely. The most problematic seemed those who were neither here nor there or who lived partly in India and partly in Pakistan due to the nature of their employment or lifestyle. These people were considered as either spies or smugglers, as such security threats that needed to be under constant surveillance. Another category of threat related to land and the next letter to the West Bengal police DIG clarifies this. The letter begins by stating that 1,859 Hindu evacuees arrived at Bongaon by train and 549 Muslims left for Pakistan by train. The letter then addresses other issues stating:

On receipt of report from Ranaghat BOP on 29.11.50 (evening) to effect that harvest from another part of Ranaghat Mouza borderlands has been removed by Pakistanis. SDPO along with SDO proceeded to Ranaghat to enquire into it on 30.11.50.

On enquiry SDPO and SDO found that about 25 bighas of land of this side of Indo-Pak border which was situated very near Pakistani village of Pokhrail and 2 1/2 miles from BOP has been devastated of the harvest. The surreptitious removal of harvest took place after night fall on 27.11.50. The special force from 1–5 from APB detachment at Bongaon had arrived at BOP in the evening of 27.11.50. The removal had been affected before they reinforced and joined in petrol work.[21]

Land was considered as extremely crucial to the formation of the nation state. Claim to land was to be rigorously upheld even at the cost of alienating ones own citizens. The police were looked upon as protectors of the nation. Pakistani police were marked as trouble makers in the official narratives. In this period the Nadia–Kushtia border continued to be tense. This was blamed on the aggressive attitude of the Pakistani authorities in the Indian official narratives. Intermittently, shots were exchanged between the police of East and West Bengal. In the Rajshahi–Murshidabad border the trouble seemed to be centred on some digging activities by the Pakistani authorities. From its inception the border was tense. This tension remained until the first few years of Bangladesh. The next report shows how such tensions continued:

> Reports of harassment of our nationals while visiting contiguous Pak villages by the Pak Muslims were also received from Nadia and Cooch Bihar. The tension over forcible occupation of a portion of Fulbari garden road, PS Rajganj Jalpaiguri by the Pak authorities has ceased gradually after our police force took possession of the land claimed by Pak authorities without any assistance. The line of demarcation of the disputed road has been agreed upon by the directors of Land Records and survey of both the states. The Pak authorities are reported to be not in favour of allowing the Hindus to live in border areas and pressure is therefore being given indirectly through the Ansars to leave the border areas.[22]

There were other causes of tension as well. Pakistani authorities' behaviour towards the refugees was one such cause. The other related to the occupation of the *chars*. In one report it was stated that, 'Pak Muslims aided by the Pak police trespassed into our territory at Char Durbarpur PS Lalgola and forcibly took away paddy to Pak territory by assaulting the labourers who were engaged in harvesting'.[23] The *chars* are archetypal no-man's-land. Claims and counterclaims over this were common phenomena. The other causes of concern were incoming flows and the rehabilitation of these refugees. A number of reports discuss meetings and protests by camp inmates of refugee camps. In one such report it was stated:

> On 13.12.53, a meeting (500) organized by the Coopers Camp, Bastuhara Samiti (CPI) was held on the Ranaghat Municipal Ground with Ramendra Narayan Khan in the Chair; the President Shib Shankar Datta (ED-CPI) Sushil Chatterjee (ED-CPI), Gaur Kundu (CPI) and others spoke in the meeting urging the refugees to unite under the

banner of the Bastuhara Samiti. They also criticized the mall administration of the camp authority as well as the police action and demanded the removal of the camp administrator, immediate rehabilitation of the refugees in West Bengal and the withdrawal of the cases against the members of the Bastuhara Samiti.[24]

The 1950s set the tone of what it meant to administer the borderland. Even today the main concerns remain with population flow. The fencing is meant to harness that flow. The other area of concern as emerged from the IB files of the 1950s is national security. The fact that remains the main area of concern needs hardly any mention. This is further reinforced by the number of cases brought in the border region under the head of rioting. Table 1.12 testifies to that fact.

In both the districts of Nadia and Murshidabad, rioting is a more frequent crime than murder and dacoity. In the case of Malda it is more common than dacoity but slightly less than murder. Concerns over rioting reflect the concern over national security in the region.

WOMEN AND BORDER: A NARRATIVE OF TRAFFICKING

As concerns over the new nation state were translated into concerns over territorial security, the same way concerns over women's security in the borders were reduced to concerns over women's trafficking for sex. If one looks at the history of the term 'trafficking' it can be traced back to 'white slave trade'. Before the Great Wars it meant the coercion or transportation of Caucasian women to the colonies to service white male officers. At that point the term did not include indentured labourers from the colonies to the plantations where often they were coerced, cheated and abused. From 1904 there were efforts to stop 'white slave trade' leading to the *Convention for the Suppression of the Traffic in Person and the Exploitation of Others* in 1949. By that time trafficking had come to be associated with transportation of women for 'immoral purposes' such as prostitution. Social scientists believe that after the wars 'women from developing countries and countries which were experiencing civil and political unrest ... were migrating to the developed world in search of a better future'.[25] Given the gender inequities

**Table 1.12 Comparison of Types of Offences Committed
in Nadia, Murshidabad and Malda**

| | 2002 | | | 2004 | | | 2006 | | |
DISTRICTS	MURDER	DACOITY	RIOT	MURDER	DACOITY	RIOT	MURDER	DACOITY	RIOT
Nadia	99	18	228	98	7	170	101	14	164
Malda	50	3	25	63	12	42	62	10	47
Murshidabad	127	14	132	99	14	139	77	6	175

Source: Government of West Bengal (2007a, 2007b).

in these countries women often entered informal sectors such as prostitution, where labour protection laws are minimal. The international community tried to combat these abuses by humanitarian legislation that addressed concerns of women's vulnerability. The term used to describe the abuse of women in the process of migration was 'trafficking'. Efforts to stop trafficking in the 1980s and '90s went hand in hand with efforts to abolish prostitution. Therefore trafficking and prostitution came to be understood as two parts of the same process. But the phenomenon of trafficking is much larger than trafficking for merely sex trade. In its myriad forms it takes place through and for marriage, sexual exploitation, begging, organ trading, armed conflicts, drug peddling, smuggling, labour, for both domestic and public consumption, adoption, entertainment and sports. In the context of the region under discussion it is likewise understood that the push factors for women's trafficking even now remain gender inequities in the country of origin, endemic poverty and political social and economic persecution. While there is no precise data, estimates provide that approximately 800,000–900,000 persons are traded annually across national borders. Of this 70 per cent are women and 50 per cent are children.[26]

'India was among the seven Asian nations put by US on its "watch list" of countries involved in human trafficking', said a newspaper report from Northeast India.[27] This is not isolated news but such statements from the West keep recurring. In the same report it was also stated, 'not only India is facing this huge problem but also has become a transit point for prostitution from nearby countries like Bangladesh, Myanmar and Nepal'.[28] India was also marked as the destination for sex tourism from Europe and United States. These reports portray that human trafficking is a thriving proposition and there are a number of routes through which women and children are trafficked into and out of this region. For a while the Assam–Siliguri route was identified as the main trafficking route through which the victims of flesh trade were transported across Northeast India.[29] But routes change and when one route is identified traffickers begin using another. Through these routes in the Northeast women from Nepal, Burma, Bangladesh, the Northeast itself and Bengal are seduced, coerced or forced into flesh trade and trafficked. This is both a procurement area and a transit area. Any report on migration in this region would remain incomplete without a stock taking of trafficking that goes on in this region because it leaves enormous consequences not just for the victims but also for the security of the region. Here we are not speaking of state security but security of people who are affected by trafficking.

This is a region of endemic poverty, social imbalance and political violence, particularly against vulnerable groups of whom women form a large part. Each part of this region is undergoing certain social and political turmoil where more and more women are getting marginalized. In Bangladesh, for example, effects of globalization, growth of fundamentalism, modernization policies such as building of dams, etc., have all contributed to violence against ethnic and religious minorities, and against women. Of course minority women are in a double bind. They are attacked both as minorities and as women. The fundamentalists who have increased their control in the political arena strive to maintain a predominantly male-dominant status quo. This strategy puts both minorities and women in general in the receiving end. Religion has come to be used by fundamentalist groups as one of the primary means by which male-dominant values and existing gender-oppressive ideologies are imposed and perpetuated. According to Meghna Guhathakurta and Suraiya Begum, 'it was advantageous therefore for the fundamentalists to target women who step outside the bounds of social norms since they represented a potential threat to the male-dominant status quo'.[30] To compound all of these developments there is endemic poverty and land alienation of poorer groups of people in *chars*. Such developments have led to widespread control and destabilization of women in the region leading to their displacement. Often displaced women find themselves in ghettos or camps. These camps are epicentres of insecurity. The living condition of the camp is deplorable. Unhealthy, damp and unhygienic, the camp is often the site for different diseases such as diarrhoea, malaria and dengue. A fall out of this is an increase in trafficking of women and children across the border.

In Dhaka, a number of recent governments have embarked on a policy of beautification and brothel eviction. One of the biggest brothels in Bangladesh is in Tanbazar in Narayanganj. This brothel started during the colonial period. Later, many internally displaced women gathered in the area and were dependent on this brothel for their livelihood. In July 1999, sex workers from this brothel were evicted by the government and sent to vagabond centres where there are evidences that they were severely mistreated. Other than brothels the government has also embarked on a policy of slum eviction.[31] In my visit to Bangladesh in 2004, I have had lengthy discussions with women directly affected by these evictions.[32] A number of women have tried to resist these developments. But many have not been able to survive such attacks and joined the ranks of the displaced. These women are particularly vulnerable to traffickers. Although any definite data as to how many women are trafficked is almost impossible to gather because of the nature of the problem, but the number of brothels in the border areas prove that this is a thriving proposition.

Women from Bangladesh are largely trafficked to India. From India they might then be taken to Pakistan or the Middle East. In a research by Sanlaap, in two red light areas of West Bengal it was revealed that most of these women migrate from one place to another. Ninety per cent of the red light areas that they have identified as places that they have worked in are situated in the states that border Bangladesh. Most of these are either in the Northeast or in West Bengal. In one particular red light area named Changrabandha about 66 per cent women said that they have come from Bangladesh. In Dinbazar many of the sex workers have said that their mothers came from Bangladesh. The report clearly states, 'The rate of trafficking in Changrabandha is remarkably higher than Dinbazar. The red-light area of Changrabandha is adjacent to Bangladesh border and women are trafficked through this border like any other commodity'.[33] Most of the women in sex work were illiterates. Many of these women entered prostitution when they were younger than 18 years of age. Most of these women came from families of either wage earners and cultivators or their mothers were sex workers as well. The mothers who are themselves sex workers find no alternative except letting their daughters take up the same profession because as children of sex workers they are stigmatized and discriminated against. They are deprived of education or even a social environment with any promise or hope. The socio-economic profiles of sex workers of at least Dinbazaar and Changrabandha portray that these women and children did not have too many options to take up other professions.

Even while in the profession their lives are never secure. Basically there are three to four modes of operation. They can work independently, or on contract basis or even under a 'madam'. Women in the third category had to give up all their earnings to the madam, and they were given room, food and some other necessities in lieu of their payments. Even on contract basis they give half of their payments to madams. The best of them earn about ₹ 5,000 per month. This takes care of their necessities and their children. Some of them even send money home. Their insecurity is portrayed by the fact that they are trafficked often from one centre to another. These women are at the mercy of both criminals and the police. Being near the border often they are forced to give shelter to criminals from either Bangladesh or India. Also, the police use them for sex without any payment. They often cater to truckers crossing zero point and to attract them they take to the roads.[34]

There are cases where women who are brought from Bangladesh to the metropolitan towns in India face tremendous brutality. One such case is that of Hamida, a young Bangladeshi girl, who was brought to India at the age of 10. She 'suffered a series of brutal rapes at the hands of the man who brought her to New Delhi, along with some of his friends who were Delhi policemen .... Only one of the accused men has served jail time'.[35] That this is a region of extreme insecurity for men and women crossing the border has been dramatically portrayed by the case of one Jayanti Bala Das of Bangladesh.[36] In January of 2003 five Bangladeshi nationals, of whom two were minor children crossed the Indo-Bangladesh border and entered India. The Border Security Force (BSF) arrested them from a Baro Bridge across the Ichhamati River. The area in which the incident took place is under the jurisdiction of the Basirhat police station in the North 24 Parganas. The Bangladeshi nationals including one Jayanti Bala Das were all taken to the Soladana BSF camp at around 5 p.m. On the same night (10 January 2003) one BSF personnel allegedly raped Jayanti Bala. Thereafter, these 'infiltrators' were put in a small boat with holes and efforts were made to push them back. Allegedly, when the boatman refused to go he was threatened at the point of a gun. The boat capsized in the middle of the river and only Jayanti Bala and her one-year-old son could save themselves. On 13 January the villagers of Bagundi, who had given her shelter, handed her over to the police of Basirhat. She was charged under Section 14 of the Foreigners Act. On 21 January a dead body was found in the Brickkiln Canal in South Basirhat. The man was identified as Jayanti's husband Basudev. When a case was lodged against five BSF personnel, the BSF men were unwilling to hand over their personnel to the Basirhat police. Although the

BSF disagreed that Jayanti was raped, the officer-in-charge of this case stated that initial examinations proved that she was molested.[37] On 27 January the SDJM of Basirhat issued warrants against five BSF men. In July Jayanti was handed over to the Sromojibi Mahila Samity for safe custody and on 15 September 2003 a writ petition was filed on her behalf. The cases are still pending.[38]

Jayanti's case reflects the situation of women who are trying to cross the border. Their status of being a foreign-born woman increases their vulnerability. No one is willing to shoulder any responsibility for these women. The state that they leave is glad to get rid of them and the state that they enter finds them unwanted. This has been proved last year when in February, 213 gypsy snake charmers who have always led a life of seasonal mobility crossing borders at certain times of the year were stopped in zero point in Satgachi in Cooch Behar. They had to remain there for days as both India and Bangladesh were unwilling to take them back until one night they just disappeared. No one knows what happened to them and even less do people care. From the Indian side we were told that they were pushed inside Bangladesh. No one even asked for evidence of what happened because this is a grey area. In such a situation women can be exploited by anyone and are therefore particularly vulnerable to traffickers. They are also vulnerable to many other crimes but often we focus on trafficking and little else. For us it is only the flows that matter. The rest can be forgotten.

The border itself is a place of endemic poverty, substantial illiteracy among women and children and enormous violence against women. Few years back in a survey undertaken in three border villages, namely, Shikarpur, Char Meghna and Nasirerpara it was found out that most women in this area are illiterate. In Shikarpur, out of 515 women only 190 had some forms of literacy; in Char Meghna, out of 590 only 100 women are literate and in Nasirerpara out of 470 women only 85 are literate.[39] These women have very few options to improve their situation. Their problems are compounded by increased militarization and criminalization of the area. Here, every other day women and children are molested or killed. On visiting the border near Char Meghna two chroniclers poignantly write:

To assert that the control of the border still belongs to them the border security on both ends sporadically do a well-orchestrated show of national safety through aggression. It is then that one witnesses the elaborate, flexing of muscles and the violent exchange of fire and mortar. On such occasions the border sky is lit up by man made conflagrations and the air swells with the sound of brutal human games. At the end of it all, what are lost on both sides are the expendable lives of common people like Baba-Hasim, and Kanakchampa and the eyesight of 6-year-old Sonia, who paid the price for playing, foolishly enough, in her own front yard.[40]

Women living in these borders live a life of extreme hardship. They are the quickest targets for both the security personnel and the criminals. 'The robbers demand women during their raids and when they get none they leave threatening dire consequences: "you can hide your livestock in the camp. You can hide your money in the bank. But where will you hide your women?"'[41] Any study on traditional security pays no attention to such insecurities, which has become part of their everyday lives.

It is true that trafficking in this region is an important phenomenon. Also, it fits in well with the state concern over population flows and women's victimhood. But sole attention to trafficking is an agenda that often obliterates the root causes of abuse against women.

If one looks at cases of offences against women in this region one finds out that although every year many such cases are reported but very few lead to actual convictions of people responsible for such violations. The case of Nadia as portrayed in Table 1.13 clearly supports my contention that all other offences against women became insignificant when posited against concerns on trafficking. In the year 2006, although 1,105 cases of offences against women were reported and 1,645 cases tried only 15 people were convicted and 1,964 people were acquitted. In Murshidabad the same year, of the 1,396 cases reported only 697 persons were tried of whom no one was convicted. In Malda, between 2003 and 2006 hardly anyone was convicted. Trafficking symbolized the two great fears of a national security state, uncontrolled flows of women with uncontrolled sexuality that might undermine the patriarchal control. Hence, in this region one is often confronted with the attitude that by stopping trafficking the state can stop all that ails women in this region. We do not consider the holistic effects of violence against women that comes from privileging a certain form of the security question. Therefore, the situation slides from bad to worse for women living under the border regime.

Table 1.13 Offences Committed against Women

DISTRICT	OFFENCES REPORTED			CASES TRIED			CONVICTED				ACQUITTED		
	'03	'04	'05	'06	'03	'04	'05	'06	'03	'04	'05	'06	'03	'04	'05	'06
Nadia	659	844	1,032	1,105	162	271	511	1,645	2	31	144	15	393	547	1,260	1,964
Murshidabad	674	1,090	1,377	1,396	236	419	7	697	12	14	–	–	167	42	7	–
Malda	145	574	521	157	145	574	521	157	–	8	–	–	–	–	–	–

Source: Government of West Bengal (2007a, 2007b).

NOTES

1. Government of Bengal (1932).
2. Chakrabarti (1918: 48–49).
3. Ibid., p. 50.
4. Ibid., p. 77.
5. *The Gazette of India* (Simla, Saturday, 22 July 1905) in Chattopadhyay (2007: 5).
6. 'The Carlyle Circular' of 10 October 1905 in Chattopadhyay (2007: 19).
7. 'Report on the Agitation' in Chattopadhyay (2007: 75).
8. Geddes (1937).
9. Ibid.
10. *West Bengal District Gazetteers* (1965: 78).
11. Ibid., p. 79.
12. Mitra (1953: XXXVII).
13. Government of West Bengal (1971: 222).
14. Government of West Bengal (2007b: 16).
15. Government of West Bengal (2007a: 13).
16. Government of West Bengal (2004: 11).
17. Government of Bengal (1932: 188–89).
18. Government of Bengal (1932: 161–62).
19. Government of Bengal (1932: 119–21).
20. 'Extract from the weekly report of the Superintendent of Police, Nadia, for the week ending 1.12.50' IB File No. 1238 A/47 (Nadia), p. 493, WB State Archives, 43 Shakespeare Sarani (hereafter WBSAIB).
21. 'To the WB Police, DIG Central Range', DIGIB. IB File No. 1238 A/47 (Nadia), Memo No. 7491 (5) / 23:50 (Tehatta), DM 24 Parganas, WBSAIB.
22. 'Fortnightly report on border incidents in West Bengal during 2nd Half of April 1951.' IB File No. 1238 A/47, Memo no. 19082/1238 A-47. For, date 7.5.1951, pp. 809–41, WBSAIB.
23. IB File No. 1238 A/47, Memo No. 25522/1238 A-47. For, date 20.6.1951, p. 867, WBSAIB.
24. 'Sushil Kr. Chatterjee S/o Upendranath of Basantapur PO, Haringhata and Gaori, Krishnanagar, Nadia,' IB File No. 1355-28, Serial No. NSP XLVI, No. 55, WBSAIB.
25. Pattanaik (2002: 218).
26. Human Rights Law Network (2006: 1).
27. *Shillong Times* (2004b).
28. Ibid.
29. *Shillong Times* (2004a).
30. Guhathakurta and Begum (2005).
31. Ibid.
32. Discussions organized by Research Institute of Bangladesh, Dhaka, 25 November 2004.
33. Sanlaap (unpublished: 18).
34. Ibid., p. 25.
35. Banerjee (1999: 64).

36. The case is registered in the Basirhat police station on 13 January 2003, under Section 376 (B)/280 of the Indian Penal Code.
37. *Anandabazar Patrika* (2003).
38. Banerjee (2003).
39. Survey undertaken by Subharati Banerjee under my supervision for her unpublished M.Phil thesis '*Bharat Bangladesh Simanta Samasya: Charmeghna, Shikarpur o Nasirerparar Porjalochona*' (Problems in Bengal Bangladesh Border: A discussion of the three villages of Charmeghna, Shikarpur and Nasirerpara), Department of South and Southeast Asian Studies, University of Calcutta, 2000–01, p. 73.
40. Banerjee and Banerjee (2003).
41. Ibid.

2

Narrated Time and Constructed Space: Remembering the Communal Violence of 1950 in Hooghly

Anasua Basu Ray Chaudhury

> *Partition was in no sense like an operation that was concluded in August 1947. The border is far from being the trace of an event long over, like a healed and fading incision scar. It is still in the process of being formed. Its creation was not merely a matter of drawing a line through a map by a qualified technocrat: it was created again and again, by a number of different agencies, on the ground through which it ran. Its shape (both literally and metaphorically) has varied, and continues to vary, through time.*
>
> Joya Chatterji[1]

Borders are not just lines in the landscape. Experts say that borders, inert elements, shape the societies and cultures that they enclose, the pre-given ground on which events take place. Borders denote a spatial dimension of social relationships that are continually being configured; in this process, the meaning of borders is produced, reconstructed, strengthened or weakened. The notion of borders in today's world is a testimony to the importance of territoriality and it also provides an insight into the nation and the sexual/gendered 'other'. The imagery of borders has become a popular metaphor in the study of socio-spatial development in post-Partition societies.

The partition of the Indian subcontinent in 1947 is not just a 'surgical metaphor'[2]—an 'operation', an 'amputation', a 'vivisection' or 'dismemberment'. It is also a line inside our heads and our hearts too. In fact, the physical fence is the manifestation of these more cognitive and emotional lines that shape our thoughts and feelings. The inner lines express who we think we are and who we affirm are not like us, whom we trust and of whom we are afraid. Cynthia Cockburn[3] has correctly pointed out that, when we are very afraid or very angry, at some identifiable moment, a line springs out and plants itself in the earth as a barrier. In that way, a geopolitical partition is not just armoured fencing, it creates differences. Against this backdrop the present chapter intends to study how the distance between Hindus and Muslims was widened by the Partition of India.

The Partition was a watershed in the history of the region. On the one hand, the erstwhile British colonies were being decolonized immediately after the World War II, and on the other, their political liberation came in a fractured state. The phenomenon of this fractured identity was not only a state affair as such. In fact, the millions living in Punjab and Bengal bore the brunt of partition in a way that still defines their existence in many ways. For Punjab, partition and exchange of population—the Hindus coming from western Punjab of Pakistan to India and the Muslims moving from eastern Punjab of India to Pakistan—were primarily a one-time affair though it was in no way peaceful or voluntary. Therefore, perhaps many would argue whether the blood-soaked partition of Punjab in 1947 resolved the growing tensions between the Hindus and Sikhs, on the one hand, and the Muslims, on the other. But, for Bengal, the partition turned out to be a messier affair that is yet to be concluded. The partition of Bengal in 1947 is a continuing process that perennially tends to influence the lives of the inhabitants on both sides of the boundary since Sir Cyril Radcliffe and his colleagues in the Bengal Boundary Commission decided to hurriedly draw an imaginary line before leaving India.

The studies on displacement due to the partition in the east of India tend to concentrate primarily on the Hindu refugees[4] from East Pakistan. These studies often overlook the other stories of partition in the East— stories of the minorities—Muslims in West Bengal.[5] In fact, the impact partition had on the minorities—on both sides of the border, who remained where they were and did not emigrate as refugees to the new nation—has not received the attention that it deserves.[6] Keeping this fact in mind in this study, we shall attempt to unravel the stories of Muslim women of Hooghly, the otherwise calm and quiet place during the turbulent years of partition. This chapter is about the twice displacement of these Muslim women, who were first displaced during partition from their homes and took refuge in Imambarah (Imam, an angel + Barah, a building to live in), a holy place for them, situated on the bank of the Hooghly River in the district of Hooghly. The violence that broke out in 1950 in different parts of West Bengal was mainly responsible for this displacement. The manager of Imambarah took initiatives to arrange a special train for these uprooted Muslims, who wanted to leave their country for the security of their lives. Crossing the newly carved international border they took shelter in a somewhat alien land in East Pakistan (earlier known as East Bengal) on the other side of the border. But then came the second displacement when they discovered, ironically, that the situation across the border was not hospitable enough for them. Therefore, these displaced Muslims from West Bengal could not assimilate themselves alongside the people of East Pakistan, who mostly belonged to the Sunni sect of Islam, while the displaced Muslims, our respondents, were primarily Shias and Urdu speaking.

To examine the social history of partition, the present study intends to capture the lives and experiences of the people who lived through that 'partitioned time',[7] of the way in which the events accompanying the partition were constructed in their minds and of the identities or uncertainties that partition created or reinforced. The main purpose of the study is twofold. First, the study would enquire on how these Muslim women negotiated borders—borders of sect, community, patriarchy and of conflicts not only in their own land but also in an alien land away from their homeland. Second, this chapter would also seek to analyse the role of Imambarah, the main witness of violence, the rescuer of thousands of Muslims at the time of communal disturbance in 1950 at Hooghly. While dealing with the inner process of 'line making' and 'line negotiating' with the help of these women's perceptions of victimhood, the study would like to focus on narratives of these Muslim women, which tend to be framed in rhetoric of Hindu–Muslim differences. It is true that these narratives may be subjective and selective in nature, but their selective memories could act as a rich archive to unfold the 'subjugated knowledge',[8] the forgotten stories of partition. For the sake of analysing we would also depend on the published government documents, unpublished letters from the proceedings of Imambarah, books, journals, newspaper clippings and local magazines published from Hooghly. At the very outset we would like to start with the stories of Imambarah.

BEING IN TIME: IMAMBARAH OF HOOGHLY REVISITED

'You know, this Imambarah saved our lives during that turbulence', Naheda *bibi* (not her real name) almost yelled out. We were sitting at Islam *bhai's* house in front of the Imambarah. Islam *bhai* is a photographer by profession. He knows Naheda *bibi* for quite a long time and when he disclosed my purpose of visit, Naheda *bibi* agreed to talk to me. She (72) was wearing a shabby printed cotton sari with a veil on her head. She stays, along with her four siblings, at Mooghaltuly, a place close to the Imambarah, a predominantly Muslim area in Hooghly. She has altogether four sons and two daughters. Two of her sons stay elsewhere. Medina, her elder daughter, is married to a rickshaw puller of the same locality. However, for the last four years Medina with her son Nasser is also staying at their mother Naheda *bibi's* place after her husband deserted her. Rafikul and Iqbal, two sons of Naheda are staying with her mother. Rafikul, also a rickshaw puller and Iqbal, a daily labour have meagre earnings. As a result, Naheda despite her old age has to work to earn a living. In her own words:

My father used to tell us that those days are gone. Therefore, we should be very cautious now and it is better to have friends from within our own community. My abbu (father) was a coachoan (coachman) and my mother was a housewife. We were five brothers and sisters altogether and I was number three in the order of the siblings. We had our own small house in the locality close to my present residence. Though our locality was predominantly Muslim however, a few Hindu families also lived in that area. We did not have any chance to go to school. But, we had many friends in our own community. My parents did not allow us to socialise with our Hindu neighbours.

I was 15 years old then. The riot took place around holi. Probably that was in the month of March. It was a very chaotic situation. Everybody in our locality kept saying that riot could break out at any moment. The situation was very tense. Soon, our area was badly hit by the riot. They looted and burnt many houses and we saw the flames from our windows. We got scared. We did not go out. Everyone in the locality became worried to save his or her own lives. However, there was no incidence of murder in our locality, although there were instances of large-scale looting and arson. Next morning, my father told us that he got the information from our relatives that they could forcibly take out many young girls from their houses and torture them. My abbu decided to leave our house as soon as possible and to take shelter in Imambarah.

We were not alone. Like us, many of our neighbours left their homes and came to Imambarah for their safety and security. As we were in a hurry, we left all our belongings except some ornaments of my mother before leaving our house. That was meagre. We were displaced from our houses. When we reached the Imambarah it was too crowded. Thousands and thousands of displaced people had taken shelter there. However, within a day or two, rations from the government reached us. We got rice and pulse. We used to cook for ourselves. But, inside the Imambarah there was no privacy. We used to share space with other families. You cannot imagine how those days were. Some families had to stay outside in open air as they reached quite late and all covered areas like rooms, long balconies, even the prayer hall were full of refugees. And, we could not go out of the premises of Imambarah fearing violence for the next two months.[9]

The main witness of those stories of violence, displacement and taking refuge is the Imambarah, the place originally belonged to Haji Muhammad Mohasin (1732–1812).[10] As he had neither children nor other relatives who would become his legal heirs, he gifted a huge area of land including Imambarah to the Trustees for the charity. In his words (translated from his deed, which is in Persian language):

[…] that the Zemindary of Pergana Kishmat Syedpur, &c., appendant to Zilla Jessore and Pergana Sobnal, also appendant to the said Zilla and one house situated in Hooghly (known and distinguished as Imambarah), Imambazar and Hat (market) also situated in Hooghly, and all the goods and chatters appertaining to the Imambarah agreeably to a separate list— the whole of these properties have developed on me by inheritance, and the proprietary possession of which I have enjoyed up to the present time; as I have no children, nor grand-children, nor other relations, who would become my legal heirs; and as I have all wish and desire to keep up and continue the useages, and charitable expenditures (Murasum-o-ukhrajat-i-husneh) of the Fateha, &c., of Hazrat (on whom be blessings and reward) which have been the established practice of this family, I therefore hereby give purely for the sake of God the whole of the above property with all its rights, immunities and privileges, whole and entire, little or much, in it, with it, or from it …[11]

As a result, a huge area surrounding Imambarah became part of waqf properties (see Map 2.1). History reveals that when Murshid Kuli Khan was the Governor of Bengal, a Persian merchant named Agha Mohamed Mutahar, who had been domiciled in India came to settle in Hooghly with his family. After settling in Hooghly he purchased the site of the present Imambarah, and built thereon an ordinary single-storied house which he dedicated to god, calling it 'Nazargah Hossein'.[12] Afterwards, his son-in-law Mirza Saleh extended the building by adding a portion which he termed 'Tazea Khana'. It was upon the ruins of this structure the Imambarah was erected. It was again renovated in 1841 under the supervision of Syed Keramat Ali.[13] (See recent photos of Imambarah; Photos 2.1a and 2.1b.)

Hooghly[14] had a fairly large Muslim settlement since a long time back. According to the 1951 census report the 1,209.2 sq. mi.[15] long district was home to about 206,230 Muslims, which constituted 8.12 per cent of the total population.[16] As elsewhere in Bengal, an overwhelming majority of Muslims of the district were Sunnis of the Hanafi sect. Shias were found in almost all areas of Muslim concentration but they were most numer-ous in and around the Hooghly–Chinsura area.[17] The area adjacent to Imambarah was predominantly inhabited by the Shias. 'Shias living in Hooghly adjacent to Imambarah are from UP and they are mostly urdu speaking. However, it is true that, after two-three generation's stay at Hooghly now we can speak Bengali fluently', proclaims Iftikar, the pre-sent *Mutawali* (manager) of Imambarah. To be precise, the areas like Mughalpura, Imambazar, Chawk Bazar, Sonatuly, Hussain Gally, Karbala, Matijil, Khagra Jhor, Mianr Ber, Kaji Danga, Ghutia Bazar, Maheshpur were Shia dominated. Besides Hooghly–Chinsura, Shias were also predominant in places like Gondolpara, Urdi Bazar, Farashdanga, Telenipara, Chapadani, Pandua, Kamal Gazi Darga of Chadernnagore and also in the Srirampore subdivisions of Hooghly district.[18] According to Jadunath Sarkar, Hooghly became a Shia colony and a centre of Shia theology and Persian culture

Map 2.1 Waqf Property Adjacent to Imambarah

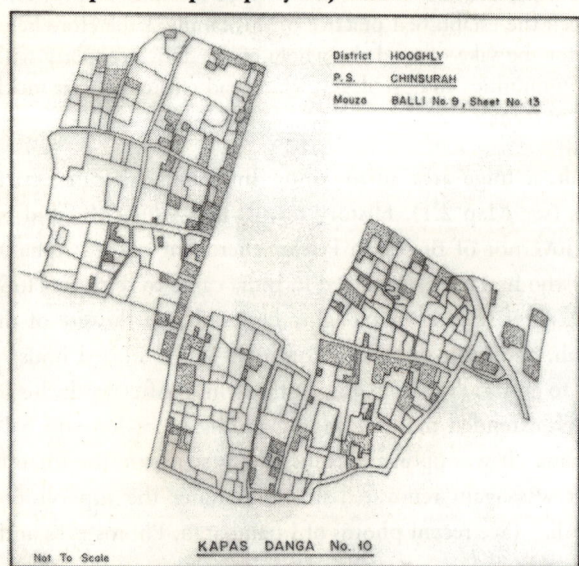

Source: Imambarah

Photos 2.1 Recent Photos of Imambarah

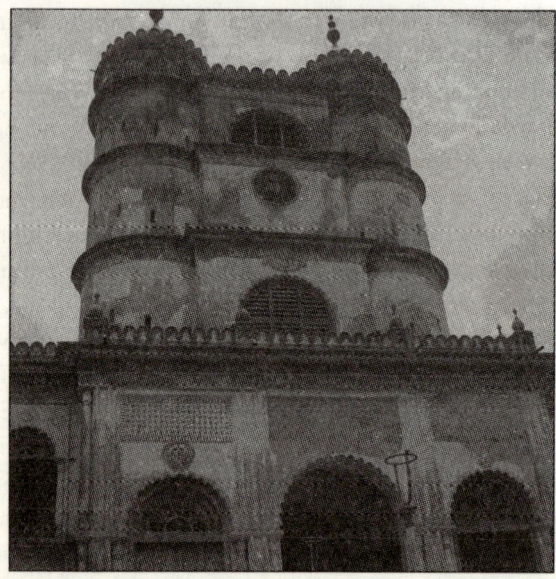

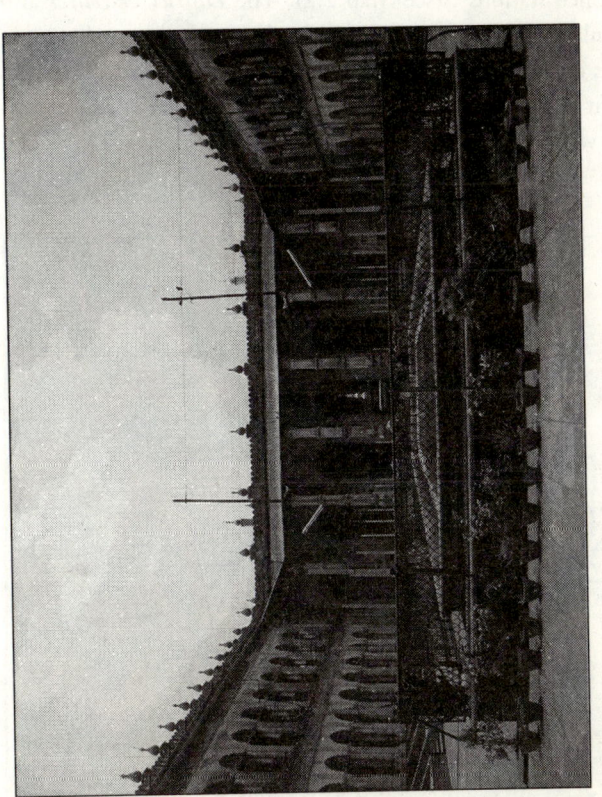

Source: Photographs taken by the author.

Note: Earlier draft of the interviews has been printed in Bagchi, Dasgupta and Ghosh (2009). The researcher would like to acknowledge her debt to Rajat Kumar Sur, Sayeed Islam Hussain and his family, Ifrikar Ali, (Manager of the Hooghly Imambarah), Haider Kareeb, Sayeed Talib Reza, Raju Mirza, Harpreet and all other staff of Imambarah. Without their help, this study would not have been possible. She wants to thank A.A. Shirazi, the Chairman, Imambarah Trust Board, Hooghly for allowing her to consult their strong room at Imambarah. The author is grateful to Ranabir Samaddar for his valuable comments.

before the full growth of Murshidabad.[19] Proportionately, affluent agricul-
turist, white-collar workers and educated persons were mostly Shias and not
Sunnis.[20] According to the *Hooghly District Gazetteer* the community had
the largest concentration in Chanditala police station, which was followed
by Pandua, Bhadreswar and Khanakul police stations. Chandannagar
and Uttarpara had the less percentage of the Muslim inhabitants in com-
pare to other police stations[21] (see Map 2.2). The *District Gazetteer* also
indicates that unlike elsewhere in India, the relations between these two
sects of Muslims in Hooghly were not marked by tension and conflict in
those days. But it is true that the Sunnis usually did not enter into matrimonial alliances with the Shias.[22]

Map 2.2 District Map of Hooghly

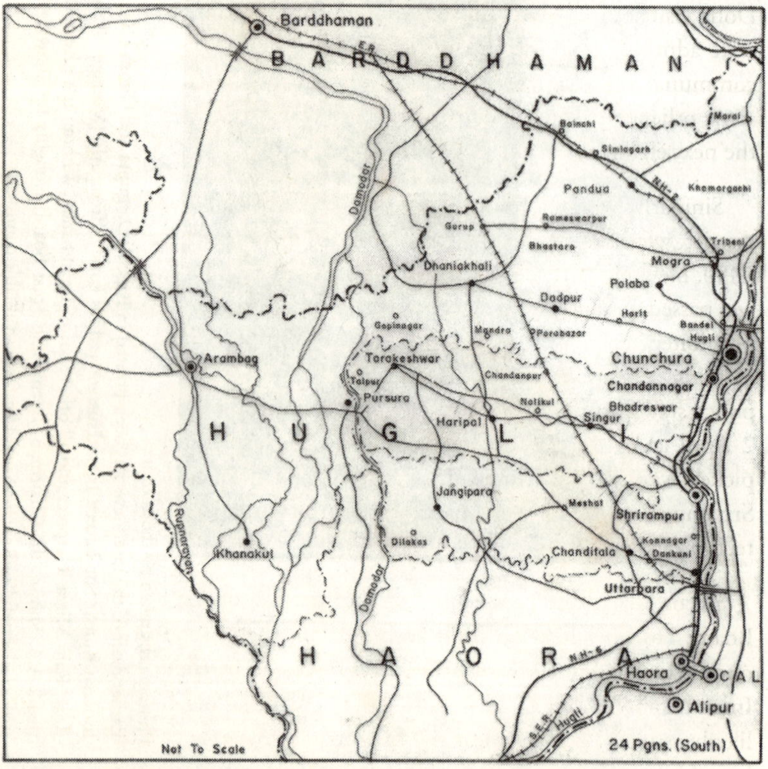

Source: Government of West Bengal (2009).

MAPPING THE VIOLENCE OF 1950

History reveals that, communal disturbances between Hindus and Muslims occurred in the area under Hooghly Municipality, Chandannagar, Srirampore, Tarakeswar subdivisions of Hooghly district from 27 February to the first week of March. According to the newspaper reports, in order to control communal violence the then district magistrate, S. Dutta Majumder imposed curfew on 27 February, which was lifted from the limits of Hooghly municipal area on 5 March. But an order under Section 144 Criminal Procedure Code (CrPC) became effective for another one week. Police patrol continued and kept monitoring the situation over all the strategic points.[23] The Pakistani Deputy High Commissioner in Calcutta (now Kolkata), accompanied by Deputy Inspector General of Police of East Bengal, *Janab* Doha visited Hooghly Imambarah, Imambarah hospital where the victims were admitted and also the 'disturbed areas', where 'certain incidents' of communal violence had occurred.[24] Immediately after their visit, due to some other unpleasant incidents the curfew was once again continued for the next eight days between 10 p.m. and 5 a.m.[25]

Similarly, Srirampore and Tarakeswar two other subdivisions of Hooghly district, were also affected by the communal disturbances of the first half of 1950. Newspaper reports identified that an order under Section 144 CrPC was passed in Tarakeswar, 36 miles away from Howrah on 29 March, which prohibited meetings, processions and assembly of more than five persons carrying of weapons, etc.[26] The curfew within the jurisdiction of Srirampore police station in Hooghly district continued from 8 p.m. to 4.30 a.m. till 2 April and in order to control the situation armed police and military pickets were posted at some important stations in the eastern railway in the Srirampore subdivision as a precautionary measure. In addition to the protection, police force provided in some trains as well.[27]

According to the proceedings of the meeting of the District Minority Board, Hooghly held on 25 February 1950, the general situation arising out of the communal disturbances was discussed by the then *Mutawali* of Imambarah, S.A. Jafri.[28] He reported that few minor incidents had occurred like bursting of crackers near the Imambarah. A peace committee consisting of influential Hindus and Muslims of the locality was formed and the situation was brought under control, but as it turned out, only temporarily.

He urged for the similar peace committee be formed in other *mohallas* of this town to restore peace and harmony within the district.[29] Again the proceedings of the District Minority Board's meeting held at the Commissioner's house on 25 May 1950 indicated that though no written complaint was received by the DM of Hooghly Abdul Wahid Sarkar, the MLA of Pandua subdivision mentioned some 'recent communal disturbances' and raised the question of rehabilitations of the displaced Muslims and issue of suitable grant to them. He also explained the urgency of giving them agricultural land and free seeds among the displaced Muslim cultivators to enable them to cultivate their land. He further narrated an incident where Muslims were 'roughly handled' and asked for police protection to save the minority community. In response, the DM mentioned that a concrete proposal had already been forwarded to the government for the sanction of suitable allotments of gratuitous grants as well as loans to be given to Muslim refugees.[30]

Hooghly was not the only place in West Bengal that was affected by the post-partition communal disturbances. Calcutta, Howrah and Murshidabad were largely affected by bitterly anti-Muslim climate of post-partition West Bengal. It is worth mentioning here that, partition dramatically changed the position and status of the Muslims of West Bengal. For a decade before 1947, Muslims had been the political masters of United Bengal, increasingly asserting themselves in the social and cultural life in even those places where Hindus outnumbered them.[31] However, the partition at a single stroke reduced the Muslim majority to be an 'exposed' and 'vulnerable minority'. After partition Muslim mass all over West Bengal lived in fear especially with occurrence of the sporadic violence which became regular feature in Calcutta, Howrah and other parts of the state. Joya Chatterji has pointed out that, the new 'Hindu mood of aggressiveness' soon spilled over to affect many Muslim public rituals, which caused communal tensions in the newly created West Bengal. Out of all examples that she has cited in her recent book *Spoils of Partition*, one is very interesting and has a similarity with the incident that took place in Hooghly in the early 1950s. She mentions a dispute that occurred in June 1949 at Kandi in Murshidabad between Hindus and Muslims. The Muslims were carrying a *tazia* (bier) in licensed procession and were refused passage by the Hindus, who did not allow them to prune a tree, sacred to them, one which prevented the *tazia* going past.

The Muslims had to back down, persuaded 'at a secret meeting' by one of their leaders that the 'authorities would redress their grievance in due course'. Chatterji further says that, every outbreak of violence and rioting, whether in Bengal or else where in India, was inevitably followed by the surrender by Muslims of more 'sacred space'.[32]

Unpleasant incidents happened near Imambarah in Hooghly during Holi in March 1950.[33] Growing animosity between Hindus and Muslims caused a sense of insecurity among the Muslims. In Saleha Begum's (73 years; staying at Sonatuly, near Imambarah) words:

There were rumours everywhere in Hooghly in those days. Everyone was interested to deposit his or her valuables at a safer place. We had a three-storied house. Apprehending an impending attack, all of us along with many of our neighbours went to the top floor of our house to seek shelter. We were gathering brickbats those days to defend ourselves. Then, one day, we saw Mooghaltuly on fire. The fire gutted almost all the houses in the locality!

As a result, the young boys in our locality started organizing night patrols. Rumour-mills were abuzz with the stories of gruesome atrocities perpetrated on women. We realized that it would not be safe for us to stay there for long. So, we decided to shift to Imambari (same as Imambara). It was already very crowded.

My father was a lawyer. He knew few people who were close to Imambari. They, in fact, helped us to get a shelter inside the Imambari. Like us, thousands of people from Tikiapara, Serampur and other places of Hooghly took shelter there. I remember that they (the majority community) had even planned to attack Imambari. But, our boys were cautions and ready with sticks near the main wooden gate of Imambari. So they could not enter into the premises of Imambari. Oh! Those days were so turbulent!

It was heard that, a train was coming from Naihati. They were trying to throw the Muslims into the river Ganga out of the train and after cutting them into pieces. They did not even show any mercy for the infants. They threw the children one by one into the river. However, those who managed to reach this side of the river were offered medical care and relief. People from Imambari provided them medicine and ice. My father and some of his associates helped the injured people. The worst victims were those who were pregnant and about to deliver. They were traumatized and were unable to move to any other place.

Our food was cooked together. We did not have much to eat. There were very few little options for us. We used to boil rice, pulses and some potatoes. The government supplied rice and pulses. There was no privacy for women. Our lives became full of uncertainty. This uncertainty increased as rumors spread.

I do not know why. Suddenly we heard that the riot could take place at any moment. The Hindus and Muslims both got frenzied and were at loggerheads with each other. But I can tell you that the trouble began at Tikiapara and then it spread to our locality. We had our own house. In our area, the Muslims were predominant. Hindus were few. We did not have a culture of modern education. Therefore, we studied at home. Some of my friends were Hindus as well. But when the riot broke out around Holi, they never avoided us. It was not expected even! My father-in-law stayed at Mahestola. A man was brutally killed with a sword. I do not remember his name anymore! It was so horrifying! I saw him lying in front of the Imambari in a pool of blood. I also witnessed tremendous violence in our locality. They killed a man and our boys rushed him to the hospital. We did not know that man.[34]

A sense of insecurity and alienation was also clear in the words of Nafisa Banu. Nafisa (nearly 80 years) has lived alone in Hooghly for more than 60 years. For the last 57 years she has lived in Imambarah itself. Her son and daughter stay in Karachi. She was born in Moradabad of Uttar Pradesh. She still recalls her village, Nougawa Saddat. Her father was a businessman. He used to lend money and he mostly conducted his business from home. They were five sisters and two brothers. She was the fourth child of her parents. Her brothers were all involved in the tea business. She claims that, her family had huge property in their village. She was wearing a *salwar-kameez* using her *dupatta* as a veil to cover her head. She seemed comfortable in Hindi though she could speak Bengali with an accent of a non-native speaker:

The condition was deteriorating everyday. They burnt a girl of our locality alive. A gardener who used to work there, a close friend of our family told us to leave that place as it had become very unsafe for us. Yeah! They beat, looted, plundered, killed and threw men into fire near Mughaltuly. But we were fortunate as we did not lose any relative in the riot.

My husband left our house with our children and my father-in-law. Finally, we came to the Imambari for our safety and security. My maternal uncle also came with us. We did not find any other option but to take refuge at the Imambari itself. Imambari was full of displaced people. Many refugees came to Imambari from Hazirnagar and Gorifa by a train from the other side of the river to escape the violence. They stayed in the Imambari for one and a half month. Syeed Jafri was the motowali at that time. The riot broke out during holi. As far as I remember it was in 1950.

More that two thousand people took shelter in the Imambari. We had to share our space with other families inside Imambari. Everyone became helpless after being uprooted. However, they were hoping to return to their houses once the riot would stop. Most of them could not carry anything with them. There was a tremendous chaos inside the Imambari. Many pregnant women gave birth to their children inside the Imambari. The women were the worst victims. I don't know why that bloody feud took place between the Muslims and Hindus ...[35]

According to Nafisa, Hindu displaced persons coming from East Bengal were the 'culprits'. 'They tried to capture vacant houses and plots of land. They also burnt many houses. Allah saved us! My father-in-law used to read Majlis[36] at Imambari. He was already too old. In spite of his age he helped so many people'. Like Nafisa two other respondents identified the Hindu refugees as the main perpetrator of the violence though they believed that the local Hindus were also responsible for the turbulence. Quoting Nilanjana Chatterjee, it can be said that East Bengali refugee settlement across West Bengal affected the minority Muslim community most adversely.[37] The East Bengalis' discourse of partition victimhood reflected their acute sense of insecurity with regard to life, livelihood and honour as a numerically and politically subordinate group in a Muslim-majority state, as much as it reflected entrenched anti-Muslim prejudice.

The major influx of Hindu displaced persons took place following the massacre in several districts of East Bengal, particularly in the villages called Kalshira in the Bagerhat subdivision of Khulna district on 20 December 1949 and in Nachole in Rajshahi district in January 1950. The violence spread to Dacca, Mymensingh, Barisal, Sylhet, Chittagong and Santhahar of East Bengal in February 1950.[38] In the massacre of February 1950, the epicentre of violence was mainly the *Namasudra*-inhabited areas, where most of the people were very poor and mostly agricultural labourers. According to the Census of India 1951, between 1946, the year before the Partition when a large-scale communal riots occurred, and February 1951, altogether 51,153 number of persons (males 26,844 and females 24,309) belonging to the minority communities in Pakistan moved on to the district of Hooghly as displaced persons. Almost all of them were from East Bengal districts like Dacca Barisal and Faridpur, although a very small number came from West Pakistan.[39] A large number of these displaced persons did not enrol themselves as 'refugees' of the Indian state. They began to resettle themselves by acquisition of land either through legal means or procedures or by occupying the vacant land owned by the government or by big land-owners. The government termed the areas of refugee settlement as 'private colonies' for the first case. But, in other cases, this process of 'collective take-over' was known as *jabar dakhal*. Particularly in the areas around Calcutta and suburb many East Bengali refugee settlements were established on land formerly inhabited by Muslim labourers and artisans who were replaced by the displaced Hindus.[40] In many places of Hooghly the incidents of captur-ing vacant space, be it vacant houses or vacant plots of land, also took place. Newspaper reports say that many peasants were arrested on charges of riot-ing, causing mischief by fire and assault in connection with their attempt to oust the refugees from plots of land belonging to their masters, which caused tensions between Hindus and Muslims as may have happened in this case in Hooghly.[41]

The narratives of our respondents clearly show a sense of 'disrespect' towards the Hindu refugees, who took shelter in Hooghly in and around partition. The way they have portrayed the Bengali Hindu displaced as the main 'culprit' for the turbulence signifies the experience of social recogni-tion which depends on a vital condition, as Axel Honneth points out, curial for the development of human identity and its denial, necessarily accom-panied by the 'sense of a threatening loss of personality'. It asserts a close connection between the kinds of violation of the normative assumption of social interaction and the moral experiences that the subjects have in their everyday communications.[42]

NEGOTIATING BORDERS: LEARNING TO SURVIVE

Due to partition a large section of Muslims left West Bengal and took shelter in East Pakistan. However, there is no accurate record of how many Muslims crossed the border from West Bengal to Eastern Pakistan. While dealing with this issue of the Muslim flight, Joya Chatterji in *Spoils of*

Partition: Bengal and India: 1947–67 has identified that, the 1951 Census of Pakistan recorded total 700,000 numbers of Muslim muhajirs in East Bengal, of whom two-thirds or 486,000 were known to be refugees from West Bengal.[43] She has further said that, imperfect records of these turbulent times leave the observers with only the roughest of ideas about who among the Muslims left, where they went and why.[44] It is true that now numbers can hardly reveal the pain, trauma and agony through which the displaced might have gone due to the ruptured economic, social and cultural ties with their original homeland; however, they are important to understand the scale and magnitude of the post-partition displacement in the Eastern part of the subcontinent.

Naheda, Saleha, Nafisa and many such Muslim women in West Bengal became refugees due to the riots accompanying the partition of 1947. They were displaced from their land, from their home where some of them could come back as 'returnees' and some could never return. They lost everything they had—home, friends, relatives and all their material belongings and had to start their lives afresh. Displacement changed their perspectives towards lives.

To them partition was an 'urban affair',[45] a distant reality until 1950. However, displacement from their own home due to communal violence converted these housewives of yesterday—the wife of a business man, a rickshaw puller or a service man respectively—into uprooted refugees leaving a deep impact on their whole psyche. They had to negotiate borders—borders of sect, community, patriarchy and of conflicts not only in their own land but also in an alien land away from their homeland.

According to Naheda:

We were at a loss. After spending some time at Imambarah, one day the Mutawali (the person in charge of the Imambarah), Jafri sahib came and enquired if we wished to go to Pakistan. In fact, that would be better for us according to him. He had already arranged a train for our journey. The train would leave at 4 in the afternoon and it would go up to Darshana, a point near India–Pakistan (now Bangladesh) border. My abbu immediately decided to go to Pakistan as he believed that it would be a safer place for us. And we were not alone. Many Muslims who took shelter in Imambarah were also willing to leave the place and go to Pakistan. So, we left our homeland and our possessions.

The train was too crowded. Everybody was jostling to find a place inside the train. Finally, we managed to get in. We went up to Darshana and from Darshana we went to Iswardi and took a steamer to move further to Dhaka.

Like Naheda, Saleha and Nafisa also spoke about the train, which was arranged by the then *Mutawali* of Hooghly Imambarah, *Janab* Jafri, to help these displaced people to cross the border to take refuge in the newly created East Pakistan. The narratives of the displaced women now living around Imambarah make it clear that an overarching sense of insecurity becomes part and parcel of the lives of these uprooted people in general and of the women in particular. Displacement due to communal tensions causes a sense of insecurity—for the woman, for her family members and for her community. Furthermore, they became worried about the effects of the uncertainty and dislocation on their children, about the psychological trauma that many of their children suffered from.

As a result, a large number of these displaced persons after coming back to Hooghly preferred to live in ghettoized clusters, mainly due to their perception that the threat to their life and property was greater when they were physically isolated from their community. Post-partition violence made them aware of their vulnerability in living with the 'enemies'. The violence of 1950 created a psychological barrier between these two communities at Hooghly. The violence left its vicious imprint on the human settlement of the *mufassal* town of Hooghly in such a way that the town that was not hitherto strictly polarized into Hindu and Muslim localities and where, in many instances, both communities lived side by side, has now become increasingly divided into 'majority' and 'minority' areas. So far as the Shias are concerned they have become 'minority among the minorities'.[46] Sixty years after the violence, today there are only eight Shia families living in the area under the jurisdiction of Chinsura Municipality of Hooghly[47] and most of these families live in the area, demarcated as waqf property, adjacent to Imambarah.

Those who left Hooghly with the expectation that they would be able to resettle themselves in East Pakistan became disillusioned very soon. Most of the displaced were Shi'ite. They were not welcomed in East Pakistan, which was predominantly Sunni inhabited. They had to negotiate the existing invisible border between these two sects of Islam, away from their original home. The situation became quite uneasy for them and soon they were again forced to leave their new-found home. They were displaced twice.

To quote Naheda:

At Dhaka, we stayed in a rented house located at Chawkbazar. But, we could not be happy at all. However, we were safe and secure in Pakistan. My abbu started pulling rickshaws and my brothers became daily labourers. But, we could not stay there beyond a couple of months. You may be surprised to hear that, but it is true. We could not adjust in the new, alien place. That was not ours. How could we stay there? The people of that place could not accept us whole-heartedly. They started thinking that we are Bihari Muslims. We did not have similarities with the Bengalis although we were Muslims. They never assured us enough to stay there. The Hindus from that side reaching here felt quite safe. But we could not feel the same way.

Within two months, we left Dhaka and returned to Hooghly, our own place. But, by that time, the Hindus had occupied our homes. We were not alone. Like us, many others lost their homes and possessions, and therefore, were forced to take shelter in the Imambarah again. My abbu went to the court to get an order to get back our house. At last, we came back to our own house from Imambarah. However, meanwhile we lost everything … Our entire household items, our furniture, everything. We had to start from the scratch.

Saleha told us that most of their relatives were staying in East Bengal at that time and they were the only ones living in West Bengal. Her father owned huge property. Hindus could not capture their house. Her elder brother protected it. She confessed that on the other hand, her in-laws were not so rich. But they were not poor either. Her father-in-law owned a house, where they stayed after her marriage. When they heard that a riot was imminent they sold their house and land at a much cheaper price. Some went to Rajshahi and others to Dhaka. Her husband Sayeed Baskuran Navi and she however initially decided to stay on at Hooghly at her parental home.

I asked her whether she ever thought of going to Pakistan at that stage or not. She replied:

It is not that, we did not consider going to Pakistan. When the riot was on the wane, Mutawali Saheb informed that all arrangements for our departure for East Pakistan had been finalized. We took that opportunity to leave our place. When the train crossed the river and reached Darshana, we saw thousands of people waiting for the vehicle to cross the border. All of them were struggling to board the connecting train. There was a huge chaos and confusion among the people. In Darshana, we were served with chira, muri, gur and dudh (milk) for children.

From Darshana we went to Rajshahi by a car. My brother-in-law was there. So we all went there. My husband, child and I stayed there for a while and then went to take refuge at my sister-in-law's place at Dhaka. We had to stay there for about a couple of months. Meanwhile, my elder brother informed us that the situation was under control in Hooghly. The turbulence had ended and all was well. My husband said that he could not get any job in Rajshahi as the place was alien to us. Besides, in Dhaka, people spoke a different dialect and had a culture of their own. We did not have much in common with them. We could not assimilate with them. So we decided to return to our own place. Thus, we came back home. However, there were not many people in the area. Everyone had left. It was true that our house was not occupied but we took all our possessions. Whenever I recall those days I feel very bad.

Our respondents left their home because of the riots of 1950. Before these riots, the female members of their families used to live in a private space of their respective houses, behind the veils. All on a sudden, the riot placed them on the streets, in the midst of the public space. When the country was partitioned and the riots broke out in Hooghly, males and females alike were on the streets. For their safety and security they had to take shelter at Imambarah with their family members, where they could not find any privacy. Moreover, when the patriarchs themselves were at risk, these women perceived themselves as insecure. Newer insecurities and uncertainties engulfed their lives when some of them got detached from the male members of their family. The self-proclaimed guardians were no more there to play the role of the protector. Patriarchal dominance became meaningless, at least for the time being, due to the forces unleashed by the partition (that was primarily an outcome of an almost all-male politics) and beyond the powers of the patriarchs. Therefore, when these women began to reconstruct their lives in an unknown territory on the other side of the border or after coming back to their known place in an unknown atmosphere, the boundaries between public and private space had already become blurred for them.[48]

In Nafisa Banu's words:

That riot forced us to learn how to survive in a post-violence situation. We did not decide to leave Imambarah as most of the shelter-seekers did. I never went to East Pakistan. We used to stay at Imambari. My husband stayed here for a couple of years. During the era of Mujib-ur-Rahman, they went to Chittagong. My children also left. But I did not go. My husband Sayad Gulam Haider, a businessman had a second wife. My husband and my children went to her. I did not want to lose my dignity. I decided to stay alone. When the bloody riot broke out during Mujib's time, probably in 1971, they went to Karachi. Earlier my husband worked here in Bhadreswar and later Baidyabati. Then he went to Chittagong to work in a British Company.

You know, when I came to Hooghly, I was only 11. When our father passed away, my mother did not have any other option and had to come to our maternal uncle's place in Hooghly. My uncle used to perform Majlis in the Imambari. I studied up to seventh or eighth standard (not in any formal school) and got married at a very young age to. When the riot broke out I was in Mirzabari—near the place of Haji Mohammad Mohsin.

When I asked her how she managed to survive alone she looked quite confident and smilingly said:

I learnt the way of performing Majlis from my uncle as well as from my father-in-law and used to practise it after the turbulence was over. I used to read in Mehfil-e-Haideri in Bowbazar on a regular basis and get ₹250 in return. In that way, I started earning and now I have a substantial amount of money in my bank account. I still do not accept any money from my son or daughter for my day-to-day survival. But, they paid for my travel to Mecca twice. I am happy. In fact, I don't want to be dependent upon anybody. So, I have already bought some land here close to Bara Imambari for my last rites.

Violence induced displacement indeed put thrust upon a fixed identity on these Muslim women as displaced. But that was not the end. The violence they encountered compelled them to negotiate with various new choices; their identities were forged through their macro-level struggles. The narratives of these women help us to realize how violence reshaped their identities and forced them to change their priorities in life; it required them to step out of their homes to earn their livelihood. In a way these are the stories of recreated space. Bodies, space, time are all inscribed and altered by violence. In the aftermath, occupying the same social space may not always be possible.[49]

In their afterlife, these doubly displaced Muslim women, as the trauma survivors, live with memories of the past and the reality of an uncertain present. This present seems to have no ending. From their perspective, it is very much real—the crude reality they cannot escape and a bitter past they cannot forget. Even their selective memories carry those bitter moments with an unbearable subtlety.

FORGOTTEN HISTORIES: PAST AS PRESENT

The narratives of these three protagonists in this chapter are basically collective memories, and are in the form of flashbacks, as envisioned by these women. This flashback relates to the idea of the past, which is remembered as reality. The existence of Imambarah acts as the only link between past and present. Moreover, their visualization of the past is a form of reconstruction. Narrative and construction bring about a similar kind of inscription, the one in the 'endurance of time', the other in the 'enduringness of materials'.[50] In fact, all memory is of past.[51] In that way, partition was of past if seen through homogeneous units of measurable time, its continued presence in people's lives (be it Hindu or Muslim) was apparent in story, gesture and conversation. Though of past, it did not have a feeling of pastness about it.[52]

According to Ranabir Samaddar, '[W]e live in Partitioned times. It is within our post-colonial being, in our agony, pessimism and our strivings …. Partition lives on in post-colonial times to such an extent that we should truly prefer the phrase "partitioned times" to the more common "post-colonial times"'.[53] With all these burdens of history, the doubly displaced Muslim women live in the 'partitioned times'. Partition lives on in the lives and times of these old women. Partition had made their homeland hostile and they started imagining that peace and security were on the other side of the border. Most of them got disillusioned crossing the border taking refuge in East Pakistan. The episodes and characters of their past remain present in their minds, mostly because they shape their identities.

In this process of remembrance, the role of Imambarah, as an institution, as a rescuer, has been revisited. Following Paul Ricoeur, we could say that, after all, we are both the readers and writers of the past; that words of the past form our narrative identity, in the sense that they tell us who we are. It is by telling and memorizing events of the past that we become and remain a historical community.[54] In this chapter we have attempted to unravel the stories of forgotten past, stories of Imambarah, the epitome of peace and security to the local Muslims of Hooghly.

This chapter is a humble attempt to listen to the 'minority of the minorities' in Hooghly keeping the fact in mind that, nowadays, speaking of the need to confront trauma has been considered central to the process of healing. Herman (1994) has argued that,

> to hold traumatic reality in consciousness requires a social context that affirms and protects the victim and that joins victim and the witness in a common alliance. For the individual victim, this social context is created by relationships with friends, lovers and family. For a larger society, the social context is created by political movements that give voice to the disempowered.[55]

The 1947 Partition of India changed the social context, which has been felt by the Muslims of Hooghly because of the violence in 1950. In this chapter the trajectory has been towards micro-histories, inflected by anthropology, sociology and theory, which have resurrected the ordinary, everyday Indian (here, Muslim women) in the picture and restore her to the past. Urvashi Butalia is right in a sense that the partition stories are personal, intensely subjective, constructed through memory, gender and ideas of self and span the subcontinent. In this chapter we have tried to unfold the stories of those Muslim women, who have come to symbolize the fate of women who saw it all—communal blaze, riots and massacres, displacement, migration to an alien land and then, finally, a return to the 'scarred roots'.

So do not even ask,
Do not ask what it is we are labouring with this time;
Dreamers remember their dreams when they are disturbed—
And you shall not escape
What we will
Of the broken piece of our lives

—Abena P.A. Busia[56]

NOTES

1. Chatterji (1999: 185–242).
2. Ibid.:185.

3. Cockburn (2004).

4. In this chapter by 'refugee' we mean a person who has been uprooted from his/her *desh*, and we shall not use the term 'refugee' as it appears in the UN Convention of 1951 or the subsequent UN Protocol of 1967. According to the 1951 UN Convention, a refugee is a person owing to a well-founded fear of being persecuted for reasons of race, religion, nationality, membership of a particular social group or political opinion, is outside the country of his nationality and is unable or, owing to such fear, is unwilling to avail himself of the protection of that country. For legal exposition of the status and rights of refugees see Hathaway (1991); Goodwin-Gill (1996) and Chimni (2002).

5. Exception is the recent publication entitled *The Trauma and the Triumph: Gender and Partition in Eastern India, Part 2* edited by Jasodhara Bagchi, Subhoranjan Dasgupta and Subhasri Ghosh, which has tried to incorporate much of the Muslim voices and experiences often taking place on the other side of the border that is erstwhile East Pakistan. At the same time they have tried to capture the voices of those who are still residing in West Bengal. See Bagchi, Dasgupta and Ghosh (2009).

6. Mushirul Hasan's book entitled *Legacy of a Divided Nation: India's Muslims since Independence*, Delhi, 1997 presents an overview of the consequences of partition for the Muslims who stayed in India. See also Kothinka Sinha-Kerkhoff's essay, 'Partition Memories, "minoritisation" and discourses of rootedness in Jharkhand: A comparison of cross-border displaced and "invisible refugees" in Jharkhand', in the paper presented at the Indo-Dutch conference on 'Displaced People in South Asia', Chennai, March 2001.

7. Samaddar (2000: 31) cited in Chaturvedi (2007: 153).

8. Foucault (2003: 7).

9. Naheda *bibi* was interviewed on 15 May 2007 in Imambazar, Hooghly.

10. De (2007: 6–7).

11. *200 Years of the Deed* (translation of the Deed of appropriation of Haji Mohummud Mohsin, dated 9th Bysakh BE, corresponding with 20 April AD 106, as cited in note 10, pp. 16–17.

12. Dey (1906: 258–81).

13. Bandyopadhyay (2007), as cited in note 10, pp. 14–15.

14. Earlier Hooghly was termed as Hugli/Hughli or Hughly. The district of Hooghly (lies between 22°36' and 23°14' north latitude, and between 87°30' and 88°30' east longitude) derived its name from the town of Hooghly situated on the west bank of Hooghly River about 40 km north of Kolkata. According to O'Malley the name Hooghly is probably derived from the *Hogla* (*Typha elephantine*), 'a tall reed which grows in abundance on the river banks and in the marshy lowlands below them'. This town was a river port in the 15th century. The first Europeans to reach this area were the Portuguese and the district of Hooghly was one of the main centres of their trading activities. In 1536 Portuguese traders obtained a permit from Sultan Mahmud Shah to trade in this area. In those days the Hooghly River was the main route for transportation and Hooghly served as an excellent trading port. Within a few decades the town of Hooghly turned into a major commercial centre and the largest port in Bengal. Later in 1579–80 a Portuguese captain Pedro Tavares founded a settlement of Hooghly, under the authority of a *farman* from

Emperor Akbar and thus Hooghly became the first European settlement in Bengal. The settlement grew rapidly and the trade and influence of the Portuguese in Bengal. The Portuguese hegemony in this region soon brought in its wake some political problems which triggered a conflict between them and the Mughals. As a result, Emperor Shah Jahan ordered the then ruler of Bengal province, Qasim Khan Juyini, to block the city of Hooghly. This eventually led to a war in which the Portuguese were defeated comprehensively and according to Jadunath Sarkar 'it was the first land battle in India in which indigenous troops and method of warfare triumphed over European troops and European leadership'. Other European powers that came to Hooghly were the Dutch, the Danish, the British, the French, the Belgians and the Germans. Dutch traders centered their activities in the town Chuchura which is just south to Hooghly. Chandannagar became the base of the French and the city remained under their control from 1816 to 1950. Similarly, the Danish established a settlement in Srirampore. All these towns are situated on the west bank of the Hooghly River and served as ports. But among these European countries, the British ultimately became most powerful. Initially the British were based in and around the city of Hooghly like other foreign traders but in 1690 Job Charnock decided to shift the British trading centre from Hooghly–Chinsura to Calcutta. The reason behind this decision was the strategically safe location of Calcutta and its proximity to the Bay of Bengal. As a result the centre of gravity of trade and commerce in the Bengal province shifted from the town of Hooghly to Calcutta and Hooghly subsequently lost its importance as Calcutta prospered. After the Battle of Buxar (1764) this region was brought under direct British rule until India's independence in 1947. After independence this district merged into the state of West Bengal. Though the city of Hooghly is more than 500 years old the district of Hooghly was formed after separation of the district from Burdwan in 1795 with the city of Hooghly as its headquarters. Later the headquarters shifted to the town of Chinsura. In 1843 the Howrah district was created from the southern portion of this district. And in 1872, the south-west portion of this district was merged into the Midnapur district. The district is bounded on the north by the district of Burdwan; on the east by the river Hooghly; on the south by Howrah; and on the west by the districts of Midnapore, Bankura and Burdwan. The river Hooghly separates the district from the Ranaghat subdivision of the Nadia district and the Barrackpore subdivision of the North 24-Parganas. For the brief history of Hooghly see O' Malley (1912); Banerjee (1972); Sudhir Kumar Mitra (1992); Kundu (2003); Mukherjee (2002) and Addha (2007).

15. Mitra (1956: 55).
16. Banerjee (1972: 221). In this context see O' Malley (1912).
17. It has been estimated that, by mid-20th century, Muslims were concentrated in two distinct regions of West Bengal. The first zone, more densely populated, was in the south, in the industrial and urban tracts around Calcutta, 24 Parganas, Howrah and Hooghly. The second belt where Muslims were at large numbers was in north Bengal, especially in the agricultural tracts in Murshidabad and beyond Malda, whereas in other parts of rural West Bengal like in Bankura, Midnapore and western Burdwan Muslims were 'few' and 'far between'. So far as Hooghly district is concerned, Urdu is by and large the mother tongue of Muslim immigrants from

Uttar Pradesh and Bihar. That should not, however, mean that all Muslims of northern India who have moved into the district invariably belong to the Urdu mother tongue group. On the contrary, many Muslim immigrants from rural areas of Bihar, where Muslim concentration is not very thick have returned with Hindi and/or Hindustani as their mother tongue. Although most of the native Muslims of the district as well as those who have migrated from elsewhere in West Bengal belong to the Bengali mother tongue group, there are certain Sayed families in the district who regard themselves as Urdu speakers. These are old families, the members of which hold considerable *aima* or rent-free agricultural lands and use the title *Ashraf* after their names. Their matrimonial relations are usually confined to identical families elsewhere in Bengal, or to Sayed families of North India. Their background prompts them to keep aloof from the common Muslim masses mostly belonging to the Sheikh community. Most of the Shia Muslims are from UP in Hooghly. Urdu speakers are mainly found in the industrial areas of the district. According to *Hooghly District Gazetteer* (1972) in Magra police station they constituted about 7.6 per cent whereas in Bhadreswar and Serampore police stations they accounted for 10 and 5 per cent of the respective populations. There were also some Urdu speakers in the rural *thanas* of Pandua and Jangipara.

18. Interview with Raju Mirza, Imambarah, 15 Januaray 2010.
19. Not only Shia teachers, but many Persian physicians and perfumers settled in hooghly, attracted by the large number of rich patrons in that town and in its neigh-bouring district, because the Arabic medical science was then in high favour all over the East. See Sarkar (1948: 469–70).
20. A. Banerjee, same as note 13.
21. Mitra (1956: 149) as in note 15.
22. Ibid.
23. *Anandabazar Patrika*, 5 March 1950, *Muffasiler Chithi* (letters from the countryside).
24. *The Statesman* (1950) . 'Curfew Reimposed in Chinsura', PTI report, *The Statesman,* 8 March.
25. *The Statesman* (1950). 'Curfew lifted in Chinsura', PTI report, *The Statesman,* 9 March.
26 . *The Statesman* (1950). 'Situation in Serampur area under control: Curfew and Sec. 144 to be in force till Sunday', UPI report, *The Statesman,* 31 March.
27. Ibid.
28. Sayed Ejaaz Hussain Jafri served his duties as *Mutawali* of Imambarah twice; 1936–38 and 1948–50.
29. Manager of Hooghly Imambarah (1949–50).
30. Ibid.
31. Joya Chatterji (1994: 213–19).
32. Chatterji (2007: 180).
33. Interview with Raju Mirza, whose family was victimized due to that incident and took shelter at Imambarah. He was interviewed on 15 January 2010.
34. The interview of Saleha Begum was taken on 16 July 2007.
35. Nafisa Banu was interviewed on 18 July 2007.
36. Majlis is the mourning session where heart-rending tales of Imam Hussain's martyrdom are narrated. A majlis or mourning ritual typically comprises a *salaam* (introductory poem), *marsiya, hadis* (sermon), and *nauha*. A notable aspect of

the mourning ritual is self beating or *ma'tam* done during the *nauhas* (elegies and lamentations) to visually express sorrow for the death of Imam Husain who was the grandson of the Prophet Muhammad. It ranges from a silent rhythmic touch to the chest in keeping with the chant of the nauha to flagellating oneself with steel chains and swords.

37. Nilanjana Chatterjee, 'Interrogating Victimhood: East Bengali Refugee Narratives of Communal Violence', cited in *http://www.pstc.brown.edu/chaterjee.pdf* (accessed on 12 January 2010).

38. *Jugantar*. 1950. 'Lauha Jabonikar Antarale Purbabonger Biponno Sankhaloghu Sampradae' (Beyond the Iron Curtain: The Vulnarable Minorities of East Bengal), PTI report, *Jugantar*, February 28 (in Bengali).

39. Amiya Kumar Banerjee, same as note 14.

40. See Bose (1968).

41. *The Statesman*, 23 March 1950.

42. Honneth (2007: 71–72).

43. *Census of Pakistan 1951*, Vol. III, East Bengal, Report and Tables, Karachi, n.d., cited in Chatterji (2007: 166).

44. Ibid.

45. Most of my respondents at Hooghly believe that partition of India was an urban affair, which did not have any direct impact on them before 1950. They are born and brought up at Hooghly. And in 1950 it was like a village without any proper communications. So what is going on in the cities took much time to reach their countryside. They first started realizing the impact of partition during the violence of 1950.

46. This is the view of Raju Mirza, who was interviewed at Imambarah on 22 January 2010. He said that most of the displaced Shias did not return to Hooghly. A large section of them went to West Pakistan.

47. Ibid.

48. Waber (2003: 64).

49. See Menon and Bhasin (1998).

50. Ricoeur (2006: 150).

51. Das (2006: 6).

52. Ibid.: 97.

53. Samaddar (2000).

54. Ricoeur, same as note 51.

55. Herman (1994).

56. Busia (1995).

Part 2

Jammu and Kashmir

Part 2

Jammu and Kashmir

3

Women's Voices: From Jammu and Kashmir

Anuradha Bhasin Jamwal and Suchismita

INTRODUCTION

It is now a well-accepted supposition that women are the major victims of warfare. One of the most obvious examples of specific victimhood of women in armed conflict is their vulnerability to sexual assault and rape. Rape and sexual abuse is nothing new in the history of warfare. Marauding armies have through different periods of history, around the globe, taken advantage of women in the course of military conquests. What is new is the role of media. Instant reporting from the field has resulted in rapid sensitization of public opinion, greatly reducing the time lapse between the perpetration of such tragedies and their responses to them.[1] However, in the case of borders, lack of access and no reportage make the consequent sensitization elusive. While stories of abuse by both men in uniform or government-sponsored armed renegades and militants have formed a dominant part of the human rights discourse in the last two decades of conflict in the interiors, there have been no voices from the borders. It is hardly unlikely that paramilitary forces that are now so deeply embedded in the interiors of Jammu and Kashmir and alleged to be involved in cases of physical abuse and torture would be so benevolent towards women in the borders, which have faced a history of repression, not just in the last 20 years but more than 60 years. In the last two decades, with huge presence of the security agencies, easy access of the militants and their supporters and guides have in their entry and exit through the Line of Control (LoC), the vulnerability of the villages, their people and essentially the women cannot be ruled out. The victimization started when the borders were carved out in 1947–48, when people living in fairly peaceful areas suddenly found themselves on the fringes of nowhere, close to places that had become simply lines drawn on a map for everybody else in South Asia. The brunt was borne not simply by women living on the borders; the prolonged trauma is also shared by women living away from the borders but affected in many ways by the sudden carving of new boundaries, dislocation and its multiple consequences.

The immediate impact of the partition has been aptly summed up by Ismat Chugtai[2]:

> The flood of communal violence came and went with all its evils, but it left a pile of living, dead and gasping corpses in its wake. It wasn't only that the country was split in two—bodies and minds were also divided. Moral beliefs were tossed aside and humanity was in shreds. Government officers and clerks along with their chairs, pens and inkpots, were distributed like the spoils of war. And whatever remained after this division was laid to waste by the benevolent hands of communal violence. Those whose bodies were whole had hearts that were splintered. Families were torn apart. One brother was allotted to Hindustan, the other to Pakistan; the mother was in Hindustan, his wife was in Pakistan. The bonds of human relationship were in tatters, and in the end many soul remained behind in Hindustan while their bodies started off for Pakistan.

The women of Jammu and Kashmir, particularly those in border areas, shared this tragic story with the women in much of the rest of the subcontinent.

The opening of traditional routes between two parts of the state and the commencement of Poonch–Rawalakote bus service has allowed many such women victims to come out with the first-hand narratives of such paradoxes and tribulations, which the invisible contours drawn by some, as per their whims, had brought in. The victims visit either side to connect the missing links of their horrifying past which keeps haunting their present too. Against this background the present study is an attempt to capture the voices of women, those who are living on the line of fire.

A VICTIM OF BORDER POLITICS

The story of Rabia alias Satya Devi[3] was one among those countless women who were direct victims of the 1947 carnage and subsequent border politics between two hostile neighbours. Last December, for the first time via Poonch–Rawalakote bus-service, she had come to Mendhar from Thakyala Badawa on the other side of border in Pakistan Administered Kashmir (PAK) along with her husband on a month-long visit to meet her family separated during the commotion of partition in 1947. Rabia or Satya had lost her way in the turbulence. She was just a 10-year-old then. There were around 200 Kumbas (families) of Brahmins in Thakyala Badawa village (presently part of PAK), 50 km from Mendhar. The turbulence had started and restlessness was there in their village too, as the word of carnage in the adjoining villages spread in Thakyala Badawa; feeling insecure, these Brahmin families too decided to migrate to the other side, to a safer place. Satya was part of the caravan, which was on the move. By a quirk of fate she got separated from the caravan being chased by the marauders. As she was moving on clueless, she was picked up by one old Muslim woman, who got her married to her son. She kept on wailing for months, but in vain. She got converted to Islam and got a new identity. Sixty years on, now she is Rabia Bi, a wife, a mother and even a grandmother.

For years Rabia did not have any contact with her family in Poonch on this side of the border. Through intelligence spies or other informers who often crossed the border, the family came to know that she was alive and was living with her new family on the other side of the border with a new identity. However, Rabia did not try to meet her family presuming that they would hate her, given her new identity. In the meantime, her parents had passed away. Through the untiring efforts of her family, she came to meet her surviving siblings (one brother and one sister) and the other members of the extended family living in Poonch. During the 1947 turbulence, Satya was not the only daughter who had been lost amongst these 200 families had lost. Her relatives in Poonch recount that 40 young girls had gone missing during that mayhem. Some Mahajan families too had lost their women (including young girls). There was no trace of the majority of them. Few others got converted to Islam, and had established their families there on the other side of the border. Now when they come exploring missing links, their dual identity bothers them:

> My name Satya reminds me of my identity which I lost over six decades ago in the corridors of the past in a swift turn of unfortunate events. Now I'm living with a dual identity. I didn't have any control over the turn of events, I was helpless. Do you hate me for that?

She left behind a question for her relatives who feel that they too had suffered an ignominious pain in her loss of identity, although during her visit with her family, her husband was treated as a revered brother-in-law by her brothers. Rabia Bi (Satya Devi) had remarked while leaving for Thakyal Brahmana in PAK:

> I'm caught by destiny in its mould. Now I've to spend the rest of my life with him (husband), and with my family there. Who knows better than us or our families that these contours have not been drawn on geographical territories but they so brutally pass through our lives…

Around 80 Dutta families, which could not migrate to safer places during turbulence, got converted to Islam and they still live in the areas of Keni, Mirpur and Kotli on the other side of the border. Amidst them still resonate the stories of the likes of Rabia Bi, as they do among others this side of the border too.

Victimization did not stop at the first generation of partition. Generations have paid a price for the geographical follies and historical blunders of those times. The brunt has been borne not by the decision-makers who stamped and endorsed those cartographic boundaries as final or disputed but by the people divided by those boundaries and those who continue to live on the edges of these boundaries on either side of the LoC and the International Boundary (deemed Working Boundary by government of Pakistan). Large-scale migrations were triggered by communal violence in the wake of the partition of the subcontinent in August 1947 or shortly thereafter by the Kabali attack in October 1947 and its counter offensive by the Indian armed forces, leading to more communal violence, killings, loot, plunder and rapes. Thousands were killed on both sides of Jammu and Kashmir and millions were rendered homeless though there are no exact figures. Even after over six decades, the wounds are still fresh as the damage caused was extensive and irreparable. Reverberations of the partition of 1947–48 are still felt with varying degrees of intensity. Many like Rabia Bi are living with dual identity although not out of choice, as the same was thrust upon them by the whims of some and a quirk of fate. For others it was quite difficult to retrieve 'individuality' following rapes and conversions during mayhem, and thus they got lost forever leaving behind the scarred memories. Many among them recall those moments as 'ignominious'.

What happened over 60 years ago transitioned into an obsession with national security and shaped the policy decisions of the two countries India and Pakistan—who deem themselves as stakeholders of two divided parts of Jammu and Kashmir on two sides of the borders. The policies of the governments in India and Pakistan to turn boundaries into zones of hostility have shaped the destinies of the people on both the sides. Some of course are more affected by the conflict and excessive militarization of the borders than the rest. The weak and the powerless are more vulnerable to victimhood—the socially and economically weak or the women naturally bearing the greater brunt, demonstrating the hierarchy of victimhood stemming from social, economic and gender factors. But the voices have been unheard because both the historical and political perspectives are always nationalist, centrist and masculine. Nothing elucidates this better than the case history of one woman from Pak-occupied-Kashmir, Shehnaz and her daughter Mubeen. This mother and daughter epitomize the plight of women living on and along borders in the state. Their case has become a reference point to delineate the susceptibilities of marginalized lot of women in the trouble-torn state.

In October 1995, Shehnaz, an inhabitant of Pak-occupied-Kashmir harassed by her husband and her in-laws attempted suicide by jumping into a river Raya Pandori.[4] However, her destiny had something else in store for her. She was swept to the Indian side by the water currents and there she was picked up by the security forces in Laam sector of Poonch–Rajouri. Shehnaz stayed in the army hospital for three days. Then she was taken for interrogation as forces were apprehensive that she could be a Pakistani spy. After sustained interrogation, she was handed over to the police in Poonch who registered a case under Section 2/3 Ingress and Internal Movement (Control) Ordinance. She was sent to judicial custody for trial and eventually sentenced to 15 months in prison for entering the country illegally. She was convicted on 15 November 1995 to undergo one-year imprisonment with a fine of ₹ 500. In default, she was asked to further undergo a sentence of three months and was lodged in District Jail Poonch.

During her detention, she was raped by the jail warden of the District Jail Poonch, Mohammed Din. Although her jail mates and some of the authorities suggested to her to go for an abortion, yet she decided against it. An investigation was launched by the then Additional Director General of Prisons Veerana Aivalli who held the inquiry and a case got registered against the jail warden for raping the woman. Meanwhile, Shehnaz gave birth to her baby girl in Nari Niketan, Jammu on 6 October 1996 and then was sent back to jail. After she completed her jail term, she was shifted to a Nari Niketan on 8 January 1997. She remained there till 8 August 2000, when authorities shifted her once again to Jammu's Central Jail. Though she was sentenced for one year, yet she remained in the jail for seven years and was released on the intervention of a lawyer A.K. Sawhney, who filed a Public Interest Litigation (PIL) for securing release of Shehnaz and her daughter (conceived during detention) in the state high court. Except for 15 months in Jammu jails, rest of her detention period was totally illegal.

Later Border Security Force (BSF) tried once to send Shehnaz to Pakistan. She was actually driven to Wagha but the Pakistani Rangers refused to take her daughter saying her daughter was an Indian citizen. Ironically, as she was not accepted by Pakistan along with her Indian-born daughter, the then Director Inspector General (DIG) Jammu wrote to SHO R.S. Pura to arrest her under Public Safety Act, in contradiction to its previous charges. She was again arrested and kept in jail. Interestingly, she had no contact with her family on the other side of the LoC. They used to send her letters initially, but all communications stopped as time passed. After a long legal and diplomatic battle by lawyers and human rights groups, particularly Pakistan Human Rights Commission and Aurat Foundation, she was granted permission to return to Pakistan along with her 'Indian daughter' in 2006. Yet that was not the happy ending to her tale of trials and tribulations. In fact, back in her home town, she had to live through yet another vicious cycle of physical and psychological agony. Stigmatized as a rape victim, like any other woman in similar circumstances in the sub-continent, she along with her 'Indian daughter' was not accepted by her husband, and his family. Her brothers supported her for her basic needs yet emotional support that was so imperative during this crucial phase of her life remained elusive. She was traumatized, both by her destiny as well as by her society where she lived; her society, where women are just a thing of desire or commodity, whose value remains restricted to her body and sexuality. She could not bear the pains anymore.

Just two years after she moved to the other side of the border (her hometown) after undergoing unimaginable suffering, she went into mental trauma and finally met a tragic end. Shehnaz belonged to the second or third generation of partition but her case is instructive of the vulnerability of women and their bodies, decades after the turbulence of 1947–48. For the majority population in India and Pakistan, the traumatic memories of partition have become historical narratives but in Jammu and Kashmir because of the disputed nature of its borders, these memories are a festering sore, which continues to bleed and make people suffer.

LIVING ON THE LINE OF CONTROL

However, the people living on the fringes have different stories altogether. Their only choice is of accepting violence and its repercussions as their fate. The worst is the plight of the border people in Jammu and Kashmir, especially those living right on the LoC. On both sides of the dividing line, people in these border areas have borne the brunt of the hostility between the armies of India and Pakistan, during wars and so-called peace times. These border areas are too heavily militarized for any semblance of normalcy and normal life. The levels of violence are not always visible, often not reported but felt psychologically, due to the build-up of troops, excessive restrictions, fenced and mined areas. The huge military presence imposes restrictions on their movement, often ends up in harassment and keeps the civilian administration away, forbidding any development to penetrate. Besides, it has encouraged a cycle of repression and also a massive number of displacements—prolonged, partial or frequent. Greater onslaughts were witnessed in 1965, 1971 and after the insurgency in 1989. Stories of killings, torture and torched villages from that period are embedded in the collective memory and psyche of the people still living on the borders. The unnatural line demarcates boundaries between India and Pakistan, especially the bloody LoC cuts through mountains, often slicing a village into two halves with people living side by side, sharing the same address in terms of the name of village but different nationalities; many families divided by a cruel twist of politics and strategic concerns. In the last two decades of militancy there have been greater incidences of hostilities along the borders. It is no longer just the gun of the soldiers on the two sides; it is also militants, counter insurgents, surrendered militants and a confusing network of their informers and agents to deal with. Thousands of people have migrated, either to the interiors or crossed the borders to the Pakistani side, many of them put up in camps set up by the Pakistani government in and around Muzaffarabad.

Identities are never simple or static; they are always multilayered. But what makes the case of the border people unique is the fragility of their national identity, which can be so easily questioned and snatched—either briefly or permanently. The women, mostly marred by illiteracy and denial of basic facilities including health care, are the worst sufferers. The shifting of the Turtuk area in 1971, in the foothills of Siachen Glacier, from the Pakistani side to the Indian side, along with its people is demonstrative of the helplessness of the entire lot. Overnight from Pakistani citizens they became Indian citizens, which they continue to be till date, but exaggerated stereotypes of 'patriotism' are often endorsed to question their loyalty. Birhuti, a village in Mendhar along the LoC, was occupied by Pakistani forces during the 1965 war. The Pakistani army withdrew after a year but the Indian forces abandoned the area for some years, and so did whatever little the local administration exists in these border areas. People had nowhere to go—no health care facilities to rely on, no schools and no government offices to turn to for any work.[5] Even today, many such areas live in the perpetual syndrome of being dislocated from their own homes, robbed off their nationality living in the no-man's-land.

KARGIL WAR AND OPERATION PARAKARAM

New technologies bring newer forms of displacement in the border areas. When Kargil War began in 1999, people in thousands were uprooted from the borders of Kargil, forced to a life of deprivation in the cold desert. The intensified war also accentuated the hostilities all along the LoC and the international borders and people throughout the border areas were forced to flee. Prominent is the case of the migrants from Palanwalla, in Akhnoor sector, some of whom are still putting up in two camps near Akhnoor, seven years hence. The biggest reason for this displacement is the large-scale mine-laying operation.

The large-scale displacement came with the near-warlike situation when Indian and Pakistani troops were mobilized all along the borders during Operation Parakaram. It left over a lakh people homeless, several thousands of them for as long as two years, on the Indian side alone. This operation was also marked by the largest ever mine-laying operation both by Indian and Pakistan armies who turned vast tracts of civilian land into perpetual minefields. Despite the claims, which are misleading, the minefields still continue to play havoc with people's lives and in Akhnoor sector, where some villagers (a thousand families) have refused to go back to their homes because the army had no plans of demining the fields, until February 2010. The administration has no plans of adequately rehabilitating these villagers or compensating them for the loss. Though the mine clearance process has begun, the villagers are still sceptical, 11 years on. They are apprehensive because in the areas that are claimed to be cleared by the army, 13 per cent landmines are still unaccounted for. Besides, they also fear massive restrictions by the army on their movement.

The proportion of those rendered handicapped by landmines is very high in the borders of Poonch; the women who take the cattle and sheep for grazing, are often at a greater risk. In Kerni alone, 35 people are maimed by landmines. Half of these are women. An unknown number of cattle have also perished due to landmines. In villages along the LoC, the Mendhar sector of Poonch district, the locals maintain that 10 per cent people have been maimed by landmines. No authentic documentation is available. There is high incidence of cattle casualties due to landmine blasts at both the IB and the LoC, but these cases go unreported and the owners get no monetary compensation for the death or injury of the cattle. A meagre compensation of ₹75,000 for deaths are allotted but that too is rare. India uses light weight plastic MM16 landmines which are targeted to blow off the limbs of the victims. For injuries, the government pays between ₹5,000–₹10,000. Besides, the Locomotive Disability Act, which can ensure jobs for the physically challenged, is not applicable to Jammu and Kashmir.

BORDER FENCING AND DISPLACEMENT

Fencing at the borders is justified by the army, quoting strategic reasons, but it seriously impacts the life of the people at the borders, especially women. With constant checking and also frisking, women are discouraged from their usual traditional jobs in their fields that are fenced out. Significantly, fencing usurps agricultural lands of the people and deprives them of their livelihood. Besides, fence imposes several restrictions. While 45 villages in the two twin districts of Rajouri and Poonch of Jammu and Kashmir were fenced out totally in 2004, the exact number of villages for which cluster colonies have come up, marking the finality of partial dislocation, is not known. The idea was first mooted after the Kargil War, when India began re-planning its strategies in civilian areas and decided to shift the villages on the fringes more to the interiors. The plan could not be wholly exercised probably in view of the lack of available land. So on an experimental basis, 14 villages were first selected for the construction of cluster colonies. (In Mendhar alone there are 10 cluster colonies.) Kerni and Birhuti in Balakote (an area of 10 border villages) are two such villages. In both these villages situated on the LoC, cluster colonies have been created 4–6 km away from the original homes and fields. Most villages in this area are sprawled across the hills and the fields are adjacent to each home, making the nearest neighbour a good kilometre or so away. It has become a nightmare for the villagers, who are expected to vacate their village before dusk and shift to the cluster colonies. Every morning they return to their homes and fields, work there and children go to schools but at night no one is allowed to stay back, thus dislocating them. Instead, they have been pushed to congested rooms in the cluster colonies. This also means a daily trek of 4–6 km for everyone, including children, aged and the infirm. It also causes economic constraints because as they say, they are unable to look after their fields at night when wild animals destroy their crop or devour their cattle. Barring Kerni, in the villages where cluster colonies have come up, the people are not expected to shuttle to and fro since summer of 2009. They have been sent back to their original village homes. But the cluster colonies still exist and the fears of being dislocated again persist as well. The idea behind setting up cluster colonies is not really known. It was deemed strategically important for the Indian defence forces, who offer no rationale behind the scheme. But it was done with the coordination of the civil administration which has located the alternate space for cluster colonies close to the villages and released money for the construction of the same.

Though army occupation, in its literal sense, cannot be defined as the direct reason for displacement, yet in the wake of armed conflicts, it is the rule of the army which prevails over civilians lives on all terms. The idea of setting up cluster colonies too was mooted by defence authorities to 'rehabilitate' the villagers away from their houses. But the villagers believe that their villages have been fenced out because the army or more specifically India does not trust them. Such beliefs are based on their personal experience of multiple displacements, over several decades. Maximum families in both Kerni and Birhuti like elsewhere in the border areas have suffered multiple displacements, i.e., in 1947, 1965, 1971 and now in 2002. Their experiences have made them believe that their religion and their proximity with the people across the border, who are their blood relations, make them 'untrustworthy' in the eyes of army.

Displacement has changed two major things for the women. The first has to do with the changing economic status, bringing in poverty and deprivation among the set of people who had previously grown enough food on their farms to meet their needs. The second change has to do with taking over the role of managing livelihood for the family while their male counterparts have slipped into acute frustration, depression and alcoholism.

Salfo Devi is a woman in her 40s at the Naiwalla camp for the border displaced living in Akhnoor. Her day begins with the hope that her husband would get some work for the day and would be able to earn something for the family. With no assured means of livelihood available to him after their fields were mined and fenced out; he goes to Akhnoor town daily, yet does not find a job everyday. Even if he gets work for the day, it's not assured that the family would get something out of his income and thus something to eat. As Salfo Devi, the mother of two, explains:

> Throughout the day, our family, me and my children, would wait for him to bring some money or food. Yet, everyday we're not lucky enough to get food. On some days he comes drunk, devouring the day's earning on liquor, we go to sleep hungry. Back in our village, there was no dearth of food, hence no question of sleeping hungry. Before the problem cropped up between India and Pakistan, following Kargil and the subsequent fencing and mining of our fields, we had enough for our needs. Life in our villages is different. In case we didn't have milk or vegetables, we could always borrow the same from our neighbours. But that's not possible here. In the camps we get everything against money. The same is true about our neighbours. Here, even wheat, rice, vegetables we have to buy at exorbitant rates, while back in the village they were available in the house itself. [6]

Her neighbour Bimla, 35, too joins her voice in narrating similar tales of woes, yet with a different perspective. Since the tents provided by the administration had literally been in tatters, most of the camp migrants constructed *kachcha* houses in the past two to three years. Her three children go to government school functioning in the camp only. The grouse of these border women presently living in the camps mainly pertains to despicable apathy of the helmsmen towards their genuine grievances:

> For them we don't exist at all. We need basic amenities; we too need to protest against our MLA. Since none is taking any initiative, not even our men, I'm exhorting the women to join together to protest outside the Tehsil office or we should also block the bridge. This is simply unbearable. There we did not have worries about the food … we would get everything … hunger was simply unknown to us … we had two buffaloes.[7]

—Bimla had much to share.

VULNERABILITY PERSISTS

For the middle-aged lot, the economic concerns overshadow even the security concerns as the recurrent migrations, persistent living in inhumane conditions under the constant glare of strangers with no space for privacy and highly militarized borders have made them reconcile with the vulnerability factor, especially sexual threats.

In fact, it is the lot of young women and girls, who are the most susceptible group as far as physical security is concerned. Although other concerns inherent in conflict situation too are very much present, like fear of sexual assault, the most common form of violence being perpetrated against the women, looms large in all situations. Ironically, they feel threatened sexually not just by the security forces and militants, but anyone and everyone (this may include even their near and dear ones, who use the body of the woman to vent out their frustration on any account). The magnitude of the vulnerability factor however varies in the border areas from the plains and the inaccessible hilly areas, depending upon the size of the population, proximity to the security forces and their religion. As in the case of border areas of Jammu, Samba and Kathua where the majority population is Hindu, the border belts are densely populated and it is presumed that the militants do not enjoy much support system among the locals, the women feel less threatened sexually. However the vulnerability factor does not diminish totally.

In the border districts of Rajouri and Poonch, women living along LoC are the most threatened lot and in their case the threat comes from both the security forces as well as from the militants. Their religious propensity and umbilical ties with the people from other sides of the border make them more susceptible. Another reason behind the higher threat perception is the topography of the scarcely populated hilly and inaccessible areas, where civil administration is almost non-existent for all practical purposes. No wonder the popular refrain in the hilly, inaccessible and militancy infested border areas of Rajouri and Poonch districts is that the militants enter the houses of civilians for two reasons—women and food. Parallel drawn between the women and food in this account, though odious, is self-explanatory. And when the militants enter a house, the security forces have a pretext to gain entry into any house, anytime and the women bear the brunt yet again.

Both security forces and militants generally use the border people as 'human shields' or 'cannon fodder'. Privacy which is so innate to the existence of women has literally become an alien expression. And this is mainly visible in the border districts of Rajouri, Poonch, Samba, Kathua, Jammu, Uri and Kupwara. Irony lies in the fact that the security personnel, who are on the border to protect the people from external aggression and intruders become a cause of internal aggression by intruding on the lives of the border people and disregarding their privacy. Violence, excesses from both security forces as well as militants, give rise to instinctive frustration among the menfolk which finds its outlet in the form of sexual violence against women. The bodies of women bear the scars of 'sexual aggression' within the family and outside, from the 'intruders' as well as the 'protectors'. No wonder the cases of incest and rapes have seen a spurt following intensified militarization of the borders in the past two decades. Paradoxically, given the border politics between India and Pakistan, majority cases of this sexual violence against border women go unreported.

Charu WaliKhanna[8] reasons that victimhood originates from the manner in which woman is defined in the masculine discourse. The term 'woman' she argues has often been dominated by intent, a meaning, a thought; in other words, by the laws of a language constructed by man. She quotes Simon de Beauvoir (*Second Sex*):

Humanity is a male and man defines woman not in herself but as relative to him, she is not regarded as an autonomous being. And she is simply what man decrees, thus she is called the 'sex' by which is meant she appears essentially to a male as a sexual being. For him she is sex-absolute sex, no less. She is defined and differentiated with reference to man and not he with reference to her, she is incidental, the inessential as opposed to the essential. He is subject, he is Absolute—She is the other.[9]

According to WaliKhanna, who endorses de Beauvoir's notion of genesis of patterned victimhood, 'perpetuation of this theory of woman as a "sexual being" makes women often strategic targets in conflict. Gender based violence during conflict is argued to be evidence of the way in which militarism and misogyny are intertwined'.

It is perhaps the same notion that inspires the abject denial of such victimhood. In Surankote tehsil in the border district of Poonch, during the mid-1990s and early 2000s, there was a massive scale of partial displacements of people from their villages. Surankote is not bang on the border, but its proximity to the borders makes the place more vulnerable. Even people living right on the fringes of the borders endorse this view:

> There is just too much surveillance of the army in our villages and difficult for the militants to either find a safe shelter or support here. They simply cross over and do not waste their time in making good their escape. They will move to villages close by where military presence is far less.

Surankote, encircled between the border villages of two border districts of Rajouri, Poonch as also parts of Kashmir Valley, thus became an ideal haven for militants during the peak years of militancy. The security forces too responded with greater militarization of these areas and increasing role of informers, many of them women. The area witnessed maximum number of renegades operating in the area. From the mid-1990s to 2002, it was extremely difficult to get anyone in Surankote to say anything in a public place. There was always the fear of being overheard. A vast majority of those co-opted as informers by both the militants and the army were women, who could be least suspected. The incidence of forced marriages has also been very high. In the summer of 2001, when army busted a hideout in Hadi Marore of Surankote area and killed the militants in an encounter, they found two women in the hideout, one pregnant with a child.[10] The women had been forcibly married to the militants. The women were first taken into custody and later let off. It is not known what happened to them later.

One year after the much publicized Hill Kaka Operation of May 2003, in which locals had enthusiastically participated as part of the counter-insurgency network, nine persons of a family including women and children were killed by militants. The incident was preceded by kidnapping of women folk from families of militants of the neighbouring village by the village defence committee members who had been part of the Hill Kaka operation. The move was defended by the Village Defence Committee (VDC) members as a defensive one, the women used as shields to protect their own men. But finally when they let the women go, the militants retaliated by killing the women and children of the VDC members.[11] Interestingly, both the Hill Kaka Operation and the incidents later in the area reflect a sharp ethnic polarization which has become the general pattern in the border districts of Rajouri and Poonch. The Hill Kaka also became the first area where massive militarization of women as members of village defence committee began.

Many men we met over a period of years maintained that the threat of either the security men and their renegades or the militants had forced them to go into hiding. Surankote tehsil, a militancy infested district of Poonch, is little away from the border and hence used to be considered as a safe hiding zone for militants. Obviously the area had heavy presence of security personnel too. The menfolk would leave the houses during night hours, or for prolonged periods, sometimes months, for safer zones due to fear of militants and security personnel who could swoop upon them anytime by making forcible entry in the houses (former for the purpose of hiding, while latter in the name of raids). Strangely, while all male members of all age groups would move out of the house, the women would be left behind in the houses. This used to be a common practice during the peak of militancy in the district. And they would validate their absurd and outrageous move with an eccentric rationale: Males are threatened, women do not have any threat hence they can stay behind. Rationale has its understandable connotation of menfolk using women's sexuality as a 'shield' and they have comfortably positioned themselves against these uncomfortable moves.

When one meets the women, one encounters absolute silence, either due to lack of ability to articulate or due to the shame and the attendant stigma.

But doctors working in Surankote maintained that there was an abnormally high incidence of medically terminated pregnancies, majority of them were cases from the far flung areas.

THE DISPLACED AND DISPOSABLE

Akhtar Jan, a mother of three in her early twenties, is a fast-weathering youth face of the population of Internally Displaced Persons (IDPs) of a fenced out village Kerni (Poonch). Carrying a few-months-old baby in her ragged shawl and tugging along yet another one and a half-year-old baby girl vacillates like a pendulum between her 'real home' and one-room tenement allotted in the scattered cluster colony constructed at a distance of 4–6 km amidst the treacherous terrains. Life lost its very meaning, when all of a sudden Akhtar Jan and other villagers were asked to leave their homes and hearths behind in Kerni following the government decision to fence out their village almost four years back to check, what the government claims as 'infiltration', which resulted in skirmishes between the hostile nations. At the break of dawn, carrying the children, after undergoing a thorough frisking, they make a move towards their houses in the village across the fence to tend to their cattle and fields, the only means of their livelihood there. After covering treacherous terrains in an hour or two, they reach their fenced out village, spend there just 3–4 hours and then start a backward journey to the cluster colony within the stipulated period. Hurriedly, as they start in the morning, sometimes they even leave their toddlers behind in the 'cluster houses' to their fate because carrying children makes their pace slow, which they certainly cannot afford. Accidental falls from the perilous heights have so far generally proved to be death-defying for children, with grave injuries in some cases and minor injuries in most of the cases.

Even among this 'invisible' population, the rules for women remain the same. The priorities are well defined; tending to their fields and cattle tops the priority list rather than attending to their own young ones. On their return journey to cluster colony, the delay, even for a few minutes, can be a cause of embarrassment and sometimes severe harassment. Although, they refrain from explaining the 'kind' and 'source' of harassment, it was not difficult to pick a clue. Another rule for the population—by the evening, no one should be there in the houses in the village. Elders, ailing, children, crippled, there is no consideration or exception made for anyone. This can be a horrid account of 'lifeless' life being lived in the near total absence of basic amenities. For this invisible population of IDPs, it would be an utter luxury if one day water, power, roads were made accessible to them.

Akhtar Jan's immediate middle-aged neighbour, Fatim Bi, 50 years old, narrates yet another tale of inexplicable torment that often afflicts the lives of particularly middle-aged women in this 'obscure community' of IDPs. Her affliction seems to be an extension of Akhtar Jan's 'unspoken distress'. Her husband breathed his last in his 'house' in the cluster colony. Even when he was gasping in the end, his indecipherable mumbling that he wanted to die in his ancestral house, was adding to the wretchedness of Fatim Bi. Fatima Bi recalled amidst her uncontrollable sobs:

> Since he was bed-ridden, he could not go to his house in the village. Before that, he trekked the treacherous distance to his 'root' with the help of his sons. As he knew, his end was imminent, he wished to stay there. But the army authorities did not allow him. He had to be brought back to the cluster colony in the evening before the expiry of deadline. As his situation worsened, the army directions restricted him to his one room shed.

Her husband's treatment cost ₹ 50,000. To meet the expenses, she borrowed ₹ 40,000 from different sources. Now, she had no monetary help available for even Darood Fateha, a ritual prayer, performed on the fourth or fifteenth or fortieth day of the death for the peace of the departed soul. Since she was busy performing the last rites of her husband, it fell on her adolescent girl to take care of the fields and cattle down the hill, all alone. For Fatima, the 'security' of her teenaged daughter was not her immediate concern. Her widowhood was not something to brood over. She cried her eyes out remembering her late husband, but the pressing needs before her did not allow her to take the weight off her feet. Her three sons are married and have families to support. So she could not depend on them.

Her elder daughter Shamim Akhtar, 30, is married and is passing through a different kind of distressing phase. Her husband cannot work since he has had his hernia operated. She has a small piece of land and miniscule livestock but her earnings are negligible as she had to manage on all fronts single-handedly with her three minor children, aged between 8 months to 3 years. So far Shamim, along with her family, has been living with her father-in-law in the cluster colony. As her family was not accorded any compensation because her husband's name was not included in the list framed in 1991 on the basis of which the amount for construction of houses in the cluster colony was distributed. Now her father-in-law heckles her to leave the house along with her family. To some extent her father-in-law too is justified on this account, because he is already sharing the little space available in one room dwelling in the cluster colony with his younger son and his family. Fatim Bi and Shamim, the distressed mother and daughter duo, both confronted with their own set of problems at this hour, cannot rally round each other.

If Akhtar and Fatim represent youth and middle-age groups respectively, 80-year-old Lal Begum of Birhuti (Balakote) is passing through the twilight phase of her life. Lal Begum maintains that life had never been different for her and other people of the village since 1965. Her assertion was actually a statement on the history of repression being perpetrated by the forces on two sides and particularly Indian forces on these villagers. Though she refrains from making any statement against the army, particularly in present context as do the other women surrounding her, yet her just one comment conveys what remains unspoken:

> We were unwanted even that time. Engaged in the security of land, the forces, on both the parts, would want us to move to other side because we, as the people, hold no meaning for either of them. Situation has not changed much. See, perhaps we have never been trusted by the forces of land we belong to. They think we help or harbour the militants. In 1965, we had been asked to leave our villages by the army. We were badly beaten up and were pushed towards the other side of the border. Army this side thought that we worked for 'enemy' force. Despite this kind of treatment time and again during those days, we used to return and get a sound thrashing. Harassment, in all its possible manifestations, was a routine affair for us.[12]

Lal Begum recalls one such incident where 'after a stand-off', they 'were not given time to take away' their 'valuables or even adequate clothes with them'. 'Cattle too remained tethered in their sheds. Winter had already set in. With no shelter around, the elders, ailing, children, we all made a move towards the forests during those hours of crisis', Lal Begum reminisces. For days together, they spent in the tents in forests as the chill in the weather increased, it became impossible for the family to stay for longer. Since the area registers snowfall up to 3–4 feet annually, after some days they took shelter in the houses of people of Manjakote village, which was situated at a higher altitude. Since 2002, despite their houses, they have been living the life of nomads. Earlier, for many days they were not allowed to visit their houses. She narrates remembering and recovering those horrendous moments:

> After repeated requests to the army authorities, when we were accorded permission to visit our houses, misfortune was awaiting us there in yet another traumatized mode. Our lifeline had been snapped. Most of our cattle had died of starvation. The spectacle was ghastly. One of the cattle had strangled itself perhaps in a bid to free itself.

They did not get any compensation for that loss. Their houses too had collapsed in the skirmishes. The same was true of almost everywhere in the village. Lal Begum concludes her narrative with a few heart wrenching reflections that represents the shared pain of these women, majority of whom are illiterate:

> Being a woman, I equate myself with cattle, herded by men and destiny. While attending to nature's call in the open with males and now even security personnel around, I just wonder if dignity and self respect are the words coined for us. I've lived my entire life with the hope that one day we would be able to live a dignified life in our own houses. After 2002, when our village was fenced out and we were forced to go through a frustrating drill from the cluster colony to the village, I made a wish at Bakr-e-Ziarat (a local place of pilgrimage)—May Allah bestow upon us His blessing! But the Day has not come yet. Appalling scene of dead cattle scares me and I think whether one day we're going to meet the same fate.[13]

These three women—Akhtar, Fatim and Lal Begum embody the predicament of the entire 'invisible' population of IDPs putting up in the cluster colonies in Poonch and Mendhar. Homeless, they already are being the victims of decades long conflict, but given the persistent and criminal administrative apathy for years, it seems like they have resigned themselves to their fate as the abandoned, unwanted thus delineating only two expressions 'desplazado' and 'desechable' (as Mia Leonin writes about the displaced community in conflict torn Columbia), i.e., displaced and disposable. These areas have always lacked on the development front. Due to huge presence

and virtual control of the army, the civil administration, also characterized by its own apathy and complacency, has little access in these areas. As
Lal Begum puts it, 'In my lifetime, I have never seen them coming here'.
Crucial issues of health and sanitation, more so in case of women, given
their particular genetic make-up, are ignored.

KERNI: THE WORST HIT VILLAGE

With the establishing of the cluster colonies, economy, agricultural and development is further threatened. Kerni appears to be the worst hit because
the cluster colonies have been created outside the border fencing. In fact
the village has been divided into two parts by the border fencing, isolating
16 families of a total of 106 families in this hamlet totally. One portion
of the village was sliced away in 1947 and is now a part of the PAK. The
fencing has further trifurcated the village (because the fence is also erected
on the gorge between the two hills over which the Kerni village spreads).
Communication between the two Indian administered parts of the village
is obstructed by this fencing where timings for crossing over have to be
strictly adhered to. Movement is not an easy task. It is further restrained by
the presence of landmines.

In Kerni, the local army unit further restricted the timings in the
summer of 2005 to shut the gate at 4 o'clock in the evening. The gate
opens at 9 o'clock every morning when villagers can move from the cluster
colonies to work in their fields and tend to their homes. But they must all
return by 4 o'clock. This timing, the villagers feel, is inadequate for their
daily chores. The army was earlier keeping the gates open till 6:00 p.m.
The change of timing came about after the discovery of a packet hung on
a tree just close to the LoC sometime in March 2005, by a villager who
brought it to the notice of the army men. The packet found in a polythene
bag contained some grenades and explosives. Villagers are unwilling to talk
about the kind of interrogation they faced following this incident by the
army and the latter's repressive measure. The army monitors their movement and actions closely and talking freely inside the village or in the cluster
colonies may be fraught with dangers. It was in Poonch town that we met
some of the people from this village and they were able to narrate the incident of finding the ill-fated packet of explosives and many more episodes
of this kind.

Close monitoring by the army on their day-to-day lives is obvious. The army personnel's presence in local traditional dress is very conspicuous. On our first visit to village Degwar, close to Poonch town and right on the LoC, three of them apparently followed us wherever we went and would either hide behind bushes or begin chatting to each other. When approached, they were unwilling to talk. On our second visit, two months later, one army man dressed in traditional dress escorted us around the village and talked about the strategic importance of wearing a local dress to fool the other side, a rationale one finds amusing and absurd after learning about how this facile disguise does not even fool the local lads. Every villager can point out the Pakistani army bunkers just over the hill overlooking this village and say, 'that's a Pakistani soldier in uniform; that is another in a civil dress'. So, it is no surprise that they are not fooled by any disguised Indian army men among them, as they are extremely adept at identifying these deliberate plants among their ranks. But, the presence of the army men inside the village also visibly sparks off a kind of fear psychosis. It was common to find villagers talking something and then deviating from the topic after spotting an army man or even a local. It is practically impossible to get them to say anything in group discussions without being superfluously sycophantic about the service being rendered by the army for civilians in their village. The same was true of the other villages along the LoC. One can find the tones changing, once in a while, when the number of people talked to are lesser. The use of locals as army informers is almost a well-known fact, though not many would talk about it. If you query, the only answer one gets is, 'yes, it happens in other villages—not in ours'. But if you talk to individuals, some of them do admit this fact. On our second visit to Degwar, after the 8 October 2005 quake, the army soldier accompanying us in civil dress was overheard talking to 60-year-old Feroz Din, 'You haven't gone across?' Flashing his toothless smile, Feroz Din replied, 'When the commander wills'. A person from the village whispered to us, 'He works for the army, if they give him the orders right now, he'll be ready to go in an hour'.

But everyone becomes tongue tied while responding to queries whether any Pakistani informers or militants cross over to this side. They plead ignorance. In fact, nobody wants to publicly acknowledge that he or she has a relative across the LoC (as stated earlier, the only exception to this rule is of mothers and fathers talking about their sons or daughters on the other side). Probably, the silence stems from a history of repression. It may not be a regular feature, but the slightest of untoward incident can provoke repression from the army. In Kerni, the timings of closing down the fence gates were preponed because of this reason. Some men from Kerni, we met in Poonch town, also narrated a recent incident about a family forced to flee to the Pakistani side because the head of the family, who was working for the army, refused to carry on with the work. He and his family were locked up in their house for two days. The family managed to give the army men a slip and ran for safety. Such, incidents, they say, are common. The army's repression can be provoked at the slightest of suspicion, sometimes quite baseless. Many of them willing to work for little monetary benefits are co-opted to participate in the espionage network, as appeared to be the case with Feroze Din. Stories abound both in villages, on the LoC and the International Border, but no one admits that he is working for the army or the militants. No one points out anybody's name. The stories are quite general with no names and addresses.

Speaking against the army is not just a crime for the villagers only because of the repression. It is also because the army is their sole provider for basic needs. The civil administration is absolutely absent. The only link is the tehsildar's office, but this office apparently is not well equipped to deal with their day-to-day grievances.

FLOWS ACROSS LOC

Coerced either by economic conditions, deprivation or extreme militarization of borders on this side, there exists a large number of the displaced persons including those who crossed the borders since 1947. A large chunk of people is said to have crossed the LoC after every war, the largest migration having taken place in 1965, many of whom returned a year later. There is no documented record of the exact number of such displaced. However, these displaced persons have been registered as refugees in Pakistan after 1990 and many of them are putting up in camps set up by the Pakistan's Azad Jammu and Kashmir (AJK) government. Since 1990, there are 35,000 unregistered refugees. According to statistics of Rehabilitation Department of AJK, this mass migration includes 11,018 persons (1,236 families).[14]

Rubina Ishaque, who has done an extensive study on the patterns of migrations across the LoC in her thesis for Quaid-i-Azam University, Islamabad, provides an insight into the causes behind crossing the boundaries and the impact. Included among these refugees are also a few families who migrated between 1985 and 1989. All these displaced persons get a paltry relief of ₹600 per person and settlement. Those who were displaced before this period got no aid from AJK or Pakistan government. Rubina has also maintained that in 1965 and 1971, 50,000 persons (9,800 families) were displaced to AJK from the Indian side of the state. She points out that there were no mass migrations past 1990, reasoning that this was owing to what she terms as 'the "sealed borders" by India & Pakistan'. Though there is no knowledge of sealed borders, there is a common perception among the displaced across the LoC that the borders were heavily mined thereafter, making both mass migrations and their return impossible.

These displaced live in 14 refugee camps in AJK-Muzaffarabad, Bagh, Kotli, Mirpur and Rawalakot. Atrocities by Indian security forces against Muslim Kashmiris are only one reason of Muslim Kashmiris' migration. It is a multi-causative phenomenon. Rubina, who met several groups of the migrants displaced from the village Keran, says that some were also forced by the Islamic freedom fighters. She writes:

Haneef Lone, an old man in the camp told me that: Freedom fighters told us to move to Azad Kashmir border, only for one week. They were sure that in one week, they will free Kashmir by attacking Indian army and then we can come back to our areas.

In many cases, the militants misled the people, asking them to join the struggle and cross the LoC. However, stories of repression by Indian army also abound. Younger boys were fed up of interrogation, checking and patrolling of Indian troops in their villages and outside. News of crackdowns and rapes from elsewhere added to the fear psychosis. Refugees maintained that in October 1990, the crisis became worse for them. They had no other option but to migrate. There were also political reasons for intimidation, especially in villages where people had supported a particular party or individual or aided militants. If few individuals felt threatened and decided to leave, the others followed one another in panic reaction. For example, a woman followed her brother. Later, her husband and children followed. Crossing the boundaries was not easy. The displaced, who crossed the LoC find themselves in a situation worse than before. Added to their vulnerability owing to involvement in crime or because of being pushed by agencies within Pakistan to work as spies, are also the economic and social problems. They are deprived of their land, property, culture and even their identity. They have no legal national identity as citizens of the host country and no ownership of land.

VIOLENCE: A CONTINUUM

The stories of Poonch in general and of Kerni in particular have helped us to understand that the issues of the border people are multiple, their causes as varied. They are indeed paying a price for political blunders and historical decisions taken from time to time and the tradition of hostility between India and Pakistan that has forced both countries to heavily militarize their respective territories, in absolute violations of the UN resolutions and basic humanitarian laws. Deprivation is absolute—physical and psychological. Neither the basic needs of human security exist, nor the basic civil liberties. Dislocation may be partial or absolute, depending on the wavering India–Pakistan relations, but it is not just physical displacement; it is also psychological. Conflict situation in the state has multiplied these susceptibilities forcing them to live under a constant shadow of fear and trepidation. Literally living on the line of fire, snatches from them any semblance of normal life; higher concentration of security personnel and the persistent fear of infiltrators and militants take out 'life' from their lives. Still they survive.

Narratives of our respondents have made it clear that violence and victimhood at the borders do not stop at the borders. They percolate further into the interiors, affecting lives of millions of people on either side of the border, often even the lives of those living miles away from these lines on the map. While what happens at the borders affects lives in the interiors and even the decision-making at the highest seats of power, the policies and decision determined at the power centres always impacts the lives of the people at the borders. This co-relation is well understood in situations of heightened hostilities, tit for tat policies followed by hostile neighbours, especially so in times of a full-fledged war. What happens at the level of high politics clearly impacts those living at the borders, not only adversely affecting their day-to-day life, but also in controlling their lives. The tragedy of the people living at the borders is far greater because of the continuum of violence they are caught in the grip of, for six decades on.

NOTES

1. Wali Khanna (2008: 4).
2. Chugtai (2001).
3. Based on interviews with Rabia Bi and her brother, taken on 22 October 2009.
4. Shehnaz's story is based on interviews with her and newspaper reportage from *Kashmir Times* and *Times of India*, that first reported about her death. Shehnaz's story has also been immortalized by a theatre group Ajoka Theatre in its much acclaimed play 'Dukh Darya'. The inaugural show was staged in Lahore on Women's Day, 8 March 2006, a year before Shehnaz died.
5. Based on interviews of a cross section of people in Birhuti on 21 October 2009.
6. Salfo Devi was interviewed on 14 September 2009.
7. Bimla Devi was interviewed on 14 September 2009.
8. Charu Wali Khanna, 'Women Silent Victims in Armed Conflict' Page 6 Interview Date, 22 January, 2010.
9. de Beauvoir, 1953.
10. Based on interviews in Surankote and news reports in *Kashmir Times*.
11. Based on interviews with some of the VDC members on 25 October 2009.
12. Lal Begum was interviewed on 21 October 2009.
13. Ibid.
14. Ishaque, unpublished.

4

Renegotiating Internal Boundaries by Women of Jammu and Kashmir

Sumona DasGupta

In this chapter, the term 'borders' is used to denote not just physical boundaries represented by de facto and de jure cartographic lines that separate the sovereign writ of one state from another, but also other fault lines generated or accentuated by a conflict. Acknowledging borders as lines that separate and delimit spaces, in this chapter we go beyond 'cartographic anxieties' and physical landscapes to 'non-cartographic anxieties'—borders that are etched on mindscapes—lines that separate 'us' from 'them'. In doing so we recognize that there can be an overlap between these two sets of anxieties and that where they intersect, fault lines come into even sharper relief. Border studies today have encompassed an area well beyond border confrontations—in fact the fall of the Berlin wall in 1989 has symbolically created a context where 'breaking the wall' has become a metaphor for discussing political and cultural boundaries that create not only conflicts but also dialogues and contemplations of the 'other'.[1] Border studies which have emerged as one of the most significant theoretical turns at the end of the last century[2] are in fact now a project that has morphed into a concern with transcending limitations of any kind—cultural, religious, spiritual, in addition to political, ethnic and national.[3] Borders—whether 'guarded' and 'fenced' on the territorial landscape or fault lines that are imprinted on people's mindscapes—can collide and coalesce, creating myriad patterns that offer room both for creative dialogues as well as violent encounters.

The physical or territorial borders in the former princely state of Jammu and Kashmir are particularly complicated given the fact that this territory has been a bone of contention between India and Pakistan since independence in 1947, and as many as four wars (1947, 1965, 1971 and 1991) have been fought over it. There are not one but several contentious cartographic borders in Jammu and Kashmir—the international border between Jammu and Kashmir and Pakistan that is known as the working border in Pakistan's terminology; the ceasefire line (CFL) of 1949 that was re-designated as the Line of Control (LoC) in 1972; the extension of the LoC beyond NJ 9842 in the Siachen sector which is known as the actual ground position line (AGPL) and finally the segment east of AGPL bordering on or controlled by China which is known as the line of actual control or LAC. However, these external borders and physical lines of contention are not the only ones that exist. There are also borders of a different kind induced or accentuated by the trajectory that the conflict has taken since the 1990s—identity fault lines that have been politicized and militarized in the course of the conflict. Juxtaposed with these various cartographic lines of contention a volatile border zone is created where the internal and external dimension of what is described as one of the world's most militarized conflicts plays itself out.

The contemporary political history of Jammu and Kashmir is well known, as is the qualitative change that took place post 1989 in that the problem 'of Kashmir' became the problem 'in Kashmir'.[4] With the outbreak of an armed openly secessionist movement in the valley supported at that time by men and women, the popular upsurge spilled out into the street. This together with the counter-insurgency operation launched by the Indian army at the behest of the civilian Indian government marked out the decade of the 1990s in Jammu and Kashmir, as a period of unprecedented direct, manifest, everyday violence which has left thousands dead, injured and displaced.[5] The dynamics and changing trajectory of the conflict, the internal–external nexus to it, *its gendered fallout*, as well as the fact that the conflict site is a border state with multiple 'lines' of de facto control, has together created several 'borderlines'.

Evidently, these borderlines are mediated by gender. Gender is used not just as a descriptive category but as an analytical tool, that is, as much about men and masculinity as it is about women and femininity.[6] A gender perspective consequently explores how men and women's roles are constructed in society and gender sensitive conflict analysis will look at ways in which gender roles, gender identities, gender ideologies and gendered power structures may be altered in the course of a protracted conflict. Informed by this, the chapter explores some of the fault lines/borderlines in the iconography of the contemporary conflict in Jammu and Kashmir, using gender as a cross cutting variable rather than as a separate issue.

URBAN–RURAL BORDERLINES

A significant borderline that was accentuated in the course of this conflict is one between the urban and rural population of the Kashmir Valley. Sharp urban–rural divides, in terms of opportunities and access, have of course always existed not just in Jammu and Kashmir but in other parts of India and South Asia as well. However, the differential manner in which the conflict in Jammu and Kashmir was experienced in the urban and rural areas in the valley brought this fault line into sharp focus. The reasons for this can be traced back to the time when the locus and epicentre of the movement were relocated from urban centres to the far-flung countryside. This happened within the first three years of the militancy with the leadership of the movement passing from the hands of the more urban-based JKLF to the rural based *Hizbul Mujahideen* and thereafter at least for sometime to non-Kashmiri *mehman mujahideen* ('guest' militants). As Alpana Kishore in her graphic account of life in the valley in the 1990s based on her first hand experiences of covering the valley in the course of that decade has pointed out, urban Kashmir raised the slogans and the temperatures and then sent its children to safer places outside while rural Kashmir bore the brunt end of the militancy losing its youth and its sources of life and livelihood.[7]

The differential impact of the armed movement in urban and rural areas of the Kashmir Valley has not been systematically documented, but the Indian census reports of 1981 and 2001 on demography for the state of Jammu and Kashmir do reveal an interesting set of pointers.[8] Among the six districts in the valley only the Srinagar district has an overwhelming urban population with more than 80 per cent of its inhabitants living in urban agglomerations. The two other districts with significant urban clusters though far below Srinagar on the urbanization index, are district Baramula with 15.8 per cent population settled in the urban clusters of Baramula town, Sopore, Bandipore, Pattan, Sumbal, Uri and Gulmarg and Anantnag district with around 13.1 per cent of its population in the growing urban agglomeration around Anantnag town itself along with Bijbehara, Doru Verinag, Kulgam and Achabal. On the other hand, the three districts with very low urban population are district Pulwama (7 per cent), district Budgam (4.6 per cent) and district Kupwara (3.9 per cent) where the inhabitants are settled in much smaller urban clusters such as Shupiyan, Tral, Chari Sharief, Hundwara as compared to the larger towns of Srinagar, Baramula, Sopore, Bandipore or Anantnag (Table 4.1).

Table 4.1 Urban Clusters in Kashmir Valley

DISTRICT	URBAN CENTRES (TOWNS)	TOTAL POPULATION OF DISTRICT	% OF POPULATION LIVING IN URBAN AREAS
Srinagar	Srinagar (988,210)	1,238,530	80.8
	Ganderbal (13,721)		
Baramula	Baramula (71,896)	1,166,722	15.8
	Sopore (59,624)		
	Bandipore (25,795)		
	Pattan (11,355)		
	Sumbal (10,655)		
	Uri (4,246)		
	Gulmarg (878)		
Anantnag	Anantnag (97,896)	1,170,013	13.1
	Bijbehara (19,794)		
	Doru Verinag (17,237)		
	Kulgam (13,136)		
	Achabal (5,834)		
Pulwama	Pulwama (14,229)	632,295	7.0
	Shupiyan (12,246)		
	Tral (11,651)		
	Avantipura (6,252)		
Budgam	Budgam (11,767)	593,768	4.6
	Chari Sharief (7,374)		
	Beerwah (6,295)		
	Khan Sahib (2,038)		
Kupwara	Kupwara (14,857)	640,013	3.9
	Handwara (10,638)		

Source: List of towns (Government of India, 2001: 1–3).

Note: Figures in brackets refer to total population of the towns. The percentage (%) of urban population has been calculated on the basis of figures available for the population of each of the designated towns in this table and the total district population as specified in the census of 2001.

The census data from 2001 indicates that other than for Kupwara the two districts with a clearly overwhelming percentage of rural population—namely Pulwama and Budgam have shown a lower average annual growth rate of population, as compared to the significantly more urbanized districts of Srinagar, Anantnag and Baramula. Given that the 2001 census reflects the trends through the decade of the 1990s—the decade where armed conflict was at its peak—this could be an indicator that the rural population was gradually coming under greater demographic stress and strain compared to their urban counterparts. An additional indicator is the data from the 1981 census (before the phase of active armed conflict in the valley). Significantly, the 1981 census figures indicate the reverse—there was a higher average annual growth rate for the districts with the greater rural population, namely Budgam and Pulwama—as compared to the more urbanized Srinagar, Anantnag and Baramula (Table 4.2). If the data from the 1981 census is read against the census data of 2001, it points towards a correlation that supports the contention that the rural areas of the valley bore the brunt of the armed conflict. Another set of statistics from the 2001 census, namely the urban–rural disaggregated sex ratio in each of the districts in the valley clearly show that the sex ratio for rural areas is far higher than urban areas (Table 4.3). This appears to suggest that once the armed conflict got under way and the rural space became increasingly militarized the men tended to migrate to the urban clusters in search of greater and more secure sources of livelihood.

Table 4.2 Annual Average Growth Rate of Population in 1981 and 2001 (District-wise Profile)

DISTRICT	1981	2001
Kupwara	1.28	3.39
Srinagar	2.30	2.83
Anantnag	2.39	2.93
Baramula	2.72	2.81
Budgam	3.16	2.43
Pulwama	2.55	2.26

Source: Figures exclude the population of Jammu and Kashmir that is now controlled by Pakistan and China. Data adapted from the Table II.4, titled 'District wise population growth in Jammu and Kashmir' in Chapter 2, Planning Commission (2003: 26). Table based on the census of India figures of 1981 and 2001.

Alluding to the 1990s, Kishore has pointed out that the security grid established by the Indian armed forces mapping every street and city in

Table 4.3 Rural and Urban Sex Ratio (Females per Thousand Males)

DISTRICT	RURAL	URBAN
Kupwara	939	708
Baramula	921	853
Srinagar	925	854
Budgam	935	794
Pulwama	950	849
Anantnag	938	833

Source: From Table II.13, Chapter 2, Planning Commission (2003: 35). Table is based on census of India figures 2001.

the valley had the militants moving from the urban areas to the mountains and jungles.[9] This not only altered the basic fabric of the movement but also had huge gendered fallout in the way rural and urban women and men were forced to come to terms with it particularly through the way in which this has reconstructed the meaning and significance of the 'home'. Feminist writings have reflected ambivalence on the subject of the centrality of the home, particularly in times of violent conflict. Some feminists have clearly cautioned against romanticizing the home, as this can also be a space where gender hierarchies and violent masculinities assert themselves with public scrutiny traditionally directed away from it in order to preserve its 'privacy'—others have pointed out that in times of violence there is a natural tendency for the home to emerge as a place of refuge—as the one constant centre in a world of violent uncertainties. Sometimes the home can also emerge as a space for resistance which challenges the militarized might of the several 'armed patriarchies' surrounding it.

In rural Kashmir the home, clearly seen as a place of refuge at least before the militancy came out into the open, became a virtual prison in the 1990s where militants could seek food and refuge and which could be searched by Indian security forces at any time. The midnight knock became a metaphor for fear and uncertainty and for women the constant threat of gendered violence including rape and domestic violence became a lived reality. The feeling of extreme vulnerability and powerlessness of women in the rural areas, particularly in the valley was enhanced by the presence of the ubiquitous 'unidentified' gunman everywhere—in agricultural fields, apple orchards, outside the house, on rooftops, in abandoned houses, and even in schools. The constant fear that the women lived with was that the children may not come home from school, or that the men may not return from the fields.

Apart from the gap in available statistics, there are also very few qualitative accounts that have focused on the impact of militarization of state and society in the rural areas. With the slogans and rallies in the urban areas grabbing media attention the steady erosion of community life in the rural remote areas hardly constituted 'news'. As a result we can only gauge the manner in which the armed conflict affected women in rural Kashmir from assessments and studies on their mental health conditions, employment and literacy over the years in which the armed conflict was at its peak. Clearly the violation of the home and community space and the personal vulnerability and feeling of insecurity that come from this has affected both urban and rural areas, and is clearly reflected in the mental health picture in the valley. Though rural–urban disaggregated data on this is not yet forthcoming, some observations by well-known mental health practitioners are revealing. A leading valley psychiatrist Mushtaq Margoob points to the tendency of elder women inducing younger ones to smoke a hookah in rural areas in order to cope with bereavement. With the easy availability of cannabis the problem of addiction has become a reality.[10] There is little doubt that this state of affairs is indicative of the manner in which the social fabric of the rural areas has steadily eroded in the course of the armed conflict.

While some of the thousands of women who have developed psychiatric disorders, stress, depression and suicidal tendencies and extensively use tranquilizers, painkillers and anti-depressants available over the counter are undoubtedly from urban centres including urban Srinagar and other urban pockets like the townships of Sopore or Baramulla; however, a significant proportion hail from rural areas where women have seen violent deaths and lost dear ones in the course of the violent phase of the conflict. Despite the fact that this has clearly emerged as a rural problem, it is those in Srinagar and other urban centres who have comparatively easier access to treatment compared to those from rural areas who have to travel far to seek this help. Apart from the Composite Rehabilitation centre located in Srinagar, the Government Psychiatric Diseases Hospital in Srinagar is also the only one to serve the valley's entire population.[11]

Acknowledging that the mental health situation in the valley's rural areas is disturbing another well-known mental health practitioner Dr Arshad Hussain points out, 'The condition of people living in the countryside was alarming as they would face tough situations on regular basis ... the prevalence of PTSD cases is more in districts other than in Srinagar and it has been noticed that fresh cases are coming from rural areas'.[12] Sociologists like Dr Bashir Ahmed Dabla who have been studying the impact of the conflict for several years also endorse this. According to Dabla:

> [A]ll through out the world, suicide rates are highest among men and more intense in urban areas, but in the Kashmir Valley, the reverse is true. Failure in school, unemployment or family problems are common reasons for suicide but the underlying factor is the conflict.[13]

Dabla's comment points to both the rural urban differential in the way the conflict has impacted lives, but also to its gendered fallout. This gender dimension is further substantiated by the study titled 'Conflict in the Indian Kashmir Valley: Psychological Impact' by a team from Medicins Sans Frontiers (MSF) which specifically stratified the data for gender.[14] Published in 2008, this survey by MSF was done to evaluate the exposure of the civilian population to violence and its consequences on mental health and is particularly significant in what it reveals about life in rural areas at the height of the armed conflict. Not surprisingly, the survey (done in 2005) was conducted in rural areas of the valley (Kupwara and Budgam districts) across 101 villages and covering 145,000 people. The results clearly revealed that it was the village that had borne the brunt of the violence and this had taken its toll on the mental health of the population.[15] Analysis from this survey when stratified by gender indicated that while one-third of the respondents were found to have symptoms of psychological distress, women scored significantly higher. While feelings of insecurity contributed to the distress for both men and women, for women this was attributed to dependency on others for daily living and the witnessing of killing and torture while for men violation of modesty, forced displacement and physical disability resulting from violence were associated with greater levels of psychological distress.[16]

In other words, and very tellingly, for women most psychological distress was associated with a feeling of powerlessness which came out of dependency on others for daily living. This again is related to the armed conflict. As Dabla in a survey submitted in 2000 indicates, women in the valley have traditionally worked in agricultural fields where they have in fact also received the minimum wages unlike the handicrafts sector where they tend to get exploited.[17] The fact that they now felt uncomfortable about leaving the confines of their home due to the armed presence all around created a sense of total dependence on the menfolk, whose security too they could not guarantee. The study also noted that for women in these rural areas the witnessing of violence was as, if not more, traumatic than experiencing the violence themselves.[18] Clearly, these findings indicate that in the phase of active armed conflict the isolated village hamlet, idealized and romanticized had emerged as 'a place without escape' where the normal rhythms of life and home were completely torn asunder.[19] This created huge boundaries redefining the space between the home and 'outside', between the individual and her/his village community and, of course, between the urban citizenry and its well-travelled prosperous elites, who articulated the sentiment of *azadi* but could afford to stay away from its violent ramification and the non-combatant rural population of the valley who were drawn into a brutal, inexorable path of no return. The latter were constantly haunted by the fear of being hunted down by either security forces or militants, since the old familial community bonds of trust and kinship had completely broken down in the midst of the violence and everyone had become suspect in the eyes of the other.[20]

Yet, ironically, despite the fact that women particularly in rural areas could no longer treat the home as a safe space, the home still seemed less predatory than the fields outside in which they had traditionally worked. The years between 1994 and 2000 were the active phase of the armed conflict, and the state as a whole recorded a negative growth of employment for women. In the rural areas where 80 per cent of the people reside, daughters were often not allowed to attend educational institutions which were located at a distance for reasons of safety.[21] The picture was less bleak in the urban centres and in Srinagar where the actions of the Armed Forces were relatively under more media scrutiny.

CARTOGRAPHIC LINES: DIVIDING LIVES AND COMMUNITIES

When cartographic anxieties caused by LoCs that divide people and communities intersect with other fault lines of community, class and gender, a unique situation of insecurity is created. Nowhere is this more evident than in Dardpora village in the Kupwara district of Kashmir Valley, where the plight of the widow and 'half widow' is even starker than in other parts of rural Kashmir. This is also the district through which the LoC passes and the pastoral Gujjar community live. In a shocking demographic change, young and able-bodied men have simply been killed or have disappeared from the face of this village either in fratricidal wars between the Al Barq and Hizbul Mujahideen who were fighting to dominate the landscape in the 1990s, or by Indian Security Forces. Here, the *private–public borders* created by a masculinized militarized society have perforce been shattered as women came out to assume new roles simply to ensure survival.[22]

Despite the fact that the village consists of female-headed households, not as a matter of choice but by accident, there has been little bond between the women in this ecologically fragile, isolated village hamlet near the LoC. Instead, a fierce spirit of competition exists. The households are dependent on firewood for fuel and light (there is no electricity in most of the households) and a zero sum game prevails with little cooperation. The 'politics and economics of firewood' has created a peculiar ambivalence in the way women view each other and this has been further accentuated by a another community fault line that separates the women from upper Dardpora (inhabited by the Gujjars who acted as porters and route indicators across the LoC during the peak of militancy) and lower Dardpora inhabited by Kashmiri speaking people. The widows and half-widows in upper and lower Dardpora simply do not communicate—in addition to the resource politics that keep them apart, they bear the political legacy of the past when their husbands belonged to rival militant groups.[23]

In the Jammu sector a different kind of 'line' creates another mosaic of insecurities. Here it is not the *line of control* but the *international boundary* that is visible with its barbed wire fence. This has also created its own gendered impact on the lives of people, particularly women cultivators, who inhabit the fertile rice growing R.S. Pura district along the international border with Pakistan. While the LoC in Kupwara district of the valley separate Indian and Pakistan administered Kashmir, the international border in R.S. Pura separates Pakistan's Punjab from Indian administered Jammu and Kashmir. The 'gates' of the two countries meet in a village called Suchetgarh on the Indian side from where the barbed fence is sharp and visible for miles.

I visited Suchetgarh in November 2009 specifically to talk to women, particularly women cultivators, in this rice rich fertile belt about the way in which the fencing had affected their lives and livelihoods. I spoke to women as they were returning from their fields, and others some of whom were working on the fields. These women shared the tribulations of having to duck bullets when cross firing happens (there is relative peace following the ceasefire but even this can be sporadically broken), the challenges of negotiating mines in the field and the everyday insecurities of the 'gate pass system' as some of their cultivable lands are on the other side of the barbed fence. Sheela Devi, a grandmother, was tending her fields when I spoke to her.[24] Sheela Devi, like many other sturdy women, cultivators of the Kashmir Valley in rural areas, multitasks, performing roles both inside and outside the household. She helps cook, packs lunch for the children of the household who have to travel a few kilometres to go to school and after her morning household tasks are done she works the fields. She said she is fortunate that her agricultural field where she grows paddy is close to her home and both are on the same side of the fence. The fields on the other side of the border in Pakistan's Punjab lie just across hers and the terrain and cultivation pattern are identical. Since the international border cuts across fertile rice bowls shelling can create havoc. Sheela Devi told us that a few years ago a neighbour could not cremate a relative as the cremation spot was out of reach due to the shelling. She also complained of 'mined' fields and the havoc it wrecked on the lives of the people and cattle with its potential to injure and kill at any time, catching people unaware. Since the danger here was more from mining and shelling, Sheela Devi did not feel that she was any more vulnerable because she was a woman.

I also talked with Puro Devi who was returning home with a cart full of fodder after the day's work along with her daughter who helps in the fields and no longer goes to school. Unlike Sheela Devi there is a considerable distance between Puro Devi's home and fields. She talked of the fenced-out fields, the gate passes and her daughter laughingly shared how adept they had all become at 'ducking bullets'.[25] In Suchetgarh, the system of 'gate passes' creates uncertainty and tension in the lives of cultivators and especially among women. The wire fence is not coterminous with the international border—between the fence and the border lie fertile paddy fields. Those who cultivate them enter through designated 'gates' and have to leave by sunset—their movements are regulated by the Border Security Force (BSF).

Both Sheela Devi and Puro Devi talked of the current temporary respite in their lives due to the ceasefire between India and Pakistan, but also referred to the constant uncertainty of having to live with violations and periods when there are no ceasefires. However, there is a qualitative difference between the kind of insecurity faced by Sheela Devi and Puro Devi in Suchetgarh along the international border and that faced by women in Dardpora along the LoC in Kashmir Valley. Sheela and Puro Devi's insecurity comes primarily from mines and shells. It does not at least overtly come from the presence of armed militants or Security Forces. Though the Security Forces (BSF) are visibly present all along the international border in this village, women cultivators did not feel particularly threatened by them—yet the presence of these same forces in the valley clearly invokes terror and insecurity among women in rural areas.

Evidently, the qualitative difference comes from the fact that the security forces in the Jammu sector along the international border (or for that matter in the Uri sector of the valley) are performing their traditional role of 'guarding the frontier'. Their constant presence in the line of duty is not needed in public spaces such as the market, the fields and certainly not in houses and schools. Consequently, their contact with civilians going about the business of life is regularized by norms of social behaviour that govern incidental everyday encounters in public spaces. On the other hand when these same security forces are employed in a counter-insurgency role in the valley and in the districts along the LoC, the very nature of their presence and their functions undergo a foundational change. Counter-insurgency operations such as cordon and search, raids on specific information, collection of real-time actionable intelligence intrude sharply on the lives of civilians and create daily physical and psychological hardships. For the non-combatant civilian population yearning to restore the normal rhythms of their lives, finding soldiers in their private and public spaces of everyday life—in field and orchards, in marketplaces, even in houses and schools—can be physically intimidating and psychologically draining. Given the situation, the possibilities of sexual violence is also much higher in areas where troops are employed in a counter-insurgency role as compared to areas where they are present at the borders in a patrolling role.

There are several cartographic lines in Jammu and Kashmir; the LoC and the international border being the most recognizable ones. Both divide people and communities. However, the manner in which they impact lives and livelihoods is qualitatively different and the types of insecurities these 'lines' cause affect men and women differently.

CONFLICT INDUCED DISPLACEMENT: CREATING NEW BORDERS

Yet another set of borderlines that have come to the surface are the ones between the displaced and settled communities, particularly in Jammu, that have sharpened in the course of the conflict. While the so-called border migrants have been present from the time of partition, the arrival of later waves of people displaced by the armed conflict—the Kashmiri Pandits and those displaced by border shelling, the border fencing project and 'war exercises' have obviously sharpened the fault lines and created new ones between the different categories of conflict induced displaced communities. Jammu—the city and its surroundings—has been home to a numbers of people and communities who have been displaced as a result of the Kashmir conflict. The Kashmiri Pandits who had left the valley en masse in the 1990s had been forced to live in miserable squalid 'camps' across Jammu such as Nagrota and Purkho to name a few. The experience of living in these camps has affected both men and women but differently—the sense of helplessness and inability to work productively despite the fact that many of the men continue to get their salaries if they had been in government employment—has resulted in the assertion of threatened masculinities, especially as women in the camps have also hinted at gendered violence.[26]

While the plight of the Pandits have attracted media attention, very little is known about another category of the displaced—those displaced from Rajouri, Poonch and Doda who were compelled to leave their homes and desert their fields once the epicentre of the militancy shifted from the valley to these areas and who live in camps around Jammu City built on empty land, over which they have no legal right despite having lived there for years. At Bellicharana camp, I met Arshida Begum, a Gujjar widowed woman who had left Poonch 11 years ago due to the constant cross-firings and shelling and had eked out an existence begging—today she resells blankets and is the provider for her family of two children in the camp.[27] Kajal's story on the other hand was a little different. She hails from Rajouri and they lived in an area relatively protected from shelling and her husband is employed by the government. When I asked why she was living in the camp, she said, her tenement had been hired/rented from another camp dweller and she preferred to live near Jammu so that her children could attend better schools. Her husband moves between this rented room and Rajouri.[28] Also displaced from Rajouri were Anju and Shakuntala who had to abandon their maize fields and cattle due to militant activities and the constant vigil of Indian Security Forces across agricultural lands. Shabnam from Doda was injured in the firing that forced her to leave home and abandon agricultural lands—she carries the scar till date. She has made an artistic home in the camp drawing on natural materials and stones and the 'house' is a *pucca* one except for the roof. She told me that the government would not allow a *pucca roof* as this would symbolize permanence of settlement.[29] I also met Gulnaaz Begum, similarly displaced from Doda, who did not even have the other rights of migrants, as no one had informed her about the registration process in the camp. Abandoned by her husband she makes a home with her daughters, son and daughter-in-law where she contributes substantially in monetary terms to the shared household while her daughter-in-law, who has studied till class 11, oversees the domestic chores. While her son drives an auto in Jammu City, Gulnaz Begum works in a medicine factory.[30]

For thousands living in these camps, with their fields burnt and destroyed, the government has not provided them with any housing on the grounds that this would encourage more migration. Though there is a tacit understanding that they will not be asked to leave the lands they have now occupied, their legal status continues to remain ambiguous. The city-dwellers and settled communities see them as a drain on resources, yet they provide vital casual labour for the city's small industries and trading concerns. In the course of my conversation with these conflict-induced displaced families, it was obvious that they feel totally disconnected from the concerns of the Jammu's trading settled communities as well as from the separatist slogans in the valley. The fact they appear to be missing from the radar of the policy-makers makes the whole issue of women in camps even more difficult to address.

Fault lines were also obviously not just between settled and migrant populations but also between different categories of the migrants who had received differential treatment in the hands of the government. The Kashmiri

Pandit camps though squalid and far removed in terms of provision of basic amenities were still relatively better off compared to the camps belonging to the migrants from Doda, Rajouri, Poonch. The resentment at this differential treatment was palpable in the interviews that I conducted with the camp dwellers from Doda, Rajouri and Poonch. Both men and women at the camps expressed similar sentiments on this issue.

It is not just in the camps for the displaced that the 'borders' are etched on mindscapes. Even among the so-called settled population, particularly in the urban city space, another kind of sub-regional borderline is increasingly becoming evident.

AMARNATH CRISIS AND THE
SHARPENING OF REGIONAL FAULT LINES

In fact, one of the sharpest 'borderlines', that now appears to be as prominent as any that can be drawn on a map is the regional divide between the three sub-divisions of the state (Kashmir Valley, Jammu and Ladakh) and indeed between sub-regions within each division such as Doda, Poonch, Rajouri within the Jammu subdivision and Leh and Kargil in Ladakh. While this is not new, the sharpening of these lines post the Amarnath crisis of 2008 has been quite unprecedented.[31] The fact that a large number of women were part of the agitations in the valley and in Jammu gestures towards the arrival of a new kind of religious-regionalism as a dominant strand of politics. A mobilization strategy based on a heady fusion of religion and region appeared to appeal across gender and class generating unprecedented hostility towards the 'other' and appearing to steamroll the political diversity within the regions particularly in Jammu, in favour of a 'unified voice' that pitted the 'Hindus of Jammu' against 'the Muslims of Kashmir'.

The roots of Jammu's discontent, which can be attributed to the perception that politics in Jammu and Kashmir has always been valley-centric, is not new and has in fact been present since the early 1950s.[32] However, the sheer scale of the agitations in 2008 and its communal overtones with Hindutva and ·Islamist slogans virtually mirroring each other in shrillness and intensity in Jammu and the valley, both the regional aspects of the divide and the ease with which street level religiosity could be used to mobilize people became evident as never before. Jammu's discontent, even as it existed since the 1950s, never found clear political expression or articulation. Unlike the valley where regional parties had emerged over the years like the National Conference, there had been no such concomitant development in the Jammu region. As a result as Rekha Chowdhary pertinently points out 'the politics of regional neglect has often been appropriated by the Hindu Right wing organizations and thus communalized in the process …'.[33] This has happened despite the fact that Jammu itself is amazingly diverse and the politics of sub-regional identity is palpable within this subdivision itself. The diversity profile of Jammu is in sharp contrast to the now much more demographically homogenized valley particularly following the mass exodus of the Kashmiri Pandit community from the valley in the 1990s.

However, it was not until the Amarnath agitation that this divergence took the shape of open hostility. Despite the accentuation of Jammu identity politics possibly as a response to the politics in the valley there had been an element of accommodation; for instance, the valley-based National Conference was forced to incorporate the regional autonomy issue in its manifesto in 1996.[34] While this put the lid, at least temporarily, on the outbreak of open animosity between the valley and Jammu, it had another unintended consequence. Sensing opportunity, the Hindu Right Wing, immediately sought to move centre stage, with its insidious politics of accentuating religious polarization by vociferously renewing the demand for the trifurcation of the state. However, the rise of coalition politics, in which Jammu was able to assert itself, relegated the politics of trifurcation to the background for the moment. All this changed dramatically with the Amarnath Land row which marked a new high in the level of open hostility between two parts of the same state—the valley and Jammu.

The demand for trifurcation of the state also gave a fillip for the assertion of regional identity politics in Ladakh with the Ladakhi Buddhist Association (LBA) demanding union territory status.[35] However, going beyond religious essentialisms, the construction of new identities in Ladakh has been examined by Ravina Agarwal with elegance and finesse in her ethnographic study of the region. The study breaks new ground by moving beyond both geopolitical boundaries to consider how social and religious boundaries are created and how these affect the lives of Buddhists and Muslims in Ladakh.

Agarwal draws on the anthropological study of international borders to tell us how the border dispute between India and Pakistan is experienced by those living along the LoC in Ladakh.[36] However, despite the stirrings in Ladakh, till date this region continues to remain liminal not just to the Indian state but to the politics of Jammu and Kashmir itself. This is in sharp contrast to the politics of assertion in Jammu.

The Jammu agitation of 2008 was also noteworthy because of the large participation of women. There were reports and images of women on rooftops showing the tricolour and black flags to leaders, defying curfew, banging on gates of police stations as part of the 'Jail Bharo' programme, chanting religious slogans, beating thalis and blowing conch shells ostensibly to 'awaken the sleeping central and state governments from deep slumber and restore the land to the shrine board'.[37] On 19 August 2008, while courting arrest women agitators were reported to have declared that they would continue with the agitation till the plot under dispute was given to the shrine board. The participation of women cut across class and caste and included several members of the faculty at Jammu University as well. Some of them shared with me reasons as to why women had placed such a large stake in this agitation.[38] In an attempt to understand the motivations and dynamics of this mass mobilization of women, I spoke to some women members of the Jammu University faculty. Three categories emerged. There were those who had clearly participated in the agitation, those who sympathized with the regional cause but stayed away from it for strategic reasons and those who saw it as a clearly communal movement with which they had no desire to remain associated. These three shades of opinion were representative of those women who appeared to have made an informed choice about participation in this agitation. For others, the swelling ranks of women agitators undoubtedly provided an avenue for participation in public life that had not been available before.

Meetings with two women members of the faculty, one of whom had actively participated in the agitation and the other who had sympathized with the cause but had stayed away, revealed that one year after the agitation in Jammu and possibly with the benefit of hindsight there is a clear attempt to downplay the overt aspects of religiosity that had given a communal colouring to the agitation. I was told that this had been a movement to ensure that the discrimination against Jammu which was the fallout of the centre 'pampering the valley' in order to keep a lid on the violent agitations there, was the primary factor that had motivated the agitation. The central issue articulated by those who participated in the agitation from among the university intellectuals was that of *delimitation*. It was because no delimitation had occurred for several years, I was told, that the balance was always skewed in favour of the valley whether in terms of Lok Sabha seats, assembly seats, public office recruitments, etc. Delimitation would ensure that the actual population is reflected and the reconfiguration of opportunities is done accordingly. While the nuances of this delimitation project may not have been understood very well outside the intellectual confines of the universities and academic circles, the consequences of the absence of delimitation was clearly understood across the board by all women. For them it translated into an area with larger population getting less representation in assembly seats and Jammu being deprived of its rightful share of jobs so that their children's future remained bleak. I was also informed that the reason why a large number of women had participated in the agitation was because they had seen it as an agitation *for their children's future*. For years they had borne the discrimination against Jammu vis-à-vis the valley and the valley-centric politics and they saw this as an opportune moment to protest.

There were other women faculty who stayed away from the agitation, despite the fact that they felt that the movement did represent genuine regional grievances because the language of discrimination which was legitimate and had resonated with the people at that time had been 'hijacked' by Hindu Right Wing forces including the BJP and they did not want to be associated with what would be seen as a communal movement. A third category of women were clear that this agitation was communally driven and spoke only to the elite and middle-class urban Jammu citizen. They asked a series of counter questions: If the agitation was truly regional why is it that the concern of other parts of the Jammu sub-division such as Rajouri, Poonch, Doda were not articulated? Why was the agitation not used to draw attention to the conditions of roads in the Chenab Valley and the state of the social infrastructure in areas that are far from Jammu City, but within the Jammu administrative sub-division? Why were the rights of migrants not alluded to? Why was the discourse loaded in favour of Hindu militant religious slogans?[39] Evidently, women who made this their informed choice were not only marginalized, but also threatened as they were seen as articulating 'anti-Jammu' sentiments.

With the abdication of the mainstream political parties who refused to play a proactive role, the complexion of the movements in Jammu as well as Kashmir changed. What could have been the politics of competing region-alisms gave way to a rabidly communal politics of competing fundamental-isms. In the valley the clarifications that this was an agitation about 'our land' did not explain why Asiya Andrabi, founder of the Islamist Dukhta-ran-e-Millat, not known for attracting a large number of women admirers even in the valley, was able to lead massive protests, and why the slogans for protecting land had to assume distinct Islamist overtones.[40] Some women intellectuals I spoke to in Srinagar admitted their discomfort with the Islamist slogans and said they had cautioned against this but once people were on the streets it was difficult to stop this. The easy appeal of religion for mobilization and for women to also actively be complicit in this turned out to be a common factor between the way the agitations were carried out in the valley and in Jammu which reverberated with 'Bum Bum Bole' as the clarion call for a supposedly regional awakening. Again much in the same way as the intellectuals in the valley, those intellectuals in Jammu who provided direction to the movement also admitted that this was not the original intent, but there was little they could do to stop the dominant sentiment.[41]

The Amarnath legacy appears to continue today even after the heat and dust of the agitations appear to have died out. In recent months, the same spirit of competitiveness that now characterizes relations between Jammu and Kashmir was also evident in the manner in which the debate over the central universities panned out. In the light of what the Amarnath agita-tion has demonstrated and its abiding legacy of competitive identity politics that persists till date, I argue, that despite the fact that the searchlights are always on the dyads of dialogues—between Srinagar (in particular with the Hurriyat) and Delhi; Delhi and Islamabad; Srinagar and Islamabad and Srinagar and Muzaffarabad—what is squarely needed is a dialogue between the different parts of the state of Jammu and Kashmir, as this will affect both the way the trajectory of the conflict unfolds and the form and direction of possible 'solutions'. With several constituencies within the three major sub-divisions asking if the political representatives in the state assembly actually represent their interests, reconciling the politics of presence with the politics of representation, will be the biggest challenge within Jammu and Kashmir. The deep regional fault lines between different parts of the state are likely to play a much more significant role in the manner in which the conflict unfolds than is perhaps cognized.

Women must be made an integral part of these intra- state/regional/sub-regional dialogues, as despite their activism in the Amarnath agitation that polarized people and communities, they have also shown the ability to transcend fault lines, whenever smaller peace initiatives across regions have been initiated. In the midst of competitive sloganeering one strand that stands out is that women in Jammu participated en masse in this agitation because they believed or were made to believe that this was for 'their children's future'. Can a shared commitment to the future of the next generation create a common platform across the divide with women proactively investing in this process? This will however remain an open question till these attempts at dialogue with women at the centre, is actually tried out.

While the Amarnath crisis represents the women's voices being subsumed in militaristic community identities, there is also another kind of quiet political activism in the Kashmir Valley that has involved the seamless transition across gendered fault lines. Led by a woman, it signifies the arrival of a new kind of politics across fault lines of class and gender though it must be acknowledged that the assumption of a leadership role by a woman does not, per se, represent the coming of age of a feminist consciousness. It is to this movement—namely the Association of Parents of Disappeared Persons (APDP) and the politics represented by—to which we now turn our attention.

CROSSING GENDERED FAULT LINES: CONVERTING THE PERSONAL INTO THE POLITICAL

In the course of the armed conflict, thousands of men have 'disappeared', picked up and possibly killed by the security forces, many of them no doubt on mere suspicion of being a militant. Alternatively, they have been killed by militants mostly on suspicions of being 'informers' (*mukhbirs*). As more and more men disappeared, and a large number of 'half-widows' and parents whose sons had 'vanished' came into existence, one woman, Parveena Ahangar, whose son Javed was picked up by security forces and then disappeared, converted her personal loss and grief into a public forum for justice. Today, the Association of Parents of Disappeared Persons (APDP), founded in 1994, is a force that is increasingly being taken note of both by members of the civil society as well as by the government. This group stands resolute in its demand for an answer from the government agencies regarding the fate of their son/husband/father in an attempt to bring a closure to their sense of loss. The personal story of Parveena Ahangar and the manner in which APDP came into existence represents how gendered borders can be crossed during times of exigencies.

In a personal interview conducted in Srinagar in 2003, just as the most violent phase of the conflict appeared to have passed on, Parveena Ahangar had talked to us, in the seclusion of her home in Batamaloo in Srinagar, about her life and why she started this association.[42] Parveena's personal transformation from a reticent homemaker whose access to education had been limited to the fifth standard, to an independent articulate woman, heading an association like the APDP has been remarkable. Married at the age of 12, already a mother at 13, Parveena's eldest son Javed (at the time a teenager), was picked up by the Security Forces on suspicion of being a militant, in what she believes was a clear case of mistaken identity. Since then this homemaker has engaged in a relentless search to find out what happened to her son—a search that has taken her to prisons across the country. This quest has altered the gendered division of labour in a typically patriarchal household. In a discussion that for us demonstrated how gender roles can change during conflict, Parveena's young daughter Saima (16 at the time we met her) told us that as her mother went hunting for her brother, she often found little time to attend to her household chores. Moreover, in these times it was her mother and even she herself who saw themselves as protectors of the family—this, despite the fact that they could not protect her brother.

Parveena's life quest—emanating from her very private grief—that impelled her not give up searching for her missing son Javed for years after he disappeared, brought her into a public space that was not consciously of her own making. Parveena's life story represents a seamless blend of the private and the public, a unique interplay of the personal and the political. We spent some time talking about her politics though she shied away from the term politics. For Parveena, the motivation behind setting up the APDP was simple—it was a simple call for justice. This is why she identified the release of political prisoners and the addressing of human rights violation as the most important priority of the government. While she showed no particular interest in discussing the notion of *azadi* or in the end the picture she had of Kashmir, she was clear about one thing at the time of our interview in 2002. The negotiating table must have representation of those who were victims of the conflict. The presence of women at the negotiating table was not the important issue. Their position as victims was in her opinion the most important marker of identity. Today, she has woven this shared identity of the members into the very fabric of the association and has also used it to ensure that the association is not hijacked by vested interests or its single one point agenda diluted in any way. In an interview in 2007, Parveena emphasized, 'APDP constitution is clear that any person who is not a victim cannot become a member'. Clearly this is to ensure that 'we will not allow anyone to exploit our cause'.[43]

Today, the government has been forced to take note of this association led by a woman who transformed her personal grief into a political instrument for justice. The APDPs methods are situated within the existing legal and constitutional system. It includes using the existing legal system to put forward their demands for justice. Members file habeas corpus in Jammu and Kashmir High Courts (which are now flooded with such petitions), undertake hunger strikes, raise funds to build a memorial for those who have disappeared and sit in *dharna* every year in Srinagar's Pratap Park on the International Day of Disappeared Persons, drawing attention to their plight with placards and photographs of missing persons. Chitra Panmanabhan poignantly and succinctly captures the spirit and significance of this tableau of loss and protest which communicates a 'life affirming aesthetic' in a public space otherwise dominated by the rhetoric of power. In embodying a living memory of the missing, 'it keeps alive the possibility of humanizing politics and its practice in public space'.[44] Parveena Ahangar's form of protest and politics is significant because of the way 'gendered borders' have been seamlessly traversed both in the private and the public spheres creating a space that challenges injustice as well as the militarization of politics by showing an alternative path 'of waging conflict non violently'.

BEYOND IDENTITY POLITICS
AND GENDERED BORDERLINES:
CAN A WOMEN'S COALITION EMERGE?

The question of whether a new politics marked by feminist consciousness can emerge in the current scenario in Jammu and Kashmir—one that transcends the identity 'borderlines' outlined in this chapter—remains a moot question. Feminist writer Urvashi Butalia talks poignantly of the importance of including the women of Kashmir in all peace initiatives and respecting their myriad experiences of the conflict. From the range of testimonies and voices in her edited book *Speaking Peace: Women's Voices from Kashmir*, it is evident that not only have men and women experienced the conflict differently but women themselves constitute no monolith. Women's gender identity has been mediated by their other identities of class, religion, caste, community, region and a repertoire of experiences come through when they 'speak peace'.[45] Rita Manchanda analyses this further pointing out that women in Kashmir should not be boxed into a victimhood discourse— pointing to instances when women have, for instance actively resisted the fundamentalist diktats of militants such as imposition of the veil.[46] Seema Kazi's recent study seeks to explain the experience of women in negotiating the militarization of both the state and the society in Kashmir.[47]

Even as we acknowledge the importance of taking into account women's diverse experiences of the conflict which must, as matter of principle, be taken into account in any dialogue process, we cannot but ask: to what extent has the fractured identity politics of Jammu and Kashmir, particularly the exacerbation of sub-regional identities prevented the dawn of a new kind of inclusive feminist politics? Why is it that the women's movement seems to have bypassed Jammu and Kashmir? Have women transcended or been held hostage to the larger politics of competing nationalisms, competing regionalisms and (now increasingly) competing religious fundamentalisms? Is the mere presence and visibility of women at rallies and *dharnas* that is now seen in both the valley and Jammu evidence of emancipation?

When different constituencies articulate their aspirations through a zero sum game where the gain of one is seen as the loss of the other, a new imaging of politics of inclusion becomes increasingly difficult. In Jammu and Kashmir, particularly in the wake of the Amarnath row, a competitive politics injected with a new militarism has emerged where Jammu's gain is seen as the valley's loss and vice versa. The game of one upmanship and the politics of triumphalism seem to have pervaded the political culture and become the manner in which identity politics has expressed itself. It is not the articulation of regional aspirations per se but the manner in which it has been articulated and the political direction it has taken that is the cause of concern. In this scenario, what is the likelihood of a new imaging of gender sensitive politics based on inclusivity and empathy?

Scholars like Rekha Chowdhary make an important point when they assert that in Jammu and Kashmir gender as a marker of identity has invariably been rendered subservient to other markers of community identities. The fractured identity politics of the state (the valley, Jammu regional identity; the sub-regional identities of Doda, Rajouri, Poonch, Leh and Kargil; the tribal identities of the Gujjar and Paharis) has prevented the assertion of a common context for sharing by women across fault lines. Despite being united in their suffering, they have not been able to articulate this in terms of their shared gender identity. It is because of the co-option of the gender identity, argues Chowdhary that the women's movement has bypassed Jammu and Kashmir.[48]

In conclusion, it is pertinent to remember that the challenges of transcending the divisiveness of identity politics to focus on what the University of Wisconsin at Madison's website describes as 'intercultural encounters and the interactive circulation of power that conditions such exchanges'[49] is evidently the space within which Border Studies increasingly locates itself. Clearly so far, gender identity has been held hostage to larger community concerns in Jammu and Kashmir. Consequently, it has not been able to mediate the sharpness of militarized identities in contemporary Jammu and Kashmir and carve out a new politics of inclusiveness that Border Studies seeks to map.

While it is true that a common identity based on a feminist consciousness does not appear to have arrived yet in Jammu and Kashmir, smaller peace initiatives by women suggest that this is not an impossibility. For instance, in a roundtable held in Delhi organized by Women in Security, Conflict Management and Peace (WISCOMP), the initial acrimonious debate based on identity fault lines did give way to a much more empathetic dialogue at the end of the process.[50] However, the extent to which

stories of personal transformation can give rise to a larger critical consciousness that would lead to political transformation, particularly in the absence
of sustained dialogue among women, does remain an open question. This
dialogue gap is possibly the lacunae that need to be addressed if a rainbow
coalition of women with shared concerns is to emerge in Jammu and
Kashmir which will be in a position to transcend identity fault lines and
influence the way the future can be charted.

Map 4.1 The Map of Jammu and Kashmir

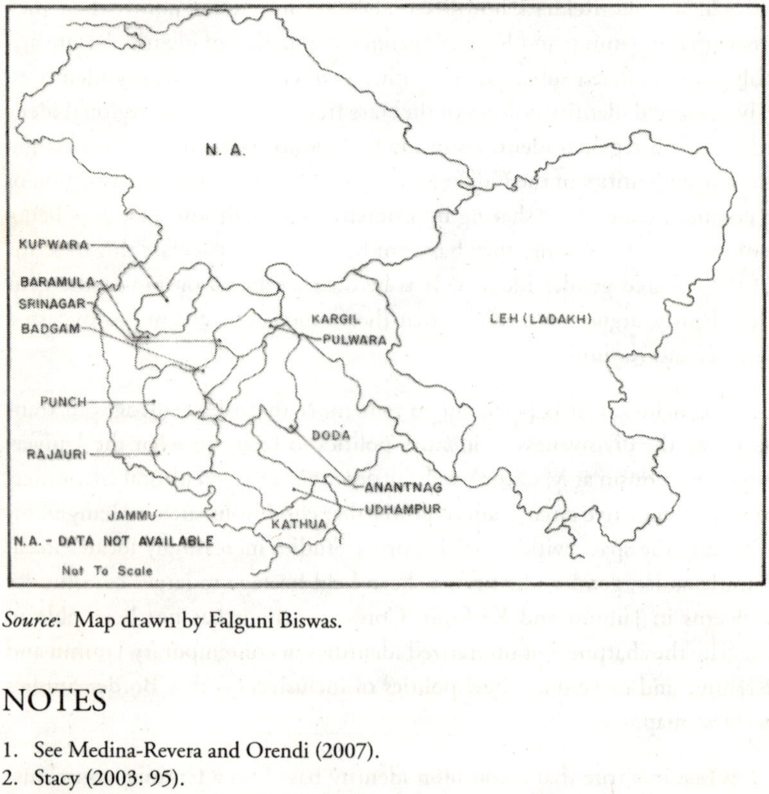

Source: Map drawn by Falguni Biswas.

NOTES

1. See Medina-Revera and Orendi (2007).
2. Stacy (2003: 95).
3. Medina-Revera and Orendi (2007).
4. Raza (1995: 39).
5. There has been a proliferation of literature on the political conflict in Kashmir.
   Some overviews that analyse the causes of the contemporary conflict/militancy are
   Bhattacharjee (1994); Bose (1997), and the more recent Bose (2003); Schofield
   (1997); Joshi (1999); Lamb (1993) and Akbar (1991).
6. Tickner (2001).

7. Kishore (2009).
8. No census was conducted in Jammu and Kashmir by the Registrar General and Census Commissioner of India entrusted to conduct the census of India every 10 years due to disturbed conditions. However, it is important to note that the figures taken from the census figures of 2001 reveal trends in the changes in the population in the 1990s which was the decade when armed conflict was at its peak though it petered out by the end of that decade. On the other hand, the figures from the census of 1981 are indicative of the trends before active armed conflict set in. Taken together the urban–rural disaggregated figures from the period 1981–2001, used with the cautionary note that census data is primary raw data that can only be read in the light of a multiplicity of socio-economic indicators and that we only have interpolated population figures for the 1980s in the absence of the 1991 census, does throw light on an interesting set of correlations.
9 Kishore (2009), same as note 8.
10. Sameer (2009).
11. Kashmir's Composite Rehabilitation Centre says an estimated 30–40 per cent of those seeking their services have been affected by the conflict.
12. Sameer (2009), same as note 11.
13. Afsana (2010).
14. de Jong et al. (2010).
15. Ibid.
16. Ibid.
17. This is revealed in a survey conducted on the multidimensional problem of women in Kashmir by Professor Bashir A. Dabla and his team of 24 researchers all from University of Kashmir, Department of Sociology, sponsored by the Ministry of Planning and Programme Implementation. The final findings of the survey were submitted to the ministry in January 2000. The unit of study of this survey was the Kashmir valley and the sample composed of 4,800 respondents [800 from each district] belonging to various economic, social, educational, demographic, age, religious, linguistic and martial groups. The summary of the survey findings can be found on http://www.mospi.gov.in/research_studies_problen_women_in_kashmir.htm (last accessed on 5 August 2010).
18. de Jong et al. (2010).
19. Kishore (2009), same as note 8.
20. Ibid.
21. Dutta (2006). While Dutta's study related to the state of Jammu and Kashmir as a whole it had a particular salience for the rural areas of Kashmir Valley where militancy had its sharpest impact.
22. DasGupta (2008); Kaul (2010).
23. DasGupta and Singh (2006).
24. Interview was taken in 2009.
25. Interview was taken in 2009.
26. Some responses on domestic violence from the camp at Purkho based on a workshop can be found in DasGupta and Sinha (2008). Reports also indicate growing divorce rates in the camps pointing to stress and strained relations arising out of living in cramped squalid quarters with little or no privacy. See Gupta, 2003.

27. Interview was taken in 2009.
28. Interview was taken in 2009.
29. Interview was taken in 2009.
30. Interview was taken in 2009.
31. The immediate triggering factor revolved around a government order diverting forest land to the Shri Amarnath Shrine Board with the right to erect pre-fabricated temporary structures for housing of the pilgrims (*yatris*) during the period of the Amarnath Yatra. The interpretation that this amounted to the land being given permanently to the Board to build permanent structures generated a massive protest in the valley where people were told that this would result in a demographic change in the valley that would alter its Muslim majority status. The order was revoked to quell the agitation and immediately a reaction was generated in Jammu where the decision was described as anti-Jammu and anti-Hindu and in favour of Muslims of the valley.
32. Puri (1983).
33. Rekha Chowdhary, 'Gender is just a Political Tool,' *Women's Feature Services,* 2008.
34. Ibid.
35. The discontent with what is perceived to be the valley-centric approach to politics in Jammu and Kashmir has been tellingly described as politics with a large Kashmir, a small Jammu and an even smaller Ladakh. For an understanding of the shape of identity politics in contemporary Ladakh, see Kaul and Kaul (1992).
36. Agarwal (2004).
37. Pargal (2009).
38. Interviews conducted with women faculty members in Jammu University by the author in November 2009, more than a year after the Amarnath agitation. The idea was to find out how the Amarnath mobilization continued to shape mindsets and politics even after the street mobilization had died out. There was unprecedented mobilization around the Amarnath crisis in the university and several women members had actually actively participated in the movement. Though they were not representative of the microcosm of the women who participated in the agitation, these interviews clarified some of the motivations and consequences (intended and unintended) of what appeared to be the largest mass mobilization in Jammu in recent years. I have not revealed the names of the faculty members I spoke to but have classified their responses into three categories.
39. Rekha Chowdhary, Professor, Department of Political Science, Jammu University for instance was clear that the diversity of opinion within Jammu subdivision was never ever addressed by the Sangharsh Samiti which also demonstrated its crisis of leadership in the course of the agitation. For an insight on the identity crisis of Jammu's Muslims see Chowdhury (2008: 11–14).
40. Arundhati Roy, writing in August 2008, while clarifying that the uprising in the valley should be seen as a catharsis rather than a vicious jihad, a reaction to years of brutal suppression of democratic freedoms of the people of the valley by the Indian state, does acknowledge, however, that the sea of green flags all around and the slogans (*Azadi ka matlab kya hai? La illaha illallah*—what is the meaning of freedom? There is no god but Allah) made it impossible to ignore the deeply Islamic flavour of the uprising. See Roy (2008).

41. For instance, I also spoke to one of the leading spokespersons of the Sangharsh Samiti, Dr Jitendra Singh. In a telephonic interview on 1 November 2008, he spoke of the cumulative feeling of hurt which found expression through an issue of faith and religion—this was not a dispute over land as the media had painted. He asserted that he had predicted something like this six months before the eruption. This, according to him, was due to the one-upmanship in the valley as the Congress, PDP and NC started their 'dangerous race before the elections over the issue of force withdrawal from the valley'. He was of the view that the 'fundamentalist vote bank in the valley generated a fundamentalist reaction in Jammu'.

42. A series of interviews were conducted by Sudha Ramachandran and Sumona DasGupta in the Kashmir valley as part of a research project on understanding the roots causes of conflict. The project titled 'Crossing Lines with a Gender Lens: Interrogating dominant narratives on causes of conflict in Kashmir', was supported by Social Science Research Council (SSRC), Washington. A summary of the findings can be found in Ramachandran, Gopinath and DasGupta (2003). Narratives of 100 women from across the various districts of the valley were collected through interviews as part of this project.

43. Bukhari (2007).

44. Panmanabhan (2010).

45. Butalia (2008).

46. Manchanda (2001).

47. Kazi (2009).

48. Chowdhary (2008).

49. Medina-Revera and Orendi (2007).

50. DasGupta (2001).

Part 3

Northeast

5

Sanitized Society and Dangerous Interlopers: Law and the Chins in Mizoram

Sahana Basavapatna

INTRODUCTION

Migration between Mizoram and the western part of Burma, specifically Chin State, Sagaing Division and Arakan State dates back to the pre-Independence period when Burma and India were part of British India and where migration of both Mizos and the Burmese[1] was a commonplace event. However, in recent history, migration, for a host of reasons, is mostly a one-sided affair, with more Chins from Chin State and Sagaing Division coming over to Mizoram and other parts of the North Eastern states of India. The developments in Burma, especially since the 1980s, changed the way migration from Burma was perceived. While those fleeing Burma following the 8-8-88 Students Revolution were considered as having genuine claim of asylum under international refugee law, the ones that came later, especially in the last decade were considered more of 'economic migrants'. Any discussion about Burmese migration to Mizoram is at once a fascinating, sensitive and disturbing topic. The porous borders have ensured that with the flow of goods, both legal and illegal, the flow of people continues despite reports of high-handedness of organizations like the Young Mizo Association and the threats and at times actual deportation of Burmese for illegal stay. It is thus fascinating for the way in which the Burmese are able to carry out business activities on a daily basis, live on in various parts of Mizoram either as daily wagers, petty gatherers or work as domestic help. This kind of migration has attracted hostility and seemingly indifferent attitude towards the Burmese, given their long history of common ethnic and religious affinity.

What emerges is that commonplace perceptions and assumptions dominate how the migration is perceived without, as it seems, the scope for transcending received notions and delving deeper into the complex nature of migration and its impact on both the Burmese community and the Mizo state. For instance, a request for access to case laws involving Burmese nationals under the Narcotic Drugs and Psychotropic Substances Act, 1985 by this researcher was turned down by the officers at the Aizwal District Court. This, the authorities perceived, would open up Mizo society to criticism and bring a bad name to Mizos.[2] Commonplace understanding of Burmese in Mizoram seems to revolve around mostly the negative impact of Burmese migration on Mizo society and culture. Examples include the fact that the Burmese commit crime and are responsible for all the drug trade. Those in authority more often than not appear to steer clear of any 'controversial' topics in this regard, be it Indo-Burma border trade, Mizoram's official policy on Burma, especially policies regarding trade and the constant flow of people. The issue is also disturbing because commonplace assumptions dominate the 'understanding' of issues, concerns and associated problems, without there being a scope for transcending these received notions and delving deeper into the complex nature of migration and its impact on both the Burmese community and the Mizo state.

In relative terms, Mizoram is predominantly an ethnically homogenous community. The majority population being Mizo, while some of the minority communities with distinct ethnic–religious and linguistic identities are the Hmars, Pawi, Lakher (or Mara), Riangs (or Brus) and Chakmas. All of these minority communities have been granted political autonomy with the establishment of Autonomous District Councils under the VI Schedule of the Constitution of India.[3] It is considered a model of peace in the North East and this has been attributed to the cohesive nature of the Mizo community.[4] The Burmese experience in Mizoram thus has to be contextualized in the social, political and economic situation of Mizoram that we see today.

Admittedly, the Burmese are foreigners in India but the borders and its dynamics problematizes identity, democracy and citizenship,[5] as a class who straddle the various fluid categories of migrants.

In the existing literature, the Burmese have been categorized either as 'refugees' or 'illegal migrants'. In trying to understand Burmese migration in the context of citizenship and what it means in the Indian context, I choose to refrain from any labelling at the outset,[6] but would use the term 'migration' referring to the act of migration. I will argue that the Mizoram experience points to the need to reconsider the flippant way in which generalizations are made to label migration of this nature either as 'refugee flow' or 'flow of economic migrants'. Very few studies focusing on the migration of Chins in Mizoram have tried to view them, for instance, as 'stateless'. The purpose for not taking on the burdens of these categories is not to lessen in any way the protection that follows this labelling. It is also not being suggested that the Burmese do not fall into either of these categories. However, I am asserting that the lines between 'economic migrants', 'refugees' and 'stateless' or any other are fine and there is every possibility of an overlap. I will argue that the Mizoram experience points to the need to reconsider the existing flippant way in which generalizations are made to label migration of this nature either as 'refugee flow' or 'flow of economic migrants'. India's refugee/immigration policy or the United Nations High Commissioner for Refugees' (UNHCR) approach to Chins would have to be kept in mind. The emerging concepts of 'mixed migration'[7] within the UNHCR or the concept of 'survival migrants' proposed by Alexander Betts[8] is arguing for the need to take these realities into consideration in inquiring into migration policy. Clearly, the international refugee regime, adopted in the 1950s is increasingly losing relevance, with its narrow definition of 'refugee' and most states ensuring that refugees do not seek asylum in their territory.

The attempt to analyse the received categories, such as the ones discussed above, forces us to look at how citizenship is constructed, considering that the nation state, which primarily has defined a citizen is itself being transformed by emerging social, political and economic changes of the contemporary times. In its classical definition, a citizen is a member of a political community who enjoys rights and assumes duties flowing from the membership.[9] Citizenship thus requires that the state provide its citizens a comprehensive package of civil, political and economic rights. At a time, when the nation state is no longer the only dominant player, the way citizenship is constructed in law and in politics has also changed.[10] For instance, Yishai Blank argues that citizenship is determined, managed and controlled in three distinct yet intertwined territorial spheres: the local, the national and the global. He further argues that sub-national territorial units as well as supranational political organizations are increasingly impacting citizenship.[11] Further, studies on how migration is impacting the rights of citizenship across the globe have also provided us rich literature on transformation in citizenship discourse as well as migrants as a category of citizens.

In India, citizenship has been constructed largely in the context of its partition in 1947 and the nation building efforts thereafter. As Ratna Kapur explains and goes on to show in the context of Bangladeshi immigration into India, 'cultural identity, increasingly conflated with religious identity, and the principle of descent and blood ties are central to the constitution of Indian citizenship'.[12] In the Constitution of India, persons who reside outside of India can register as Indian citizens if they or either of their parents or grandparents were born in India.[13] However, no person is entitled to become a citizen of India if he or she has voluntarily acquired the citizenship of a foreign state.[14] The courts have also held that a person who migrated to Pakistan after 1 March 1947, and acquired Pakistani nationality could not subsequently claim Indian citizenship.[15] The project of building a Hindu nation in India, as Samaddar explains, has been 'reflexive'.[16] He argues, 'India is predominantly nationalistic with reference to Pakistan or Bangladesh and not with reference to the US or the United Kingdom'. He then goes on to argue that 'It makes ethnic suppression and sufferings due to forced migration tolerable to the ethics of a nation'.[17] This has meant, in the context of North East, that contests for identity and citizenship in much of the North Eastern states have been ignored. Only with its Look East Policy, which was adopted in the mid-1990s, has the government focused on this frontier region as it can aid in India's economic and political ambitions. Even so, the North East hardly figures in India's national imagination. What this has meant is that the contests over territory and identity between the various tribes in the North East and how these are changing the citizenship discourse in India is relatively unknown in most parts of 'mainstream' India.

In this context, this essay is an attempt to bring out the various ways in which the Chins and Mizos interact with each other. How does one understand this migration across borders? How has the Chin–Mizo relationship and Mizoram's recent political history impact the Chins? What does the easy permeability of the borders say about migration in this region? Does it help in understanding the traditional notions of citizenship in India/South Asia? The borders play a significant role in not only limiting executive decision-making, but are also exploited by a variety of actors in the act of 'crossing over', of people and goods alike. A further dynamic of the changing economic fabric of Mizoram has consequences for the Chin–Mizo relationship that oscillates between convenience and hostility. How are the Chins viewed not only by the laity, but also by those in authority? Does law prove a useful medium of protection, given the changes in the economic and political context? On a normative level, what should be the response of both Mizoram and India towards Chins? Should they be deported because they cross over illegally or be accepted as members of the community by legalizing their stay? Does this particular experience add to the debate about refugees in India? These issues are the subject of the discussion in this chapter. This research is based on primary and secondary literature. Experts from academics, government officials, lawyers, officers of the judiciary, staff from the non-governmental organization (NGO) and current and past functionaries of the Young Mizo Association were interviewed on several aspects of the Chin migration.

In the next section, I explain Burmese migration in the economic, social and political context in Mizoram, highlighting the role played by some of the prominent community organizations in keeping Mizoram a 'cohesive society'. Thereafter, the various issues of Burmese migration in Mizoram are highlighted. In a subsequent section, I attempt to comprehend experiences of Burmese women in seeking to use law as an instrument of protection. This is followed by the conclusion, where I attempt to answer some of the questions raised in the 'Introduction'.

HISTORICAL OVERVIEW OF THE CHIN–MIZO RELATIONSHIP AND MIGRATION ACROSS BORDERS

It would be pertinent to introduce the Chins in Mizoram in the context of political and economic developments in the region over the last 60 years.

This includes an overview of the shared relationship between the Mizos and Chins, Mizoram's history of development (political, economic, cultural and social) that plays a significant part in impacting the Chin population, and a sketch of India's policy on refugees and migrants.

The Chin–Mizo relationship as we understand now can be traced quite a way back. Both the Chins and the Mizos believe in a similar origin myth. According to the Mizo oral tradition, their ancestors are believed to have emerged from a cave or rock known as 'Chhinlung', believed to be in present day China. This population then moved on through what is now Tibet into the Hukwang Valley in Burma and over time moved to Kubaw Valley (in west of Sagaing Division of present Burma) to enter into what was then called Lushai Hills in the 18th century.[18] Lian Sakhong, in drawing a picture of the Chin ethnicity, describes the accepted myth of common descent and notes, 'All sources of Chin traditions maintain that their ancestors originated from "Chinglung" or "Cin-lung"'.[19] However, the decade of the 1940s, which lead to the creation of independent states of Burma/Myanmar and India, is significant to understand the recent trends we witness in Mizoram and the more complex dynamics at work. While a common descent is invoked by the two communities in relating to each other ('they are our brothers'), the break-up of the territory that lay to the north-east of British India in 1947 lead to an identity contest.[20] This contest to claim a superior status over each other also manifests itself in the claim for the dominant identity that continues to impact the relationship between several sub-tribes, including between the Mizos and the Chins. Thus, for instance, the Kukis do not identify themselves with the Chins and seek a separate territory within Burma, the Chins believe that they are the original inhabitants of the region and thus call the Mizos as 'chins living in *western Chinram*'.[21] The Mizos on the other hand, believe that Chins are a sub-tribe of the Mizos. This contest continues to this day, albeit in a different form and forms a factor in the Chin–Mizo relationship in Mizoram.

India and Burma were British colonies until they gained independence in 1947 and 1948 respectively. The creation of Burma as a separate dominion under the Government of India Act, 1935 led to the division of the Lushai population across the geographical region[22] that we now call the 'north-east'. The Treaty of Yandaboo drew the boundary line between India and Burma in 1937.[23] By this time, the Lushai population that was found across the 'north-east' was now divided between three countries, India, Burma and Bangladesh. Chungkhosei Baite, in *Independence of India and Burma: Its Impact on Chin People*, gives an account of the break-up:[24]

> [A]bout 5,00,000 in Manipur, about 8,00,000 in Mizoram, about 50,000 in Tripura and about 2,00,000 in Cachar and North Cachar Hills of Assam in India, about 2,00,000 in the Chittagong Hill Tracts of Bangladesh and about 30,00,000 in Chin Hills Matu area, Khumi area, Mara area and Arakan in Burma.[25]

It is thus highly conceivable that migration of Burmese and the Mizos in areas that are now divided by official boundaries was commonplace. In fact, Mizo historians argue that the Mizos were in the Chin Hills of present-day Burma from the 15th to the 18th century before they migrated to what is now the North Eastern region in India, including Manipur, Assam, Bangladesh (Chittagong Hill Tracts) and Burma due to 'the pressure of the Chin or the stronger clans of Burma and the pressure of over population'.[26] Keeping this historical fact in mind, it is difficult to argue for a closed society that can stop the movement of people.

MIGRATION IN CONTEMPORARY TIMES

In relatively more recent times, specifically, the end of the decade of the 1980s, Burmese migration has been characterized differently from the previous decades.[27] The increase in the military strength of the junta during this period and its gaining of control over the ethnic states that were otherwise autonomous, led to large-scale internal displacement.[28] A large number of Burmese nationals are now known to have escaped to and sought asylum in countries in the neighbouring South and South East Asia.[29] The increase in the strength of the military junta by more than twice its size since 1988 lead to setting up of camps throughout the ethnic states. Bhaumik, for instance, notes that the Burmese junta's control over the south-western region of Burma, which includes Chin State and Sagaing Division 'resulted in the establishment of over 20 new battalions of soldiers throughout this remote and mountainous area', essentially leading to '... growing persecution and impoverishment of the local people' (Bhaumik, 2003: 204).[30]

The characterization of the Chin migration has been a factor in the political relationship between the two countries. While initially, India was welcoming of Burmese nationals who fled following the student demonstrations in the late 1980s, this was not so in the late 1990s, when its foreign policy considerations in the region changed.[31] Burmese nationals living in Delhi and recognized by the Office of the UNHCR are issued Residence Permits and thus tacitly recognized by the Indian government, but those in Mizoram are still believed to be largely 'economic migrants'.

This brings us to another essential factor that impacts the Mizo–Chin relationship and revolves around the political, economic, social and cultural factors that make up Mizoram. Mizoram is largely a homogenous Christian community with smaller minority tribes comprising the Chakmas, the Hmars and the Brus who, as per the Sixth Schedule of the Constitution of India, administer their affairs through Autonomous District Councils.[32] Politically, Mizoram witnessed about two decades of insurgency demanding a sovereign state before it was granted statehood in 1987.[33] In terms of the social and economic development, numerous changes have taken place since the last two decades and the existing economic policy in the form of the 'Look East Policy' and the border trade would lead to further changes. Mizoram boasts of the second highest literacy rate in the country after Kerala at 88 per cent and generally low poverty levels.[34] The Look East Policy is being received with enthusiasm and the border trade is believed to have become an essential feature of Mizoram's economy.[35] Emerging changes also include a transition from shifting cultivation to a semi-settled agricultural system which has led to significant and substantial changes in the rural agricultural economy among others, in the form of change in the agrarian structure from common ownership of land to private ownership, cultivation for subsistence to commercial production.[36] Changes have also been visible in the structures of rights institutions and the legal system. The system of chieftainship where the Chief held powers of village administration, as well as, administration of justice according to customary laws was abolished by the establishment of the District Councils in 1952 (which in turn had legislative, executive, financial and judicial powers).[37] A decision to separate the executive from the judiciary was taken in 2002 and was effectuated in 2009.

CHIN NATIONALS IN MIZORAM

There is little agreement on the number of Chin nationals living in Mizoram. However, rough estimates suggest the Burmese[38] population is between 70,000 and 100,000, apart from a smaller number of Nepali and Bangladeshi population. A large number of the Chins work in the informal labour market, in weaving units, tenant farming, quarries, road construction, trade, housekeeping and domestic work[39] and in government services. It is generally agreed that the Burmese are able to work in any circumstances and take up all kinds of employment given the overwhelming need to earn. Over the years, Burmese organizations such as Women's League of Chinland (WLC) and Human Rights and Education Institute of Burma (HREIB) have set up bases in Mizoram focusing on legal protection, health care, advocacy and training. Some of the Mizo organizations that have played a role in the Chin–Mizo relationship include the Young Mizo Association (YMA), Mizo Zirlai Pawl (MZP) and Mizoram Hmeichhe Insuihkham Pawl (MHIP). There are also a number of NGOs, such as, Ferrando Integrated Women's Development Centre (Peace Home),[40] that works with Burmese domestic workers, the Centre for Peace and Development (CPD),[41] which as a Service Provider under the Protection of Women from Domestic Violence Act has intervened in matrimonial issues involving the Burmese, Grassroots Development Network[42] that provides a safe house for women facing domestic violence, and Human Rights & Law Network (HR&LN) that has focused on human rights education, advocacy and intervention.

As an organization that claims to have 3.5 lakh members, 750 branches spread all over Mizoram and in the other neighbouring states of Assam, Manipur, Meghalaya, Nagaland and Tripura,[43] YMA is one of the strongest non-political voluntary organizations and defines its role, as also noted on its website as 'running adult education centres, afforestation, construction of houses for the rural poor, conservation of Mizo culture and heritage, cleanliness drive, campaign on health and sanitation, running public libraries and campaign against the evils of drugs and alcohol'.[44] Although claiming to be a social organization, a number of YMA functionaries and members are either associated with political parties or hold positions within

the government, casting doubts on its identity purely as a 'social organization'. The influence that YMA wields in Mizoram is enormous, including
in politics, economy and social life. Among some others was the MHIP,
established in 1974 as a Mizoram government programme 'to facilitate ...
the work of SSWAB [State Social Welfare Advisory Board][45] and the various government departments' and works for the 'upliftment of women and
children'.[46] Reaching out to women without 'discriminating between caste,
creed or religion', its activities are similar to those of the YMA, with particular focus on women, fighting against atrocities against women, championing
the cause of destitute women, counselling, leadership training and social
integration. It seeks to build its image as the 'mother of social, economic
and cultural liberty'.[47]

Studies on the Chin population in Mizoram and their status in law
done by Mizo academics or activists are scarce.[48] An unpublished MPhil
dissertation of the Department of Economics, Mizoram University, titled
'The Pattern of Migration and its Effects on Economic Development with
Special Reference to Mizoram' gives a perspective of how Burmese migration is viewed in Mizoram. It notes, '... Myanmar alone contributes as
high as 84.08 percentage of the total international migration (to Mizoram)
while Nepal and Bangladesh contribute 9.61 per cent and 6.01 per cent
respectively'.[49] A large number of these people live in Aizawl, in smaller
towns along the border as well as in the south, including Champhai, Saiha,
Lunglei and Lawngtlai.[50] It argues, like most others, that the Burmese are
'illegal migrants' and concludes that 'work or employment opportunity is
the main reason of migration for external migrants'.[51] On the basis of data
taken from Census 2001 Government of India, the author notes that 'the
most important reason for migration is family', accounting for 40.04 per
cent of the total international migrants while '26.38 per cent do not specify
their reasons for migration'.[52] Relying on this data, he argues that a high
percentage of the population moving because of 'family' and 'unspecified
reasons' indicate that Mizoram receives a good number of illegal migrants
from other countries'. He further adds, 'family is an important reason for
migration of females'.[53] To begin with, to classify all those migrating to
Mizoram, including the Burmese, Nepali and Bangladeshi nationals as 'migrants for work' is to take a narrow view of the complex nature of migration.
Further, even if true, the Census data relied upon in this instance is insuf-
ficient in itself to lead to such a conclusion. The categories that the author

relies on, 'family' and 'unspecified', is broad and fails to capture other factors that result in migration. Lastly, and importantly, migration as a phenomenon cannot be explained by oversimplified variables such as the ones adopted in the Census data. In similar vein, dominant perceptions, some of which run the risk of being mere opinions in the absence of a holistic study, hold the Chins responsible for smuggling, alcohol abuse, illegal trade, entry without identity documents, violation of laws and 'misuse of freedoms they have in Mizoram'.[54] Crimes allegedly committed by the Burmese such as theft,[55] rape, smuggling of arms[56] and such others have also been reported. The Mizo police as well as organizations such as the YMA also arrest and initiate legal action against the Burmese involved in these crimes and are what clearly appears as selective arrests of 'illegal' Burmese nationals.[57]

Research carried out by some organizations, academics and journalists that are based outside of Mizoram give an account of the various aspects of Chin migration into India. The report by Human Rights Watch in 2009 while focusing on protection and livelihood problems faced by the Chin refugees highlight the 'discrimination and abuses Chin face in Mizoram State in India at the hands of voluntary associations and Mizoram authorities, and the continuing lack of protection for Chin refugees', '… the abuses, severe discrimination, and religious repression' faced by the Chins and 'serious obstacles to finding jobs, housing, and affordable education' because of discrimination and lack of legal status. They also note the periodic 'anti-foreigner' campaigns and the targeting by Mizo voluntary associations and Mizoram state authorities.[58] The Centre for Refugee Research, University of New South Wales, Australia carried out a survey where it interviewed 48 women and 10 men in November 2008.[59] The objective was to understand two aspects, 'the risks and issues of concern for refugees living in Mizoram and Manipur and the description of the situation of ongoing persecution in Chin State which is causing refugees to flee and to have a fear of forced return'.[60] The study revealed that because of the difficulty in finding employment, women have taken to sex work. It also brought out the problems associated with domestic work, including low wages and sexual violence, domestic violence, and the inability to access education, health care and political rights. It further notes that Chin women:

… are particularly at risk working in abusive and exploitative environments in Mizoram. Many are employed as traditional hand-loom weavers,

where they are often required by their employers to work very long hours
and live at the workplace. Most Chin weavers are not paid salaries, but
instead receive low wages on a piece-by-piece basis. Their wages typically depend on the intricacy of the weaving pattern and how much the
weaving is sold for, decisions decided upon by the employer. Although
exact wages depend on many factors, most Chin weavers receive 150 Rupees
(US$3.50) for completing four to five weavings a day. Chin weavers in
Mizoram typically work in small, cramped rooms with limited natural
light. As handloom machines take up a considerable amount of space,
there is little room to sleep. In some instances, weavers must sleep on their
machines. Domestic work, according to the report, employs women and
girls aged between 12 and 20 years and involve often work very long hours
for little pay. The exact wages often depends on the employer, but Chin
domestic workers typically earn 200 to 1,500 Rupees (US$4.50 to $35)
per month for 16-hour days. The risk of abuse and exploitation, including
rape and sexual violence, beatings, failure to receive promised wages, and
other problems, is high.[61]

The social and economic context that animates the life of the Chins indicates that exploitative conditions are a result of the illegal status of Chins,
who in turn, due to this factor, keep a low profile of themselves.[62] Articulation by the collective community in a way that criticizes the local authorities runs the real risk of a clamp down on them, as recent experience
suggests. The Human Rights Watch released its report on the Chin population in Mizoram in 2009 (as mentioned above). Among others, it concludes
that Chin nationals in Mizoram lack basic protection of their rights and
adequate humanitarian assistance. It goes on to state that the Government
of India, despite not being a signatory to the 1951 Convention on the Status
of Refugees and the 1967 Protocol, is bound by the principle of non-
refoulement. In its assessment, the government has failed to protect refugees
as per international law. Further, in Mizoram, the Chin nationals face discrimination and threats of 'forced return' by 'Mizo voluntary associations in
collusion with the Mizoram authorities'.[63] The report was not well received
by several organizations, some of whom noted that Human Rights Watch
misrepresented the situation. The General Secretary of Central YMA was of
the opinion that not all facts were taken into consideration and the report
was biased. When asked if he could give an example, he stated that contrary
to what is stated in the report,[64] the situation is not as bad as is made out
to be.[65] Another YMA functionary noted that the HRW report considered

information from only 'one side' and 'hurt the sentiments of Mizos'.[66] He stated that while some information provided by the report was true, 'people have to be careful about reporting the conflict; otherwise it will lead to an undesirable situation'.[67] Following its publication, the YMA held a meeting with all Chin Associations and asked them to publicly apologise for it. It also decided to undertake a census of the Chin population in the entire Mizoram. At the time of the interview, out of a total of 772 YMA branches, 173 had submitted their reports.[68] Although the General Secretary of YMA did not explain the purpose of the census, the President of the MZP, V.L. Krosshnehzova, stated that the Census would aid in addressing the 'social problem' of Chin nationals getting into illegal activities.[69]

LEGAL AND SOCIAL INSTITUTIONS: BURMESE WOMEN'S EXPERIENCES

From the previous section, three specific issues may be flagged for further discussion. These issues include the way Chins are perceived in Mizoram, their legal status, basic protection and the efforts made to overcome discrimination and lack of rights. As the law stands, the entry, stay and exit of a foreigner arriving in India is regulated under the Foreigners Act, 1946, the Constitution of India, the Registration of Foreigners Act, 1939 and the Passports Act, 1967. The Government of India has plenary power to pass executive orders on any issue concerning foreigners, as the subject falls under the Union List of the Constitution of India. India's policy towards refugees has been, at a minimum, an adherence to the principle of non-refoulement (but as in the case of Mizoram, even this principle has been violated by India). Burmese nationals who apply for asylum in Delhi with the Office of the UNHCR have been tacitly recognized by the government of India once they are given refugee status by the refugee agency. This is the current practice as refugees get Residence Permits from the Foreigners Regional Registration Office (FRRO). Under the Foreigners Act, 1946, a foreigner entering India is required to hold valid passport and visa and a permit from the local authorities.

Chin women who live in Mizoram often do not have valid legal identity papers. Usually Chins arrive in cities like Aizawl or the bordering towns either for a short duration or for a longer haul. Entry into Mizoram is easy as border trade is also encouraged. Moreover, it is not easy to distinguish a Chin from a Mizo. In the case of Mizoram, notifications issued by the state government in 2003 laid down the guidelines 'for the regulation of entry etc., of Myanmar Nationals in Mizoram'.[70] They required that a Burmese national 'ordinarily resident in any area within 40 km on the Myanmar side of the Indo-Myanmar frontier, entering into India across the said frontier after ... July 1968' should possess 'a permit or other like document' by the Myanmarese authority and 'a permit ... by the authorities' in the State of Mizoram.[71] Burmese nationals could thus travel within Mizoram within a 40 km radius from the border, but travel 'which is beyond the 40 kilometres from the crossing-point along the aforesaid border' would require the Burmese to have a valid passport and visa under the Indian Passports Act, 1920 and the Passports Act, 1967. This notification was suspended by the Government of Mizoram in 2006[72] following complaints by the Assam Rifles of arms smuggling across the borders.[73] The significance of this notification must, however, be understood. Burmese nationals could, under this law, apply for a 'Temporary Stay Permit' under Guideline 8(1), but would need to specify a sponsor, who is 'a bona fide indigenous resident of Mizoram residing within 40 (forty) kilometres of the Indo-Myanmar Border'.[74] The Form II, specified in the notification, is required to be filled in by the applicant along with an 'Undertaking by the Sponsor', who would be required by law to assist Mizo authorities in arranging deportation of the permit holder when he is 'no longer require[d] for his service' to the job he or she was doing in Mizoram. Thus, this notification not only regulated the entry, stay and exit of Burmese in Mizoram, but also amounted to a temporary work permit. No further notification has however replaced this law.

To the extent that the Chins do not have valid documents, they are 'illegal' entrants in Mizoram and run the risk of deportation and abuse by the police. Employment although easily found, is exploitative and affordable housing or education is also not easily found.[75] However, the fact that they are 'illegal' in law only partially explains the situation. The precarious legal status of Chins in Mizoram makes it difficult, if not impossible to claim basic rights, either of education, or humane conditions of work or access to employment. Under the law, the Chins entering Mizoram without valid identity documents and visa are illegal migrants, against whom proceedings under the Foreigners Act and other legislations can be initiated. However, Chins have also been granted refugee status by the United

Nations High Commissioner for Refugees (UNHCR) and tacit recognition by the Government of India, by way of Residence Permits for recognized refugees in Delhi. The Chins in Mizoram, however, are caught in the situation where it is not possible to make a clear distinction as to their legal status. In sum, the Mizo's response to Chin's social, economic and political status is one of focusing for instance, on the 'illegal acts' of the Chins while at the same time, perceiving them as 'brothers'. For instance, the Chairperson of the State Women's Commission, Ms Rozami argues that Chins commit illegal activities ('the Burmese steal and run away'), such as drug trafficking and other criminal activities that may attract state action criminal laws. This, according to her is the direct result of the poor economic situation of Chins.[76] No logical explanation is given as to the real connection between these two factors. Perhaps, it is meant that the dire situation in the Chin state forces them to commit crimes like theft or drug trafficking, as an easy way to overcome their impoverished status. She continues that despite their 'criminal activities', the government of Mizoram cares for the Chins and therefore does not initiate legal action against them. Similarly, the President of the MZP, on being asked about the legal status of the Chins stated that 'one cannot say that Chins are illegal because they are brothers'. He added that 'they are refugees and risk their lives to survive'.[77] The repeated invocation of these two opposing factors in explaining The Mizo relationship with the Chins is commonplace amongst the Mizos generally and the Mizo (and non-Mizo) authorities interviewed for the purposes of this research.

Thus, despite the existing uncertainty—the inability to implement the laws, the inability to differentiate between a Mizo and a Chin, and the inability to stop people from crossing over the borders—many examples of varying kinds indicate a mixed response. Burmese nationals are often arrested, threatened with deportation and at times 'left near the borders' (who then return back).[78] Every news report detailing the arrest notes that the Burmese are 'illegal' or that it has lead to disturbance of the social fabric and thus is intended to drive home the point that a 'peaceful' and 'clean' Mizo society cannot be allowed to be contaminated by non-Mizos. This function of maintaining law and order is carried out by the YMA,[79] apart from the state authorities who by law have been entrusted with this mandate. As pointed out by a YMA functionary, the idea is to separate the 'good' Chin, who are 'good citizens' of Mizoram, from the 'bad' ones.[80]

In the words of one member of YMA, the issuance of a quit notice or the action to deport a Chin is merely a 'request' and not an order.[81] What could it mean to call a 'good' Burmese a 'citizen'? Does it refer to the ethnic and religious ties that continue to partly define how they view each other? If it is so, then there is a constant switching between rejection of the Burmese and their identification as one of 'our' own. And at the very local level, does it mean that 'citizenship' itself is constantly defined and redefined, indicating that formal citizenship is not static and is unable to explain the experiences of a large number of migrants?

However, it would be unfair to judge the Chin situation in Mizoram and the response of the Mizos as one of constant opposition. While to a large extent women are unable to access protection under existing laws, two examples are given below that explain how women use laws to protect themselves. The first example, unique in many respects involves a case of domestic violence against a Chin woman. The second involves issues of employment and the efforts of an organization that seeks to secure rights for domestic workers. In a case of domestic violence, the complainant approached the court under the Protection of Women from the Domestic Violence Act, 2005 seeking an Order prohibiting the respondent from committing an act of domestic violence (physical violence) under Sec.18, custody of her daughter under Sec. 21, an order for compensation under Sec. 22 and monetary relief under Sec. 20. In this case, the respondent was a Mizo while complainant was a Chin, who having come to Aizawl for a visit, married the respondent and had a child aged about a year and a half at the time of filing the complaint. The complainant alleged that the respondent has been physically violent, 'abused the complainant verbally and emotionally by calling her names and looking down at her because of her family background and also due to the native place where the complainant has come from'.[82] It was further alleged that the respondent 'prevented her from taking up any kind of job and that the complainant is living in constant fear'. The respondent denied these allegations and stated 'that he was never married to her under any provision of law'[83] but accepted that 'they were living together'. The complainant decided to initiate legal action despite threats from the respondent that he would complain to the police that she was a Chin and therefore illegally staying in Aizawl. The Centre for Peace and Development, one of the Service Providers under the DV Act had helped the complainant file a Domestic Incident Report under the Act and facilitated counselling for both parties on the direction of the court. It submitted its report stating that 'despite' four rounds of counselling, the parties had opted for divorce.[84] On the basis of all the facts put before her, the judge held in favour of the complainant and ordered the respondent under Sec. 18 to reframe from 'causing any sort of physical hurt to the complainant',[85] 'using obscene words',[86] 'entering in the house where the complainant presently lives',[87] 'causing any obstruction to the complainant from her going to different places where she desires'[88] and 'causing any hardships to the minor child at any time'.[89] The respondent was also ordered under Sec. 20 to 'pay a monthly allowance of ₹ 2000 and pay maintenance to his child till the minor attains the age of majority'.[90] The custody of the child was given to the complainant under Sec. 21 'till the said minor attains the age of 3 years in accordance with the customary practice'.[91] Although the Centre for Peace and Development was aware that the complainant was a Chin, it did not disclose it in the DIR. The Magistrate, Sylvie Ralte who heard the case was also aware of this fact, but as stated in her order that 'the purpose of the Act is to give protection to the aggrieved woman from domestic violence',[92] did not consider this a material fact given the circumstances and thus, proceeded to make the order in favour of the complainant.

The second case under discussion in this chapter is related to the issues of employment. Ferrando Integrated Women's Development Centre (hereafter Ferrando Centre), is an organization that focuses on domestic workers and in addition, runs a weaving and tailoring centre, a piggery and pottery centre, an embroidery centre, drug treatment centre and has drop-in-centres in Aizawl, Champhai and Saiha. A majority of Ferrando Centre's clients are Chin women. A total of 30 staff members are responsible for five projects, including projects on drugs/HIV, skills development, disabilities and domestic workers. As none of the Mizo women acknowledge that they are 'domestic workers', any talk about domestic workers more often than not involves the Chins. A large number of Chin women work as domestic workers in Mizoram. According to figures cited in the Annual Report, National Domestic Workers' Movement, North East Region for the years 2006–07, 65 per cent of those registered with the organization, amounting to 1,187 women are Chin and the rest of about 645 women are Mizo. The feeling of being looked down upon by the Mizos, discrimination, low wages, non-payment of wages, verbal, physical and sexual harassment and abuse, excessive work over that which is allowed by labour laws, lack of security in the place for accommodation, inability to find employment and inadequate nutrition—were identified as problems that women reported to the organization.[93]

As a response to the problems identified, Ferrando Centre registers domestic workers, which is a first step in attempting to exercise their rights. In explaining some ground realities of Burmese domestic workers, Sister Rose Paite states that it is sheer survival that prevents women from negotiating for their rights. However, women who register with the NGO are found employment, and a contract is signed between the employee and the employer, attempting to put in place a framework of relationship that has the potential to ensure rights, including appropriate pay, hours of work and weekly leave in the contract. Those who are registered are also asked to inform Ferrando Centre of any problem arising in the workplace, who then takes the necessary action. This according to Sr Rose is an improvement, considering that women were subject to more exploitation in the past. For instance, she notes that while earlier Burmese women had to settle for anywhere between ₹400 and ₹800 as monthly salary, they now do not have to agree to work unless they are paid at least ₹1,500. Another advantage of registration is that trainings are regularly conducted on legal rights and negotiation skills and weekly meetings are held every Sunday so that women have a forum to share their concerns. These problems are then raised with the concerned employers.[94] While the organization is among the few that focuses on legal rights of Chin women who work as domestic help, a large part of its interventions also concentrates on rehabilitation of women and provision of opportunities for vocational training. Thus, given the focus on assistance as opposed to legal interventions, the organization is limited in its efforts to make an intervention on workers rights and migration.

These preceding two examples suggest that there are some instances where recourse to the law is the only option, for instance in case of rape or sexual assault. Sexual abuse, including harassment and rape are rampant; however, women hardly complain or choose to initiate legal action. In their experience, even when a rape case is filed, the fact that Sr Rose has to accompany the complainant personally during the hearing and the possibility of a trial dragging on for years often results in inaction. Thus, not all instances get reported, let alone investigated and charges framed against the perpetrator. Some of the non-legal ways of improving the situation of migrant women have been the training of women to negotiate for their rights at the time they start working. For instance, where earlier women ended up agreeing to working long hours, seven days a week and for low wages, now they insist on a weekend off and an assurance of a minimum salary (without which they do not agree to take up the employment and share their experiences in a regular weekly meeting in Fernando integrated centre). According to Sr Rose, this has raised the level of confidence among women. Some inferences can be drawn from these two examples. The case of a Chin woman seeking protection under the Domestic Violence Act seems to be the first such case and indicates that the complainant was seen not as an illegal migrant, but as a survivor of domestic violence and in need of immediate assistance. This is a significant order, considering that Chin women are often subject to violence without being able to access the legal system even if they are theoretically entitled to take recourse to the law. Employment, however, is a more sensitive issue in Mizoram. A large number of domestic workers are Chin women, and reports suggest that the Mizos have come to be dependent on them as not many Mizos take to this nature of work. At the same time, the fact that the Chins are forced by survival needs to take up any employment under the most trying circumstances make this kind of employment exploitative. At an informal level, therefore, the space to negotiate with the existing system exists and is aided by Mizo individuals and organizations as in the two instances shown above. Significantly, numerous examples also suggest that legal protection is not easily available and therefore these examples may be exceptions.

Thus, there is an element of truth in the argument that '… the integration of Chins in Mizo society oscillates between rejection, solidarity and dependency'.[95] At the cost of stretching the argument, there is yet another inference that I wish to draw. Both these cases, where the importance of protection and entitlement dominate over concerns of formal citizenship, is an example of the notion that although illegal, there is something more fundamental that needs to be factored into, in understanding that the illegal migrant is also a rights bearing subject. The Constitution of India may be said to recognize this in Articles 14 and 21, which extend to all persons and not just citizens in India. Linda Bosniak, for instance, calls this 'ethical citizenship'[96] where she argues that '… a person's physical presence within the territory of a state—whether a national or supranational state—should be the basis for extending them important rights and recognition'.[97] She further argues that a 'territorialist commitment is a constitutive part of the law of many liberal democratic states'[98] and 'ethical territoriality correctly treats membership as matter of social fact rather than as legal formality and it honours egalitarian and anti-caste commitments that liberal democracy purports to stand for—does stand for at its best'. How does this reality impact our notions of citizenship? India as a post-colonial state, in defining its policy towards foreigners has displayed 'cartographic anxiety', especially in relation to its neighbours. As B.S. Chimni explains, 'This cartographic anxiety has been accentuated by porous borders and the fact that states in South Asia have been carved out of people's inhabiting a "common space" for long periods in history'.[99] This cartographic anxiety is true of Mizoram, with numerous instances of demarcating the insider from the outsider. Mizoram displays this through a strong sense of identity, visible in its relationship with the Chakmas or the Brus (which also run the risk of turning antagonistic), or in the mandate of social organizations such as the YMA.[100]

Fundamentally, how may one explain such a response where on one hand, there is a clear show of solidarity and recognition of the factors underlying the flight of Chins to Mizoram and at the same time, this solidarity is conspicuous by its absence if one recognizes that the Mizo response to allegation of illegal acts is usually by way of threat or actual deportation? Further, how are the law and legal enforcement institutions used in their application in the context of Chin 'immigration'? It is submitted that there is an *incorrect* understanding or perhaps indifference to how existing law applies to refugees in India. This has a bearing in its impact on the Chins, even if it is argued that not all of them are 'refugees' under existing law. A few examples would clarify this point. The chairperson of the State Women's Commission in Mizoram argues that the Chins 'reach Delhi and get a lot of money from the UN after which they come back and continue with illegal work'.[101] Yet another interviewee, a lawyer practising in the Aizawl district court, notes that the Burmese are given refugee status by the Government of India. It is thus clear, that the presence of the Chins or others from Burma in Mizoram is characterized as illegal without a clear understanding of how the law operates vis-à-vis the Burmese nationals. For instance, Paula Banerjee argues, in the context of trafficking of people across borders, that women from Chin State who survive sexual harassment are not given refugee status, as that is one a ground for asylum (Banerjee, 2009: 442–63): 'Denied citizenship by the Myanmar government and refugee status by the Government of India (GoI) these women become stateless'.[102] It is for this reason that it is difficult to characterize the Chins as 'refugees' or 'migrants' conclusively. These legal terminologies, while they admittedly serve the purpose of ensuring protection, also run the risk of misuse in a context that serves a specific political purpose. In the Chin context, as has been substantiated in this chapter, the Mizos acknowledge that Chins face 'hardships' in Burma and therefore are compelled to flee; however, this argument is not translated in the legal discourse which continues to stress on 'political' persecution as a standard for refugee status. If there is a tacit recognition that the Chins continue to flee owing to the political situation and the economic conditions that are precipitated by Burma's political situation, it is imperative that a mechanism be developed to give an opportunity for those seeking asylum to do so, after which a decision on an asylum claim can be made. In the context where India's policy is ad hoc and therefore subject to the plenary powers of the executive, to consider 'a large part' of the Chins as 'illegal migrants' not only leads to violence, but is a selective use of law that only serves the purposes of real politics.

CONCLUSION

One often wonders what it would take for the Chin–Mizo brotherhood and ties between the two communities to be acknowledged, the reality of migration to be clearly articulated as a problem and international relations between Mizoram/India and Burma to be ultimately valorized? This question points out at and forces us to look at the various factors at play. As has been raised earlier, as non-citizens, are the Burmese to be deported for illegal stay? Or does their experience suggest the various ways in which the Burmese have already been able to work the system in Mizoram? Deportation in this case is not only selectively carried out, but is also difficult for a variety of reasons. Suggestions that a strengthening of the border forces and the police forces would resolve this issue also do not provide answers. The social, political and economic context sketched in this chapter is equally important to make meaningful conclusions of the nature of the Chin–Mizo relationship. What can be noted from the Chin–Mizo relationship is solidarity, on account of ethnic similarities but also hostility, owning to the political and economic implications of the migration. Law and legal institutions are inadequate in protecting the Chins, and are not the only instruments that Chins have employed in ensuring protection in Mizoram. At times, as the examples above suggest, law has been used as a means of claiming rights, but non-legal factors, such as invocation of ethnic similarities also play a role. On the other hand, voluntary organizations such as the YMA, and their mandate to create a cohesive and peaceful Mizo society where all are integrated into the way of life, results in the taking of law into their own hands.

In almost every interview done and most literature referred to, there is an acknowledgement and acceptance of the fact that the Chins are unable to survive in Chin State/Sagaing Division because of the deteriorating political, economic situation. Given Burma's history, a radical change is also unlikely in the short term. Thus, while India is keen to trade with Burma, it would be forced to consider the growing (predominantly) Chin population both in Mizoram, other North Eastern states, as well as metropolitan centres like Delhi. Seen in a national security perspective, Chins are then problematized and although a desire to control the movement of people is articulated, the nature of the borders clearly makes the task difficult. Mizoram itself is undergoing far-reaching transformation; the agrarian structures are changing with new modes of production resulting in new legal systems. What was traditionally a classless society now has to grapple with private property, the landed and the landless. The number of people in big cities like Aizawl is likely to grow for the opportunities for livelihood it has the potential to provide in the coming decades. However, it is well-known that the Chins are concentrated in Aizawl, which also raises the possibility of more tensions. Could a society continue to deal with its migrant population without factoring in these changes? What would a policy on migration have to consider? I wish to make two points by way of suggestions in this conclusion. The debate about how we understand migration and how the various categories of migration are constructed becomes relevant. In refusing to be trapped in either of the categories at the start of this chapter, the objective was to understand if the characteristics of one construction are found in another. From the Mizoram experience, it is evident that these categories are at best convenient, but do not suggest anything conclusive. The second points relates to the everyday experiences of migrants and the conception of citizenship that dominates a particular social and political context. The argument that geographical presence should be the basis of membership in a community needs to be explored further in the scenario that Mizoram presents us.

NOTES

1. Among the Burmese who are known to migrate to India, the Chins, Kachins, Nagas of Burmese origin, Burmans and the Rahkine (from Arakan State) are known to migrate between India and Burma. For the purposes of this chapter, the term 'Burmese' is used to refer only to the Chins.
2. The rising use of drugs amongst the Mizo population is attributed to the increasing access to drugs through the Burmese who bring it with them from the Chin State/Sagaing Division in Burma. Mizos argue that they are the 'victims' of drug trafficking wholly controlled and promoted by the Burmese, without conceding that they are also part of this trade. This makes any talk about drug trafficking in Mizoram a sensitive topic.
3. Patnaik (2008: 74).
4. Ibid.: 20.
5. Doty, undated.
6. In case of Bangladeshi immigration into India, Samaddar, 1999 pursues a project of comprehending how borders turn our conception of nation states on their head. Such a project, in my understanding, also problematizes received categories of legal and illegal. See also, Agamben (undated) where he brings out the fluidity of the categories of stateless people and refugees in the context of the collapse of the Russian, Astro-Hungarian and Ottoman empires.
7. Crisp (2008).
8. Betts (2010).
9. Leydet (2006). 'Citizenship', *Stanford Encyclopedia of Philosophy*, http://plato.stanford.edu/entries/citizenship (accessed on January 2010).
10. Sassen (2006).
11. Blank (2007: 114–49).
12. Kapur (2007: 544).
13. Refer Article 5, Constitution of India, Government of India.
14. Refer Article 9, Constitution of India, Government of India.
15. Refer Article 7, Constitution of India, Government of India.
16. Samaddar (1999: 28).
17. Ibid.
18. Sakhong (2003: 8–17).
19. Ibid.: 6.
20. Robin K. (2009: xv–xxiii).
21. Supra note 19, pp. xiii–xxi.
22. Robin K., same as note 20, p. 341.
23. Ibid.

24. It is however not clear if the estimation of the population is recent or belongs to the time the borders were drawn.

25. Ibid. Supra note 23.

26. Patnaik (2008: 3).

27. Samaddar (2003: 182).

28. Banerjee et al. (2005: 216).

29. Ibid.: 222.

30. Supra note 28, p. 204.

31. Ibid.: 196–204.

32. Patnaik (2008: 74–90).

33. Patnaik (2008: 72–83).

34. Ibid.: 17.

35. Levesque and Rehman (2008).

36. Patnaik (2008: 91–125).

37. Thanhranga (2007); see also Patnaik (2008: 206–17).

38. See for instance, Levesque and Rehman (2008); National Coalition Government of the Union of Burma (2008: 946–71); Human Rights Watch (2009: 65); WLB and Centre for Refugee Research (2007: 3).

39. Interview with Sr Rose Piate, Ferrando Integrated Women's Development Centre (Peace Home), 3 December 2009, Aizawl.

40. See the website of National Domestic Workers Movement (NDWM), of which Ferrando Integrated Women's Development Centre (Peace Home) is a member. The website is as follows: http://fiwdcpeacehome.org/More-about-FIWDC.html (accessed on 15 March 2010).

41. Interview with Ms Diana Hmingthanpari, Centre for Peace and Development (CPD), 1 December 2009, Aizawl.

42. The Foundation for Social Transformation and Department of Social Work, 2008.

43. *Young Mizo Association, A Profile*, Pamphlet (undated).

44. The website is as follows: http://centralyma.org.in (accessed in January 2010).

45. The State Social Welfare Advisory Board (MHIP page of the Mizoram Government website) was set up in 1972 by the then Union Territory of Mizoram to carry out various activities to promote the welfare of women and children.

46. Patnaik (2008: 340–78) at p. 366.

47. Ibid.

48. Some research has been done on the Burmese migration, such as the dissertation by Z. Zirnunsanga referred in this chapter. However, there is little systematic study of the Chin migration that analyses the phenomenon from the perspective of Mizo history. The existing literature, in the form of media reporting, etc., dwells on issues such as 'illegal migration' of the Chins, thus being narrow in its approach. Interestingly, none of the contributions to the two recent publications brought out by the University of Mizoram (and referred extensively in this chapter) consider it important to focus on this issue, despite Chin migration being such a sensitive issue in the state.

49. An unpublished MPhil dissertation of the Department of Economics, Mizoram University, titled 'The Pattern of Migration and its Effects on Economic Development with Special Reference to Mizoram'. The study, however, does not indicate the total population of migrants from these countries.

50. Ibid.: 120.
51. Ibid.: 212.
52. Government of India (2001).
53. The Census, 2001 data however is not helpful in coming to this conclusion as it does not give enough disaggregated data.
54. Interview with Mimi Khar, Journalist, Mizzima News (and Consultant for the British Broadcasting Corportation), August 2009, Aizawl.
55. *Khonumthung News*, 2 March 2009.
56. *Khonumthung News*, 24 March 2009.
57. *Khonumthung News*, 15 June 2009. This reported the arrest of 54 Chin people who worked in a restaurant and handloom factories. The arrests were made on the grounds of illegal stay but were released on payment of fine. While a large number of Burmese are known to live illegally, it is baffling that the police is selective in its arrests.
58. Human Rights Watch (2009).
59. WLB and Centre for Refugee Research (2007).
60. Ibid.: 8.
61. Ibid.: 75–76.
62. Although it is widely known that Chins arrive in Mizoram, live in different parts for varying periods of time, carry on trade, etc., a number of Chins this author was able to speak to during a visit in 2006 note that they keep a low profile as it is impossible to tell when one might be deported or sent to the borders.
63. Supra note 59, http://www.hrw.org/en/node/79892/section/4 (accessed in May 2010).
64. The report quotes a Chin national 'The way [the Mizos] think is that killing a Chin person is like killing a dog. It is not that serious.'
65. Interview with Pu Lalbiakzuala, General Secretary, Central Young Mizo Association, 2 December 2009, CYMA Office, Aizawl.
66. Interview with Pu Lalkhama, NC State Planning Board, Government of Mizoram.
67. Ibid.
68. According to these reports, there are 6,912 Chins living in Mizoram making them 877 families. The rest of them are yet to submit the report. The census was supposed to be completed by April 2009 but because 'some are active branches and some are not', the census is still not complete.
69. In specific reference to the report of the Human Rights Watch and the manner in which it was received in Mizoram, Pu Krosshnehzova also noted that while they are aware of Chins living in Mizoram for business, etc., some others, in his opinion are into illegal activities, which has turned into a social problem. In his view, the YMA may have felt that it is important to eradicate this problem and Census may aid in towards this purpose.
70. Government of Mizoram (2003).
71. Ibid. Part-A: Issue of Permit, Guideline 1(a) and 1(b).
72. Interview with Pu Lalbiakzuala, General Secretary, Central Young Mizo Association, 2 December 2009, CYMA Office, Aizawl.
73. Interview with Pu Lalhriathpuia, Home Department, Government of Mizoram, 2009.
74. Supra note 71, Guideline 8.2.
75. Human Rights Watch (2009).

76. Interview with Ms Rozami, Chairperson, Mizoram State Women's Commission, Government of Mizoram, 1 December 2009, Aizawl.
77. Interview with V.L. Krosshnehzova, President, Mizo Zirlai Pawl, 2 December 2009, MZP Office, Aizawl.
78. The often quoted joke is that even if Chins are left near the borders, they get back faster than the police!
79. Lalneihzovi (2006: 63).
80. Supra note 63.
81. Supra note 68.
82. Order of JMFC dated 22 October 2009, in connection with Criminal Complaint No. 96 of 2009 (parties) (Domestic Violence), para 10.
83. Order passed by the Judicial Magistrate First Class in Criminal Complaint No. 96 of 2009, para 11.
84. Ibid., para 13.
85. Ibid., para 15(1).
86. Ibid., para 15(2).
87. Ibid., para 15(3).
88. Ibid., para 15(4).
89. Ibid., para 15(5).
90. Ibid., para 16.
91. Ibid., para 17.
92. Ibid., para 14.
93. Government of India (2006–07: 20).
94. Interview with Sr Rose Paite, Ferrando Integrated Women's Development Centre (Peace Home), 3 December 2009, Aizawl.
95. Levesque and Rehman (2008).
96. Bosniak (2008).
97. Ibid.
98. Ibid.: 3.
99. Bhargava and Reifeld (2005: 290).
100. See for instance, the pamphlet 'Check List for Identifying NGOs/CBOs/ Traditional Institutions, YMA Note' (undated) Copy with the author. An example is the decision taken by YMA to declare each year dedicated to various issues. While some have been dedicated to the promotion of education, cleanliness, wild life protection, the years 1998 to 2002 and 2004 were declared as 'Ram leh Hnam humhalh-Preservation/protection of mizoram and its Identity'. The notes do not explain its programmes or activities done towards this objective.
101. Supra note 72.
102. Roohi et al. (2009: 442–63).

6

Engendered Lives: Women in the West Garo Hills

*Anjuman Ara Begum**

Partition is conceptually distinct from population transfer, though in most cases, it is accompanied by substantial sorting of populations.[1] Partition is a political outcome that impacts social life tremendously. With partition the border creeps in, creating lines that divide people, society and nation. The border becomes physically visible when it is fenced. Fences along the border-lines make the border a concrete and fixed structure representing control of land and people. Border gives birth to the extremities of particular forms of violence that are enacted in the name of security and well-being—check-points, walls, fences, technologies of surveillance and governance.[2] At such a criss-cross of bordered existence, different particularities of border—such as territorial, disciplinary, religious and intellectual—intrude into funda-mental concepts like democracy, sovereignty, rights and belonging, which characterize human beings as social beings.

Since the nation state fails to bring the lives along the borders into the mainstream domain, the obvious imaginary concept of the communities within a geographical territory appears hollow. Moreover, in many cases the people living on and by the border prefer to belong to their brethren

*The author is indebted to Subhra Sankar Roy Choudhury, Sulema Khatun, Noor Banu Begum, Jamat Miah, Saidur Rahman, Erik de Maakar, Nokma of Chapahati, Nunu Sangma and borderlanders who shared their experiences.

on the other side of the fence. Such realities essentially heat up the barbed wire and cement that *Baul* Singer Fakir Lalan Shah has immortalized in this verse, 'The winged soul trapped inside a cage only flies off; no one knows how'.[3] As the lyrics of the Baul song resonate with the drawing of a forced shadow line, the exodus cannot be stopped. Free souls despite being vulnerable to repressive agencies of discipline and punish, just sneak into a newly unknown territory. Borders exist everywhere, between life and death, between the believer and the atheist, between the dweller and the neighbour and between the void and the fullness.[4]

Keeping these under consideration, this chapter deals with a fenced geopolitical space known as the West Garo Hills bordering Bangladesh with an area of 3,714 sq. km. and population of 518,390 as per the census report of 2001.

Known as one of the most massive convulsions of human history, the Indian subcontinent witnessed partition in 1947 with the creation of two states, namely India and Pakistan (East and West). The horror of this epochal event could hardly even ebb away, when history faded again into a ripple with the creation of Bangladesh in 1971. Fresh borderlines began to be drawn. As a consequence Garo Hills was mapped into this fencing mission. From 1980 onwards, several borders were carved out in Garo Hills. These borders visibly demarcated and divided the plain and hill population, majority and minority, indigenous and non-indigenous, original inhabitants and migrant population. The great divide ultimately led to armed conflict and a sudden spurt of nationalistic sentiments. It created borderlines among the different ethnic and religious communities, engendering the lives along the borders. The agents of history ruthlessly dismembered and mutilated territorial as well as anatomical body with the heat of poverty, anarchy and repression equally felt by both men and women.

From political demagogue to local moneylenders, from the security personnel to the scar-faced ringleader of the cattle herd smugglers, it is a tightrope walk on a scary altitude with no life support, where a small mistake could prove lethal. Nevertheless, the murky ambience that the womenfolk live in surprisingly by sheer resilience and adaptive power, continue to nestle the home and the micro-world of their own. Women's lives in the borderlines of West Garo Hills reflect their sheer resilience, silent tears and a burning desire to put a step outside the line called 'border'. Heat of the barbed wire constructing the border melted their lives and inevitably morphed their lives into a different shape.

HOW THE BARBED WIRE CAME IN THE INDO-BANGLA BORDER

Several countries in the world have constructed fencing along the international border in the last century, in an attempt to counter illegal flows, cross-border terrorism, smuggling, etc. The Mexico–US border, Spain–Morocco border, India–Pakistan border, etc., can be quoted as examples. In the sub-continent, borders have become a part of life after the partition in 1947. Citizens of both the nascent states accepted it as inevitable, with much pain in their hearts. Families got divided into two countries and borders became barriers. According to Berg and Ethin (2008), 'borders ... are conceptual and concrete points of reference for establishing what is internal and what is external, what can come in and what must stay out. The logic of this selection is inevitably socially constructed—the creation of borders can thus be regarded as a process through which "imagined communities" define their "imagined territories".[5]

The idea of protecting the border with a fence was not new.[6] Demand for fencing or 'complete sealing' of the border along the East Pakistan border was echoed in 1964[7] which grew much louder after the Assam agitation in the 1980s. In 1986, the Government of India approved the construction of fences along the Indo-Bangladesh border. The Indo-Bangladesh border extends to a total length of 4,095 km. Of this, West Bengal has a border length of 2,216 km, Tripura 856 km, Meghalaya 443 km, Mizoram 318 km and Assam 262 km. It was rationalized that the 'barbed wire fencing would be very effective to check trans-border movement of terrorists, infiltration and border crimes'.[8]

As the entire Indo-Bangladesh border has been prone to large scale illegal immigration/infiltration from Bangladesh, the Government of India sanctioned the Indo-Bangladesh Border Roads & Fence project in 1986 at a cost of ₹371.74 crore with a view to preventing infiltration by Bangladesh nationals. The cost of the project was subsequently revised to ₹831.17 crore in 1992.[9]

Fencing was constructed in two phases. In 2001, the director general of the Border Road Organization calculated that 1 km of border fence cost ₹ 2.2 million and 1 km of border road ₹ 4.5 million.[10] In October 2004, Government of India decided to continue fencing the border. The UPA government allocated funds for border fencing, road and maintenance, as well as for boats and aircraft for the Border Security Force (BSF). The government spent ₹ 2,404.7 million for fencing the Indo-Bangladesh border. In 2007, India decided to replace the entire 861 km of fence constructed under Phase I in West Bengal, Assam and Meghalaya, as most of this fence had been damaged by adverse climatic conditions and repeated submergence. The replacement work has already commenced in the states of Assam and West Bengal. A total of 193.70 km of fencing has been replaced so far.[11] The fencing now has a concrete base with barbed wire and is also equipped for passing mild electricity.

One of the discontents between the two 'friendly countries,' India and Bangladesh, was the clause of an agreement signed between the two countries in 1974. The clause puts a prohibition on the construction of any objects within 150 yards of zero line in the border.[12] However, the construction of fencing along the Bangladesh frontier, leaving 150 yards between the zero line and the fencing, became impossible in many places because of geographical and sometimes historical reasons. Sometimes, places of worship located right near the zero line or the river made it impossible to construct the fencing 150 yards away from the zero line. In a preliminary survey, the Home Ministry and the BSF have stumbled upon 46 such patches where the fencing cannot be constructed as per the India–Bangladesh agreement of 1974.[13] Apart from this the issue, the matter of adverse possession of land along the India–Bangladesh frontier has caused many political wild fires. The Infamous Pyrdiwah and Boroibari incident is still fresh in the minds of people. About 551 acres of Bangladesh land is under adverse possession of India while 226 acres of Indian land is under adverse possession of Bangladesh, along the Assam–Meghalaya sector international border.[14] Construction of fencing along the international border remained slow since its initiation. An editorial note published in local daily commented:

> Slow progress of construction of roads and fencing along the international border with Bangladesh has seriously affected border management and the Centre must take adequate steps to ensure that the work is completed

within a specific time frame. The Centre has sanctioned construction of
fencing in a stretch of 565.428 kilometres along the international border
in Assam–Meghalaya sector, but so far, fencing is completed only in
a stretch of 157.102 kilometres and work is in progress in a stretch of
133.735 kilometres. At this rate, no one knows as to when the job will be
completed ...[15]

In addition to the above quoted passage from the editorial section of a
local daily, my research also revealed that the inspector general of the BSF
(Assam and Meghalaya Frontier), Prithvi Raj too clearly informed the media
on 23 August 2009[16] about the reasons for delay in the construction of fences:

We are facing problems in about 270 kilometers due to various reasons.
But we are persuading the construction agencies to speed up the work.
The construction agencies are facing problems due to objection by the
Bangladesh Rifles at places, hostile terrain and weather, and opposition by
locals who fear their land would fall outside the fence.

Newspapers also reported that according to a Union Home Ministry report,
3,437 km border of the total 4,095 km India–Bangladesh border was to be
fenced by March 2010. 'Work has so far been completed along a 2,800 km
stretch and construction on the remaining portion is on'.[17]

RELATION BETWEEN THE GAROS
AND NON-GAROS IN WEST GARO HILLS

Relationship between the people of the borderlands in West Garo Hills
is an important factor to understand the area. Creation of the border has
had much thrust on the social life as well. It is observed that border has
created many social borders within the region. It created borders between
people, culture, language, traditions and practices. The total population of
Meghalaya on 1 March 2001 is 2,306,069 as per the results of the Census
2001. About 85 per cent of Meghalaya's population constitutes the tribal
people. In interior reaches of the Garo Hills, the percentage of tribal population is as high as 97 per cent. The Khasis are the largest group, followed
by the Garos. Other groups include the Jaintias, Koch, Hajong, Dimasa,
Hmar, Kuki, Lakher, Mikir, Rabha. Only 15 per cent of the population is
non-tribal which includes about 54,000 Bengalis and 49,000 Muslims.[18]

During the Mughal period, some Bengalis were in contact with the Garos[19] of the border areas through trade of essential commodities like salt, rice, kerosene, garments, etc. They were then employed by the zamindars of Bijni, Mechpara and Gauripur to cultivate the marshy lands and resettled some of them. When the British came, more of them were brought as labourers and traders in the weekly markets. The Muslims found in the plain area of West Garo Hills are mainly from present Bangladesh, where Dhaka was the eastern-most outpost of the Mughal empire.[20] The successive invasions of the Muslims against the Ahoms left behind a sprinkling of the Muslim population at the plain foothills of Garo Hills. Later on, they were also drawn into these areas as they found that there were lots of virgin soils, while some of them came as petty traders and labourers.

Meghalaya was created on 21 February 1971 vide the North Eastern Area (Reorganisation) Act 1971 with the assertion of preserving indigenity and ethnic identity of the tribals in the state. All the five districts of the state (now seven states) were already placed under the sixth schedule. As a result, democratic limitations were placed upon the non-tribals of the states. Out of the 60 assembly seats, 55 seats were reserved for the tribals to contest and 5 seats were kept open for the non-tribes to contest. A fact-finding report published by North East People's Initiative on 'Police firing on demonstrations in Garo Hills' articulates:

> ... several developments since 1972 have given serious set back to the hopes of the indigenous people who assumed that separate statehood was all they needed to accelerate their socio-economic advance while preserving their cultural identities. First, with the government setting up district councils under sixth schedule of the Indian constitution, conflict arose between the traditional tribal bodies and the newly instituted official councils. Secondly, boundary disputes cropped up between local tribal landowners and central government establishments and army cantonments. Thirdly, the new state with its abundant natural resources attracted a huge number of non-tribal investors and businessmen. The last factor created tensions between the tribals and non-tribals.

Explaining the socio-political scenario in Garo Hills, Rajesh Dev wrote:

> ... issue that has dominated ... in Meghalaya, which is similar in most of the states of the region, is the concern for the preservation of indigenous identity given the popular perception about the 'sustained exodus and

influence of non-indigenous communities' upon the fragile socio-economic and cultural fabric of the state.[21]

Marriages between the Garos and the non-tribals are treated as an invasion to the indigenity of the Garos.

> With partition some people fell in India or Hindustan and some fell under Pakistan. Border emerged and we saw state authorities putting pillars and marking the border. There was one place where the river was very deep and labourers could not erect pillar there. Instead, they put the pillar on the embankment. Later the pillar was stolen by some East Pakistanis. I heard there is pillar sign in the map, but not in reality. *This created confusion…* [emphasis added]. This is how the river came under Bangladesh today. Now with the fencing coming in, we feel that we are trapped. We cannot enter Bangladesh freely like before. We are a sort of refugees now, *separated from our relatives who are in Bangladesh due to border* [emphasis added]. The Garos are not giving us equal status.[22]

Social relationship between the Garos and the non-tribals in Garo Hills is ever changing with time and situation. It fluctuates from 'peaceful' to 'violent'. Mutual distrust and uncertainty prevails and is the chemistry of this relationship. *Garo noi karo* (Garo is for no one) is the popular punch used by the non-tribal residents along the borderlines of West Garo Hills, which is intended to depict the 'selfishness character of the Garos', as observed by the borderland non-tribals. On the other hand, the Garos believe that non-tribals or 'bangals' as addressed by the Garos, have enough land to accommodate themselves outside Garo Hills, as they don't constitute the aboriginal people of Garo Hills. An ordinary villager in Chapahati said 'Garo Hills is the land of the Garos and not for others. If others keep pouring in Garo Hills then where shall we go?' The Garo nationalism intensified after the nationalist movement spearheaded by Achik National Volunteers Council (ANVC). In the 1990s, the group was very active, carried out widespread extortion, kidnapping and killings for ransom. Several youths from non-tribal areas of West Garo Hills left their job in fear. A typical case could be quoted here:

> We were happily settled in Tura [headquarter of West Garo Hills] for ages. My mother was a Garo married to a Muslim man. I was brought up as Garo. I married a Muslim man from Mahendraganj and we had 7 children. My husband was a well settled contractor and had a good business.

We had all the comfort in life. Suddenly, one day in 1987, I don't remember the date but it was Friday, there was a riot. The cause of the riot
was the beating of the principal of a college by a non-tribal boy from
Mankachar, Assam. At around 2 pm, riot started in Tura. Several Garo
youths attacked our house at around 8 pm and asked for my husband.
They said that since my husband is non-tribal, I should hand him over
to them and rest of us can live in Tura as I am a Garo. How can I hand
over my husband to them? They started beating us. My son is handicapped. He was severally beaten and my daughters were molested. All
our household things were taken away by our Garo neighbours. We ran
away to save ourselves and reached police station. We found one of my
daughters was missing. We stayed there for the whole night. Next day the
police arranged for buses and we were to leave for Mankachar in Assam.
There were about 22 buses and all the affected non-tribals boarded the
buses and suddenly we found our daughter in one of the buses. We had
lost everything, but I was happy to see our daughter. We all wept together.
We stayed in Mankachar for 15 days. Then we shifted to a small plot of
land that we bought in Mahendraganj long back. Since then we are settled
here. In that riot six members of our family and relatives were killed by the
Garos. Our housemaid's deadbody was lying there under the bed and we
heard that people saw worms coming out of her brain. The loss incurred
by us on that day was never compensated, neither by any individual nor
by the state. There was no investigation too. About 50 non-tribal people
were killed during that riot.[23]

Now, even riots among the non-tribals themselves are occasionally experienced. On 10 October 1997, clashes erupted when an immersion procession was passing through a place of Muslim worship, a mosque, in a village
in Mahendraganj. Two persons were killed, houses were torched on both
sides and about 100 were wounded. Curfew prevailed for three days
continuously and officials brought the situation 'under control'.[24] Non-
tribals' perspectives about the Garos vary. Positive aspect of their perspective is that Garos are simple, honest and hardworking, while the negative
aspects brand Garos as dictators, aggressive and repressive by nature, who
lack fellow-feeling. Non-tribals view themselves as the sons of the soil, as
they were here since time immemorial and they think that they should be
provided the privilege of equal rights. The bitterness of the relationship is
much enhanced because of the mutual suspicion which is influenced by
several social and political factors. Non-tribals are sometimes dependent on

the Garos for their economic gain, natural resources, and so on. The Garos
too are dependent on the non-tribals for their skill-based works and business skills.

FACTORS THAT IMPACTED WOMEN'S LIVES IN FENCED BORDERLANDS OF WEST GARO HILLS

Several factors impacted women's life in the borderlands of West Garo
Hills. These factors ranging from social, political or economic reflect the
patriarchal control over women. Border regime itself is a system of control,
regulating behaviour at the borders.[25] Control over borders has traditionally
been an important attribute of the nation state, intimately linked to issues
of sovereignty and independence.[26] Fencing the border is a means of control over the flow of goods, human and animal movement and to regulate
human behaviour in the borderlands and this gives rise to 'border management'. Fencing is seen as a major deterrent for the 'infiltrators' and a great
help to the BSF in improving border management.[27]

The most immediate impact of fencing in the West Garo Hills is the loss
of agricultural land. It's a loss that resulted in no adequate compensation
and rehabilitation till today, though out of insecurity and fear psychosis it
displaced the residents who formerly lived along the 150 yards along the
border line. 'In 1954, when there was "allah hu akbar",[28] we crossed the
border and took shelter in East Pakistan. This is not possible now. If a group
wants, they can really eliminate us as fencing is there as a barrier', said Abu
Hussain.[29] Fencing also proved detrimental for those who were dependent
on cross-border trades, both legal and illegal. Above all, fencing created a
feeling of being trapped in one's own land. In the borderlands of the West
Garo Hills, it became almost impossible to cultivate the lands that fell outside of the fenced area. Local people complained that 'there is inadequate
guard along the fencing and dacoits from Bangladesh would cut and grab
our paddy once it is ready for harvesting and this forced many to stop cultivating their lands falling outside the fenced area.'[30] Sometimes there were
inadequate openings or 'border gates' along the fencing lines that prevented
cultivators from reaching their land. Similar concerns were even echoed
by the Meghalaya chief minister. The then Chief Minister, Lapang said,
'His government will take into account the survival needs for the people

**Photos 6.1 Two Photographs of Fencing under Construction
and a Border Road along with Fencing in West Garo Hills**

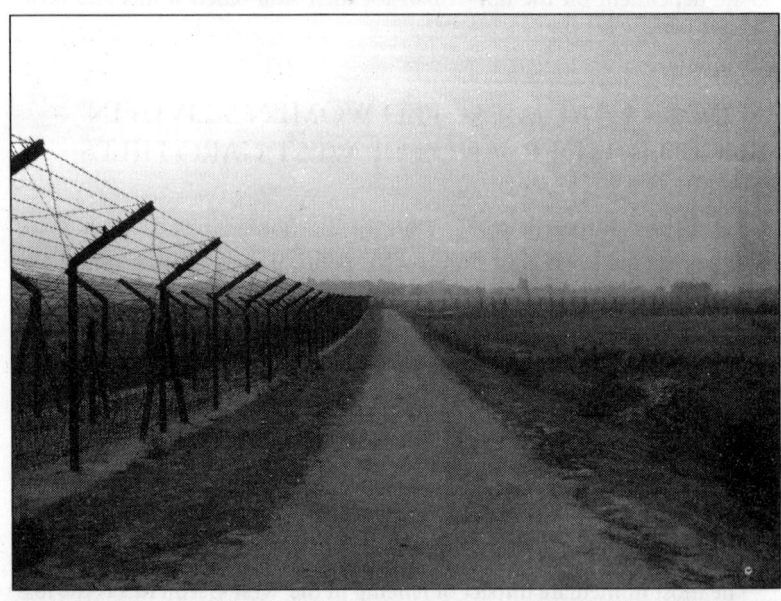

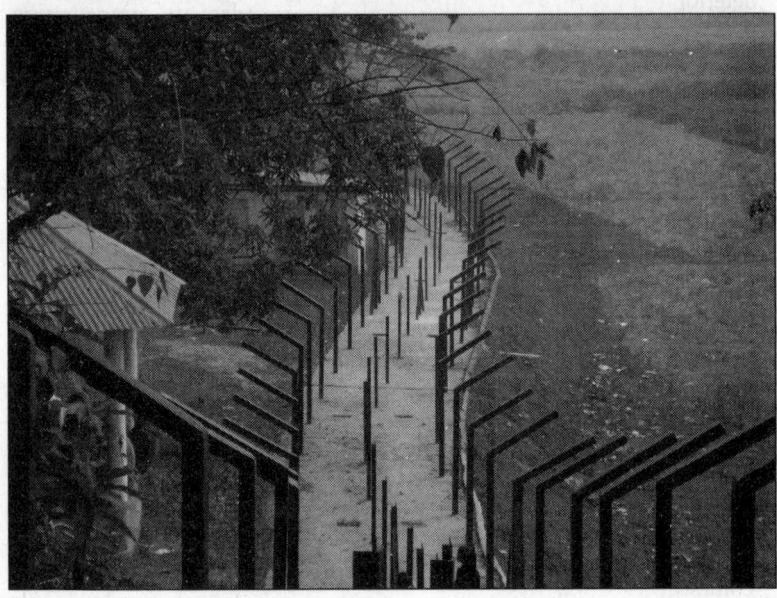

residing along the border ... Instead of fencing, better roads for smooth running of vehicles are required to check infiltration.'[31] Women landowners whose lands fall beyond the fencing have completely given up cultivating their lands in the border lands of West Garo Hills.

The issue of Land rights in West Garo Hills is unique considering its sixth schedule status. The official website of the district[32] traces the history of contact between the British and the Garos which started towards the close of the 18th century after the British East India Company had secured the Diwani of Bengal from the Mughal Emperor.[33] Consequently, all the estates bordering Garo Hills, which for all practical purposes had been semi-independent, were brought under the control of the British. History reveals that though political control had passed from the Mughals to the British, the latter, like Mughals, had no desire to control the estates or their tributaries directly. The zamindars were not disturbed in the internal management of their estates. In fact, they were entrusted, as they had been by the Mughals, with the responsibility of keeping the Garo Hills in check with help of their retainers. Thus in the beginning, the intermittent conflict between the zamindars and the Garos went on unabated until the situation deteriorated to the extent that the British were forced to take notice. This development led ultimately to the annexation of the Garo Hills in 1873. Captain Williamson was the first deputy commissioner of the unified district. The district was bifurcated into two districts viz. East Garo Hills and West Garo Hills districts in October 1979. Immediately after the formation of Meghalaya state on 21 February 1971, government of Meghalaya passed Meghalaya Transfer of Property Act 1971. As a result, transfer of lands from tribals to non-tribals became illegal. For instance, during the 1977 parliamentary elections, the Congress 'issued a press note reminding the people that unauthorised transfer of land ... from tribals to nontribals and from non-tribals to *others* was illegal, void and punishable under the Meghalaya Transfer of Land Act 1971'.[34]

Women in the borderlands of West Garo Hills are found to be the owners of land resources, but only on paper. Male members of their family enjoy the possession and overall control over the resources. Women are denied of their legitimate rights over their own land. The denial of rights comes from their 'own' family members and the state follows a policy of

non-interference without helping these women. A typical case study can
be cited here:

> I got married at an early age in 1968 probably. My husband was a
> tailor by profession. After marriage we shifted to Tura for business pur-
> pose. After sometime 'liberation war' (liberation war of Bangladesh)
> prevented us moving to Mahendraganj. After the declaration of indepen-
> dence of Bangladesh, my husband was served a notice of 'quit India' as he
> was found to be a 'Bangladeshi'. I wanted to move and relocate with him
> in Bangladesh. But my father interrupted and said that he cannot allow
> anyone to take away his daughter. My husband left me. Life became ter-
> rible, as there was no one to look after me. My remarriage was arranged
> with a local man in Mahendraganj. I got remarried to this man who
> had another wife and children. Life became more terrible after the second
> marriage. My husband's first wife wanted to poison me. I left my second
> husband's home after two years. Then I lived with my younger sister for
> 17 years. My second husband gave me land as 'mehr' (dower) during my
> remarriage. He never handed over the possession of this land. Later these
> lands fell outside the fenced area. I tried a lot to get the possession of this
> land. I complained to the local leaders. No one could help me. Then I left
> Garo hills and decided to go back to my first husband. I started living in
> a border village in Assam. Fencing was already erected in the border and
> it became difficult to cross the border. Somehow I managed to go through
> and finally met my husband after years. My husband had remarried in
> Bangladesh and had made a big family. I stayed there for six months and
> then he died. I came back to India. And now I have no one in this world.
> I stay in a village in Assam and teach Arabic and Quran to students. This
> gives me a livelihood—Zubeida Khatun.[35]

BORDER TRADE AND EXTRA NATIONAL INTEREST

Border trade whether legal or illegal is always a source of income and livelihood for many. Fencing proved barriers for the people who were dependent
on the barter system of border trade. Barter system is the preferred mode
of trade, as money exchange booths are still unknown not only for security reasons, but also for the fact that these are some of the most remote
areas in the subcontinent. This kind of economic exchange is an important

means of livelihood for the people along the borderland of West Garo Hills. A police official requesting anonymity informed, 'sometime we allow such activities to continue as people are left with very little options for livelihood'. People's protest obstructed the construction of fencing for quite some time. Meghalaya government is yet to approve of the construction of fencing in some parts of the international border.[36]

In barter trade, people usually exchange food, cloths, dry fish, mosquito net, utensils, gold, silver, etc. After fencing this type of cross-border trade became illegal and is now know as informal trade, black marketing, illegal trade or smuggling and persons carrying out such business are commonly called 'blackers' or '*blackdari*'. It was estimated that informal trade resulting through smuggling is worth ₹200 crore annually, while formal trade through Meghalaya border with Bangladesh was around ₹170 to 200 crore a year.[37] The total volume of informal trade is higher than the formal trade. It is observed that the majority of 'blackers' were women. A local resident informed:

> Now after fencing, smuggling has come under control. Women, who were earning good money through door to door sale of smuggled items, now have become domestic labourers. One woman named Sahera was very close to me. She expired. Government paid compensation about 50 thousand INR per bigha for the lands that fall outside the fenced area'.[38] 'These women are now working as domestic workers or under NREGA (National Rural Employment Guarantee Act 2005) or otherwise. But none of them are into 'business' now.[39]

The importance of the border trade and the adverse impact of its sudden closure is reflected in the fact that both India and Bangladesh agreed to reopen the border *haat*s (weekly markets) in October 2009. Border *haat*s were functional from the Mughal period. Bahadur kata, Sherpur, Purakhasia, Dalu, Mankachar Mahendraganj, etc., were important border *haat*s for years till the border fencing came in. Most of the border *haat*s were closed down by 1971 though some had managed to remain open until 1974. Of late, discussions on reopening of transit points and passages have been very much revived,[40] which signifies its importance. Reopening of these century old *haat*s would provide livelihood opportunities for women and their families along the borderlines.

PEOPLE AND SECURITY FORCES
ALONG THE FENCING

As a matter of policy, border is necessarily 'armed', well protected with trained armed security personnel. Security personnel target and are sometimes targeted often at the cost of their lives. On 14 April 1987, the Rishi Community of the Baghmara (now in South Garo Hills district) town was celebrating Charak Puja in the Primary School building. The establishment anticipated some disturbance to peace and tranquillity in the town, therefore, alerted the law enforcement agencies. Within a few hours after Puja, the town experienced serious communal disturbance. A senior sub-inspector (Sardul Singh) of BSF stationed in the town opened fire on a crowd near a place called MT garage at 9:15 p.m. Several persons were injured as a result of the firing.

The most terrific incident of brutality along the Indo-Bangla border is that of 15 BSF jawans who were taken hostage by the (Bangladesh Rifles) BDR from Boroibari in Assam's Mankachar sector bordering West Garo Hills on 18 April 2001. All of these captured 15 BSF jawans were killed. Their bodies were returned to the BSF on 20 April at Mahendraganj checkpoint on the Indo-Bangladesh border, 26 km from Assam's Mankachar town. It was termed as 'murder in cold blood' by the Indian authority and they even refused to accept the badly mutilated bodies of their BSF. Only seven bodies could be identified as those of the BSF men, while the rest were disfigured beyond recognition.[41] It was reported that during the exchange of fire in the Mankachar region on 18 April, a patrol of 16 BSF jawans reportedly got separated from the rest of the troops and fell into the hands of the Bangladeshis. Director General of the BSF, Gurbachan Jagat, said, 'One of our patrols strayed and got caught by the Bangladesh Rifles or Bangladeshi villagers on the other side of the border'. However, the BDR claimed that it was not responsible for the death of the captured BSF jawans and added that the marks on the bodies indicated that it was the work of a mob of Bangladeshi villagers. A probe team led by a former BSF director general is investigating the circumstances that led to the death of the BSF jawans.[42] A senior BSF officer, who requested anonymity stated:

> The actual fact of the case never came out. The real incident is that a small river island surfaced in the river between India and Bangladesh.

Some families from Bangladesh settled there. BSF used to extort money from them saying that the island falls under Indian Territory. This incident is a result of their greed.[43]

Occasional tension on both sides of the border is a constant phenomenon. 'Flag meetings' are organized quite often to negotiate the difference between the border security forces of both the countries.

India and Bangladesh share a 4,096 km frontier, regarded as one of the world's most fluid borders. More than 1,500 miles of the border have been fenced with barbed wire and concrete under the 1.2 billion dollar project during the past seven years.[44] It is pertinent to mention here that, not only smuggling or cattle lifting, the West Garo Hills border is also a transit point for insurgent groups having their base camps across the border. As many as 479 infiltrators were captured on the Indo-Bangladesh border in Meghalaya and Assam in 2009, while nine people were killed. The nine deaths were reported to be caused by the apparent firing by forces between January and 22 December 2009. The BSF was quoted in a statement that was reported to newspapers that 32 militants and 42 linkmen of different militant groups

Photo 6.2 Woman Seen Fetching Water from a Pond Near the Fencing

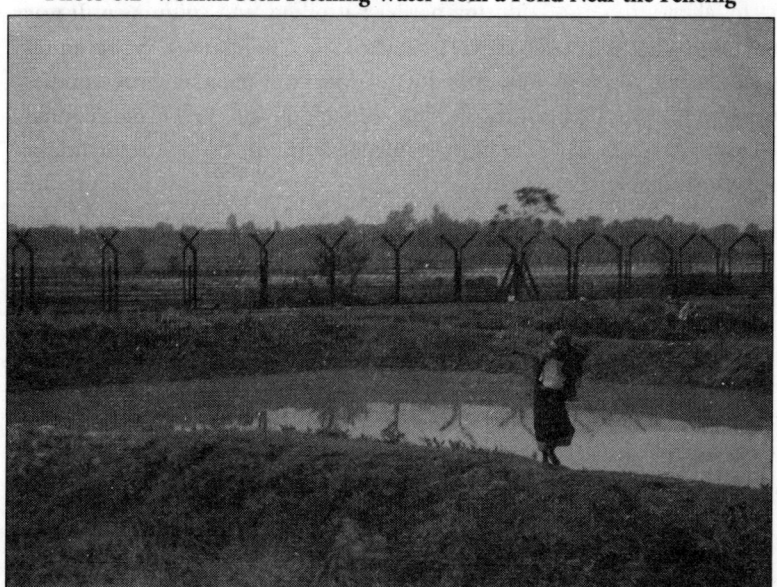

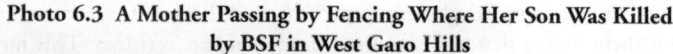

Photo 6.3 A Mother Passing by Fencing Where Her Son Was Killed by BSF in West Garo Hills

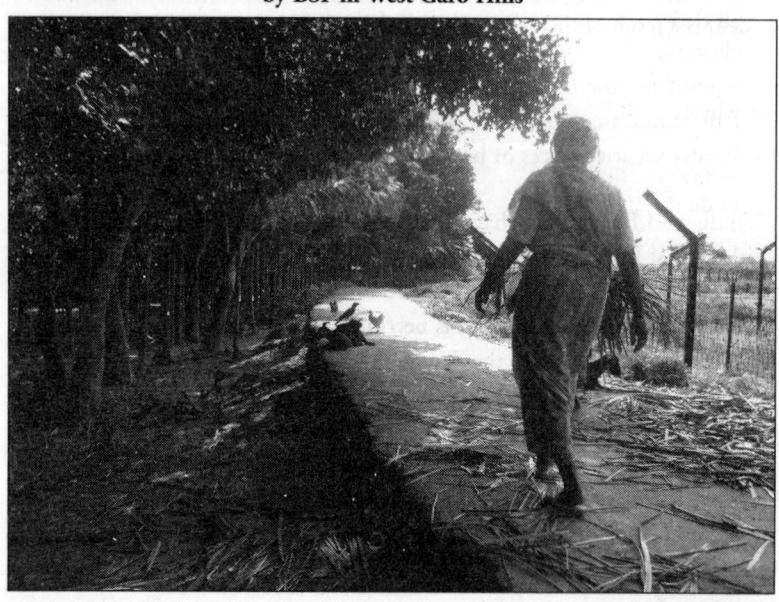

were taken into custody during border patrolling, and counter-insurgency operations in Assam–Meghalaya frontiers. Ten militants gave up around the time. As many as nine militants of Muslim fundamentalist organizations were also caught in the border and various arms and explosives were recovered from them.[45] Though completely different versions of such claims are also available:

> I thought the fencing would act as the boundary wall for me and protect my family. But it proved to be a killing site. BSF first arrested my son while crossing the border. First they took to the camp and then brought him back near the fencing and shot him dead. Many of my neighbours witnessed it. Later BSF told us that he was trying to flee into Bangladesh with some contraband substance and BSF personnels were forced to open fire. Everyone fled. No one gave true witness about the incident. I contacted the local MLA. MLA gave 1500 INR and asked me to keep silent. We are poor people. My son was the only earning member. I cannot work anymore. There is no possibility of justice for my son. They branded him as a 'smuggler'. We have friends and families in Bangladesh. Once the border appeared we could not meet them. Tell me how my son can refuse if somebody calls to share a bidi while working in the field? It would be

impolite and indecent. We have land on the other side of the fencing. Sometime BSF allow us to go and at other times they refuse use entry, all depending upon their mood. Sometime they will allow going if we clean the area surrounding their watch tower. Sometime they ask to show identity card to go to the other side of the border and work. Now, from where we will get an identity card? We had voter's card, but we have had to change our house several times and we lost these documents. Many stopped cultivating their lands that fall outside the fencing. May be I have to do that as well.... Gumeljan Bewa.[46]

NARRATIVES OF 'TRAPPED WOMEN' IN THE BORDER LANDS OF WEST GARO HILLS

Kadamphool, daughter of Kodu Sheikh and Naychan Khatun, was only 14 years old when she got married in 1946. She belonged to the village Dhanua, Kamalpur, now in Bangladesh. She said:

I could visit my parents for two years freely. Then the issue of the border came in 1947. Once the border was created, my husband would take me to the border and my parents would receive me from the other side. This continued for two years only. Since then I haven't visited my parents or my siblings. Now with the fencing coming in, my heart pains and my soul weeps as I will never be able to see my relatives or my place of birth. There is no restriction for birds of the two countries, why is there restrictions for human being? I live the life of a maid for my husband and if he divorces me, I have no place to go.[47]

With the border and now the issue of fencing, women along the border lines of West Garo Hills feel that they have been trapped, as their movement is heavily restricted. These women have compromised with everything in life and often have had to face domestic violence silently. Some other women migrated to Garo Hills due to the communal riots during partition with a feeling that there is no reprieve for them and after migrating the restrictions imposed on their lives by the border and the fencing makes them feel further disempowered. The border and the fencing almost become a literal manifestation of their lives of entrapment, violence, abuse, attrition and neglect. Sharashi Prabha Das who belonged to Akoa village of Mynmensing district (now Bangladesh) was only 15 years old when she got married. Her husband Naresh Das has land properties in Garo Hills that helped them to shift during communal riot in 1952:

Photo 6.4a Arfina along with Her Mother

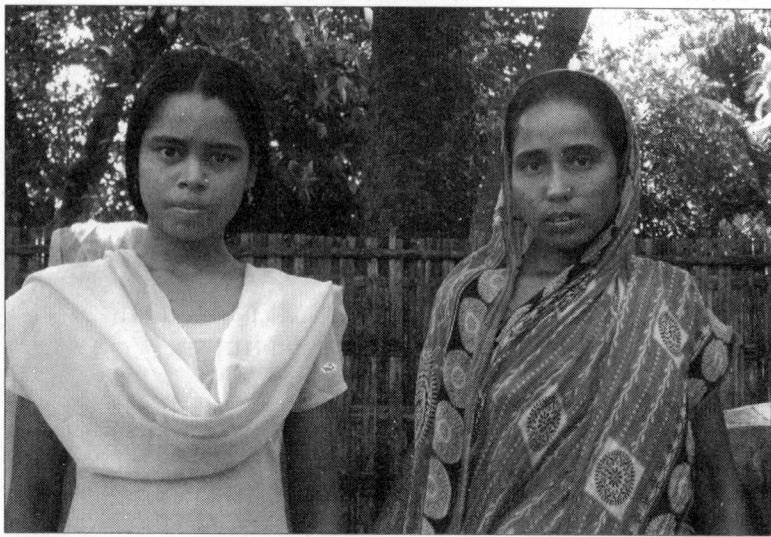

Note: Her father was killed by the BSF in 2002.

Photo 6.4b Photo of Gumeljan Bewa

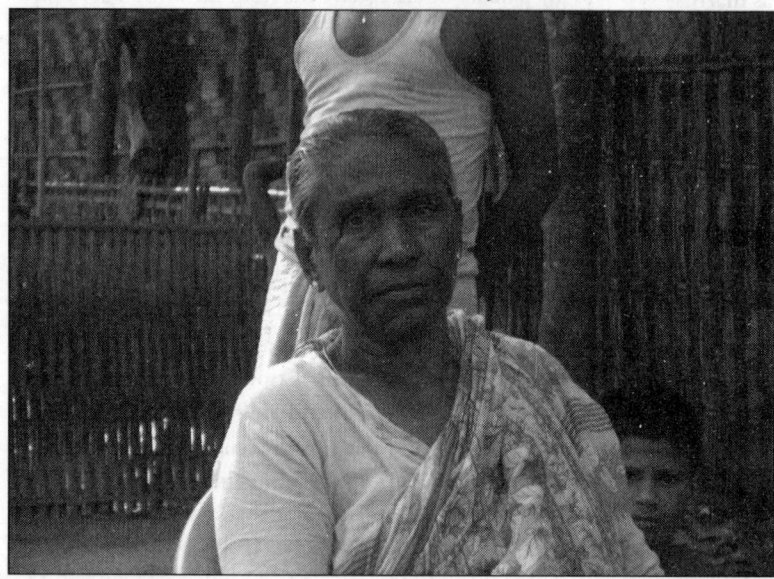

Note: Gumeljan Bewa's son was tied with the fencing and shot dead by BSF on being a suspected smuggler.

Due to riot I couldn't meet my parents and never could see them after that. They died. I never met any of my family members since I left my place of birth. Today I can only shed tears for them. With border and fencing I am restricted now. I can't move freely like before.[48]

Similar situations are experienced by many women. Saraswati Das, daughter of Manindra Das and Priyabal Das of Kailapatti, Sirajganj (now Bangladesh) was married to Ramen Das at the age of 14:

I along with my husband migrated to Kolkata soon after partition in 1947. After that for 30 years I didn't hear anything about my parents. Later I came to know that my father died thinking of me all the time. It was only after 1971 that I came to know about it. Many developments took place in between. The border became very 'strict' and fencing came in 2009. I felt fine I could connect with my family after 40 years and then I heard that my mother too had died six years back.[49]

Border crossing became a part of women's daily life after 1947. Border crossing was easy till the fencing came in. In the case of Lalphool, daughter of Lalchan Bepari of Mahendraganj the border proved favourable. Lalphool was married in 1971. In that year people from East Pakistan moved towards the Garo Hills area. One boy from East Pakistan took shelter in her house. She fell in love with this boy and she eloped in 1972. They crossed the border and lived with the boy's family in Bangladesh. Lalphool faced heavy domestic violence that forced her to come back to India. Fencing came in 1986 and it was difficult for her to cross border. Finally she managed to do so. Her ex-husband accepted her back and she had three children later.[50]

Women are also affected by the cattle lifting and raids by dacoits which became a daily phenomenon until border fencing controlled the menace to some extent in border areas of West Garo Hills. But occasional theft and raids by dacoit are continuing even today. Cattle smuggling too remain a lucrative 'trade' among the border, though fencing was supposedly aimed to prevent this. In 2008, the BSF seized contraband goods and cattle worth ₹155 million[51] and in 2009, BSF seized smuggled goods including cattle, forest products, ganja and other contraband items worth ₹53.80 crore.[52] Same news media also reported that the seizure of fake Indian currency of the face value of ₹1.07 lakh Bangladeshi taka, which is worth 2.60 lakh and Indian currency worth ₹39.76 lakh along the international border.

Cattle lifting is common in borderlands of West Garo Hills but lifting of woman was somewhat unheard of until the abduction of a female from Hallidayganj, a small business place in West Garo Hills. Mafusa Begum,[53] aged about 22 years was forcefully abducted by about 15–16 men from Bangladesh. Her husband, a school teacher narrates the incident as follows:

On that fateful night, January 21, 2004, I and my wife were sleeping in our bedroom. Around 1:15 am, dacoits numbering about 15–16 encircled our house. We are joint family. My elder brother, Nurul Hasan's house too shares the same courtyard. On January 20, 2004, I organized a Hepatitis B vaccination camp and sold the injection at a discounted rate. Such camp was very new in our village. Probably the dacoits got information that I collected lots of money. They first entered my elder brother's house by breaking the door. I think probably they planned to attack my home instantaneously. It was not well planned as they mistook my elder brother's house as mine. In 2004, there was no cell phone service, but land lines were there. I had land line connection. That night I watched TV till 12 midnight. I was sleeping soundly. Suddenly I woke up hearing a loud cry from my brother's house. I made out that dacoits have come. I asked my wife Mafuja who was in 'half dress' (sleeping dress) to wear proper cloths. I tried to call a friend from the landline. But my friend did not pick up. I went to the door and peeped through the hole and found that a man standing at the door step. I was worried about my wife and she is not so brave. I pretended as if there is no one in the room. Soon after two three minutes, someone shouted 'open the door'. I did not open. They tried to break the door. Then I opened the door. Immediately, two or three persons entered the room and asked for money. I said that I have no money. You can check the safe. I told them that I work in a private college and get 750 INR as salary. They searched everywhere in my house. Initially I was afraid of the dacoits, but soon I gained my courage and was answering them. There was a fat man among the group. He was overseeing the activities. After sometime he ordered, them to 'hurry up'. One of them put the torch at my wife's face, but no one behaved badly with her. The fat man ordered one of his companions, 'that if there is no money, then they should take her'. After hearing this, I asked my wife, to 'pray to Allah'. One of the men took her on his shoulder and all of the dacoits left immediately. Before leaving they locked me in. After they left everyone came and rescued me. I went out running and called her name. I called all the villagers. Some came out and informed me that they had no clue as to where the dacoits could have taken my wife. I ran around looking for her until it was 5 am. I got no clue as to where my wife could be. She disappeared in the fog.

After about 48 hours of this incident, Mafuja was rescued by the locals in Bangladesh and was handed over to the BSF stationed near Hallidayganj. Mafuja, still traumatized remembers her ordeal and narrates:

…as soon as they took me out of the house, I became unconscious. They took me on their shoulders. After sometime I could hear my husband calling me. Then his voice seemed to fade in the fog. Next morning I found myself in a house with tin roofs. My captors went behind the house and were whispering among themselves. I saw some women and children. I went near them and asked for help. 'Please rescue me', I requested. They replied, 'they are devils. They don't know humanity and have no mercy. You take allah's name'. I was surprised to see that no woman asked me anything about why I was brought here. Day light got brighter. I gained my courage. One captor came close to me and proposed marriage to me. He said, 'your husband did not try to save you. I have lots of money. Be my wife.' I replied that 'I will kill myself before marrying you'. I was crying all the time. After sometime, they asked for a burqa from the women and asked me to wear it. Then they put me on a cycle rickshaw. As the rickshaw was passing, I could see people moving around. They are all in lungis. Before reaching Rowmari, I saw three men in trousers standing near a motorcycle. I decided that I will ask their help. Before reaching the men, the chain of the cycle rickshaw fell down. I thought this is the chance to run away, but could not gather courage. The cycle started moving again. I thought I missed the golden opportunity to rescue myself. As we were passing the men, again the chain fell from the cycle rickshaw. I immediately gathered courage and jumped from the rickshaw and caught hold of the three men standing there and all I could utter was 'please save me'. One of men said that 'you are like my sister. Don't worry, we will help you.' I discovered that I am in Bangladesh, not India. The three men were teachers in a college. They took me to the house of the chairman and explained how I was kidnapped from India. The chairman has two daughters and the eldest one is of my age. The chairman adopted me as his daughter and promised to help. That whole day and night I stayed in his house. Chairman scolded the dacoits and asked them not to do this ever again. Next day with the help of the BDR and BSF, I reached the border and saw that my husband had come to receive me. After a day and a night, I finally returned home. This incident has scarred me for the rest of my life.

Similar real-life stories of women are found echoing in the area and are usually met with silence and tears. These women have no space to be vocal about their sufferings.

IN LIEU OF CONCLUSION

In these barbed regions oppression knows no boundary. People are perennially victimized, either in the name of development or underdevelopment. Only 5 per cent seats of 60-member legislative assembly are kept open for the non-dominant, non-tribals. With fences coming in, non-tribals, especially women tend to become more vulnerable. In this socio-political space gender, ethnicity and subjectivity are interlinked. Women's lives and aspirations retard in the abyss of gendered politics. They remain as the silent mass visible only in voter lists. Women belong to the category of the left outs, their sufferings continue and their voices are muted by the strings of poverty, gender discrimination and religious sedimentation and above all by the fenced borderline. To add to the nefarious power structure surrounding them, another vicious structure which often restricts the growth of the women is religion. Instead of the supposed protection inscribed in the sacred texts, wrong and false interpretation by the oligarchs subjugates them more. Often the women are pushed to a state of increasing anaemia, continuous pregnancies, multiple divorces and a mimetic self of her true existence, who perhaps are not fit enough to figure in the welfare programmes run by the government.

Here gender is interwoven with fixated boundary and gendered fixation is always on the run. Women are seen as moving between different worlds, jobs and places either by being restricted to an imagined geography or being part of perennial flows between locations.

In such socio-political sphere nationalism, fundamentalism and racism meet and complement each other. The denial of political and social rights for women is a matter of bureaucratic convenience. Fencing has restricted the mobility of women the only thing that could have given them a way out of poverty, conflict, social pressure and other adverse conditions. But still women are resisting and their resistance will continue as their hopes of survival remains not withstanding government control, fencing or violence.

Map 6.1 Political Map of West Garo Hills

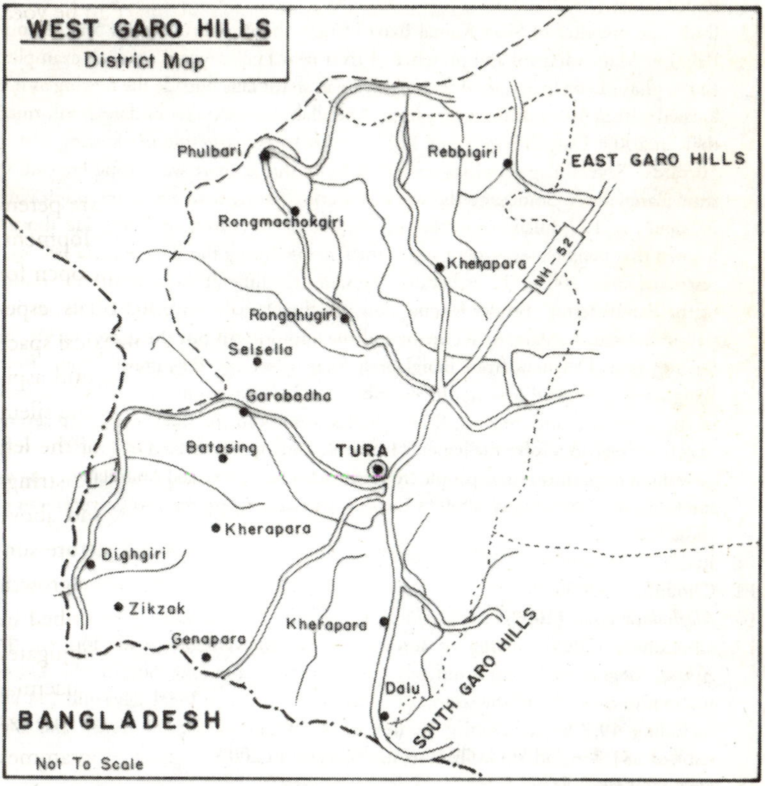

Source: Map drawn by Falguni Biswas.

NOTES

1. Sambanis and Schulhofer-Wohl (2009: 82–118).
2. Devadas and Mummery (2008).
3. http://en.wikipedia.org/wiki/Lalon (accessed on 16 January 2010).
4. Virilio (1997: 1).
5. Berg and Ethin (2008).
6. Schendel (2005: 212).
7. Ibid.: 212.
8. The statement of G.M. Srivastava, the then DGP of Tripura in Agartala, cited in IANS (2010).
9. *The Assam Tribune*, 10 December 1998.
10. Shamshad (2008).

11. Government of India (2008: 3).

12. Rediff News (2009).

13. Ibid. The presence of Shah Kamal Baba Dargah sheriff, (shrine of Pir Shah Kamal Baba) in Mahendraganj and presence of river near Hallidayganj are such examples. In the phase-I construction of fencing, Dargah sharif falls outside the fencing as it is located within 50 yards from zero lines. Abdullah, the caretaker of dargah informed that 'in 2009, Dargah was "taken inside" India by constructing the fencing within 50 yards. 'Several flag meetings were held to fix this as there was strong opposition from Bangladesh. Sometime the workers worked at night to avoid any unpleasant incident', said Abdullah, care taker of Dargah on 30 November 2009. He also informed that people's movement across the fencing during the 'dargah mela' has been restricted since 2007. This is because, he said, it's 'difficult to guarantee the return of the Bangladeshis'. Border fencing now put the Dargah inside India. The fencing passed behind the dargah. We requested the authority to put the graves inside the fencing area. Devotees from Bangladesh long to see the Pir's grave. People from Bangladesh protested fencing the dargah site as it will prevent them to have a look of the grave and offer prayers. Border forces from both the sides conducted several 'flag meetings' to resolve the issue. 'The whole fencing was erected in a rush to avoid unwanted opposition from people from the other side', revealed Abdullah during an interview on 2 November 2009 at Dargah, Mahendraganj; see also Government of India (2008).

14. Rediff News (2009).

15. Choudhury (2009).

16. *Meghalaya Times* (2009).

17. Choudhury (2009). Giving an account of the achievements of the force in the Assam–Meghalaya frontier, officials said that the troops take care of 557 km of international border in the sector, of which, 443 km are in Meghalaya and 134 km including 49.7 km of riverine border are in Dhubri district of Assam and BSF nabbed 181 Bangladeshi infiltrators in the sector in 2009.

18. www.westgarohills.nic.in (accessed on 2 June 2010).

19. Sangma (2010).

20. Ibid.

21. Rajesh, Dev, same as note 34.

22. Interview with Abu Hussain, aged about 80 years, resident of Mahandraganj, on 20 November 2009.

23. Interview with Nur Jahan T. Sangma and her family on 6 January 2010.

24. Rediff News (2010).

25. Berg and Ehin (2008: 53–71).

26. Ibid.

27. *The Assam Tribune*, same as note 17.

28. Many residents of Mahendraganj referred to *Allah hu akbar* of 1950s. It is not clear what happened in that year. It seems there was a sort of communal riot and during this riot Muslims shouted *allah hu akbar* to seek help from other Muslims. In all probability, it could be the time of Language movement of 1952 in East Pakistan.

29. Interview on 28 November 2009.

30. Interview with Abu Hussain, Ayub Ali and others at Mahendraganj and Mankachar, 30 October 2009.

31. Schendel (2005); same as note 6.

32. www.westgarohills.nic.in as on 1 January 2010.

33. http://westGarohills.gov.in/history.htm as on 2 January 2010.

34. Rajesh Dev (2010).

35. Interview with Zubeida Khatun in Agia, Assam on 27 November 2009. Name changed on request.

36. *The Assam Tribune*, same as note 17.

37. *The Shillong Times*, 23 October 2009.

38. Interview with a female ex-smuggler in Nandichar on 25 October 2009.

39. Interview with Anowara Bewa, Mahendraganj on 23 August 2009.

40. *The Assam Tribune*, 10–12 January 2010. Several news items and editorials were published on the importance of opening of border haats.

41. Choudhury (2001).

42. Ibid.

43. A senior officer of BSF requesting anonymity informed the researcher in Guwahati on 15 November 2009.

44. Ibid.

45. http://www.india-server.com/news/479-infiltrator-captured-along-the-18401.html (accessed on 2 June 2010).

46. Interview with Gumeljan Bewa on 25 October 2009.

47. Interview with Kadamphool at Mahendraganj on 7 May 2010.

48. Interview with Sharashi Praba Das at Mahendraganj on 7 May 2010.

49. Interview with Saraswati Das on 8 May 2010.

50. Interview with Anowara Bewa on 21 October 2009.

51. Sinlung (2009).

52. Ibid.

53. Interview with Mafuja Begum and her husband on 29 November 2009 at Hallidayganj.

Part 4

Voices

7

Voices of Women in the Borderlands

*Aditi Bhaduri**

One of the most difficult international borders to be manned and secured is the Indo-Bangladesh border. Both closed and porous, it defies all established political norms and security measures. The total length of Indo-Bangladesh border is 4,096 km. Of this length, almost three-fourth has been fenced. However, the fencing is not continuous or contiguous. There are villages right on the zero line and within 150 yards of the international border. The border is also criss-crossed by the river Padma, which makes it difficult to fence the entire length.

The border region between India and Bangladesh is densely populated and is a region of endemic poverty and social imbalance. Borders also unite and bridge divides, provide passages and transits. The result is that there is a steady movement of people and goods across the border, both legal and illegal. The borderland is a site of multiple forms of violence as well as

*This chapter would not have been possible without the help of the Border Security Force, South Bengal Frontier and thanks in particular to Mr Vikash Chandra, DIG (G), BSF, SBF, Kolkata, and to Mr B.D. Sharma, Inspector in General, Prisons, West Bengal. Thanks also to Sabir Ahmed, Gautam Middha, Bongaon, Petrapole Simanta Unnayan Samiti, Zakir Mallik, Chapra Social and Economic Welfare Association, Benjir, Hatkhola and Hatkhola Gram Panchayat, and to the many women and men residing on the borderlands between India and Bangladesh, who willingly shared their lives with me.

contestations. Women form a particularly vulnerable group as they often cross the border in search of livelihood, security, or are simply trafficked, and become victims of multiple forms of violence. Yet, these women do not only embrace or affirm an identity of victimhood, they are also agents of their lives. In 2009 alone, for instance, 147 women have been held for smuggling contraband across the border. Thousands of narratives unfold daily in the borderlands between India and Bangladesh, and there are multiple realities of life here. Too often discourses are either only rights based or only security based. The reality is far more complex and the lived experience is that women inhabiting these areas engage in manifold negotiations with numerous agencies.

Keeping these facts in mind I have tried to capture voices from the borderland to portray the everydayness of life, as it is lived and experienced by women living in these borderlands. Interviews were deliberately not conducted with any victim-survivor of trafficking (which is rampant across the borders) or with any female sex worker, as these issues have received widespread coverage in academia and in the media. These interviews were conducted with women living in villages of Jayantipur, Hatkhola, Petrapole, Shutiya, as well as, with women serving sentence in correctional facilities in Kolkata.

Mukti Shahji
Village: Petrapole

I grew up near Haringhata which is also a border village, but it was different. Here it's far more developed because of Petrapole border crossing. In my childhood it was common to see people go over to what is now Bangladesh. I thought it was all one village. That village would be just part of our village. But later we understood differently, as slowly more security people moved in on both sides. Then I got married and came here where my husband worked on some land owned by his sister- and brother-in-law. Afterwards he opened a small business. Here too there were not so many security people like they are now. Over the years they have grown, and now I see this place is swarming with them. See that pond, we would all bathe there. Across the pond that is Bangladesh. Can you see one Bangladesh Rifles (BDR) man is sitting there? With so many Border Security Force (BSF) people on this side and BDR on that side, we had to discontinue using the pond. Now we bathe here in this place that we have made.

We are living in fear all the time. The BSF people keep coming and measuring the land. They came last week too. They want to fence this place for security. What will happen to us then? We will be fenced out. We do not want that. It is bad enough living in a border village. We cannot have people visit us or move out from our homes after 7 p.m. If someone comes to visit me from my village they have to leave by 7 p.m., as after that time movement becomes difficult. And at times when the BSF clamp curfew we cannot move out even after 5 p.m. We had to return home by evening. If we need to move after 7:30 p.m., the BSF asks us several questions—which often turn into interrogation. It is the same if any relative comes to our place after 7 p.m.; they are questioned for hours on end, their bags are searched, and they feel humiliated. At times if they are shoot-outs or the BSF suspects someone smuggling something, or if any intruder from Bangladesh comes here then we have had it. They come knocking, search our homes, and turn it upside down, with no respect for anyone or anything. If sometimes that happens at night, we just lock ourselves in, pretend to be sleeping, not knowing anything. We do not like to get caught in such stuff.

But, in spite of everything we do not want this place to be fenced off. The BSF presence has also resulted in some sense of safety and security. We do not have thefts or robberies, which used to take place earlier. Earlier, when there was less presence, we had more freedom to move around, but people from the other side would keep coming and stealing harvests, cattle, even household goods. I have heard once my sister-in-law had food that was being cooked on the fire-pit that got stolen by people from Bangladesh. They are something else. We are also Muslims, but we are not as daring as them; they have the nerves and guts to do such desperately daring things. If we are fenced out, we will lose the protection of the BSF. We will be exposed and vulnerable to people from that other side and left at the mercy of the BDR. We do not want that. It is not that there is no problem with the BSF here. See they are all over the place. We had much greenery and gardens around our house, but now see the land is bare. That's because we cannot grow plants and trees higher than three feet from the ground. They have cut down all the mango and coconut trees here. At nights they keep watch there, and when my neighbours have gone out to the toilet, they have been harassed. No one will tell you that it has happened to them, but it has happened to all of us. But of course we do not want to get into trouble.

My elder daughter goes to the school—it's a government school and I am always uneasy from the moment she leaves home until she is safely back.

She has to pass all these constables, sometimes they call out and sing songs, and tease her. They don't understand Bengali and I think they don't like Bengali people. My daughter has to show her identity card while going to school and while coming back. But if we are fenced out, it will become even worse. We will have to submit our identity cards all the time. Even now if we return a little late, we have to answer so many questions and show papers. I cannot imagine what will happen then. Our lands for cultivation will be on that side. When we visit the other side of the fencing for cultivation, we would need to submit voter card/ration card, etc., at the BSF camps. They work for the protection of national security; on the other hand they violate the rights of people living on the border.

The hospital is in Bongaon at least 7 km from here, and imagine if something is to happen suddenly to us at night, the gates would be closed by 6 p.m. And if they fence this place they would also take away the land from us. They have offered very cheap price. The BDO came once and he offered only ₹5,000 for one bigha. Just imagine! And we are very poor people. We do not have money to buy land on the other side, as the price of which will be considerably more. On this side we will be devoid of all security and protection as the BSF will move within the fenced area. We really do not know what will happen. We have submitted a petition to the BDO not to fence this place, but we have heard nothing. We live in mortal fear that any day that will happen.

We belong to lower middle class. We face various kinds of difficulties—especially economic stress—throughout the year. Now the NGO Petrapole Simanta Unayyan Samiti is helping us. I am the head of this group of 25 women. We save ₹60 per month (₹180 in three months). After three months a woman is eligible to receive ₹1,000 as loan amount. After every three months, she gets additional ₹500 upon repayment. Loans are provided to women after careful examination of her business proposal and feasibility. Women are becoming self sufficient with the help of their small enterprises. I have bought some chicken and engage in poultry. I sell the eggs to my neighbours and that helps me complement our income. We have three daughters, and as you know everything is becoming more expensive. I have given birth to all my daughters at home, as the nearest maternity home is in Bongaon. Now, two of them go to school. My youngest one is just two years old and she stays at home with me. There are no ICDCs in this village. So you see it would be doubly difficult for us if the village is fenced out. We only pray that the government does not fence this area. Please pray for us.

Parweena Bibi
Village: Hatkhola
District: Nadia

I was born and brought up in this village. My natal house is down the other side, about a kilometre or two away. I live here with my seven children and husband. I have been married for almost 20 years. Our fields are on the other side of the fence, and I tell you what a problem it is for me to tend to them. To go out to the other side, we have to keep our IDs with the border (security) people. When our children go to school, they have to keep their IDs. When my husband goes to tend to the fields, he has to submit the ID. When I take him some lunch, I have to keep my ID with them. When people come to visit us from the other side, they have to keep their ID with them. If we go to the market, the hospital, or any other place it's the same. At 6 p.m. they close the gates, and life for the day ends for us. Not that we go out much. All over this border area as you know the day is over by 6–7 p.m. But when we have an emergency, it's terrible. Worst is the attitude of the guards. On and off they check us. We are women, but they do not spare us. They take their weapon and nudge us with it, feel us up to see if we are hiding anything on our person. As if! But no one will complain. No one will speak up. We are at their mercy, if we speak up then it's our fault and we have to bear the consequences. They just behave as they want to. There is a gate close to my house, but they can close it at their mercy and I have to trudge all the way to the main gate which is almost 2 km away from here. Same is true of my children experience when they return from school. Sometimes they find the gate nearby closed and they have to walk all that way to the main gate and then from the main gate to our house here.

We cannot cultivate the more lucrative items like papaya, which fetches a good price. No, everything has to be just three feet tall, so we have 'path' and paddy. During harvest, we have to specify the number of sacks of harvest we will be collecting and have to enter them in their register. Now, just tell me, is it possible to be absolutely accurate? Sometimes we may enter a certain number and then have a sack or two extra, but that will just be confiscated by them. I cannot tell you how many times they have done this. Sometimes, if they are hungry they will just take away stuff to eat; maybe a chicken and they won't even pay for them. We are poor people and farming is all we have. So many of our youth are now leaving this place; they want a better life, not this horrible sad border village life. Many of them would go to Mumbai, now. We have two of our youth in Kuwait; for the first time someone from our village is living in the Arab countries. There was an agency in Chapra that was scouting for workers. We don't know how they are, and what life they are leading. We are looking forward to hearing their news. For here there is no future. Also, Mohameddans we hear find it difficult to find jobs in other places.

But here life is really horrible; it was not so earlier. People would come here from that other village. See across this khal, that is Bangladesh on the other side. Earlier they would come over here, cross the khal, and buy things from us. See, there you can see the BDR men. In front of us are the BSF men, they are there every 10–20 feet. It's such a nuisance, all the time we are surrounded by strange men. At least the BSF people move around. They turn and sit with their backs to us. They face the other side, but these BDR men just sit and stare this side, they don't move at all. I don't know why.

People do try to sell some things from this side to that side of course. I don't know exactly what. I know they like to buy fruits from here, and sometimes some cattle; but my family does not sell anything, so I do not know. But it's true, that many things are sent from here, and things come from there too. And people came from that side too, earlier. Of course, people from Bangladesh liked to visit India but it has stopped and it is of no use to us. We are not involved in that. We just need to lead a peaceful life. Earlier it used to be better, but now with this fence it's really difficult. We feel so abandoned, as no one cares for us. If someone suddenly goes to that side, the BDR people catch him and thrash him, while here the BSF are always so suspicious of us. They don't treat us like humans. They make fun of us. They don't speak Bengali. I don't think they even like Bengalis. Some of them tease the young girls and women, you know. Now see, no one will tell you that something has happened to them, but I am telling you that all have had some kind of unpleasant experience. We live here and that seems to be our crime. We are always looked upon with suspicion, as if we are all criminals doing something illegal. Now many of our friends from the other side have stopped visiting us. So we stand and chat with each other through the fence, but these men keep standing, so we always have company.

We feel unsafe sometimes because our husbands are away tending to the fields and we are all alone. I'm telling you life here is hard, very hard. You do not know the hardships we face. Our hardship comes from this side and from that side; it's as if we do not belong to any side. Which is our home? Which is our land?

Which is our country? We are scared of people from that side. Earlier they would come and take away our harvest, i.e., before the fence was made. Now our fields are safe because they lie within the fence, but our household goods and cattle are not. Deep in the night they sometimes come here and rob things from our house. We have no one to complain to, or no one to turn to for protection. I do not like the people from the other side. They talk sweet, but they harm you. Once, a couple of our village boys went that side. The people over there informed the BDR, and they arrested the boys. Our poor boys! That's how people are; you cannot trust anyone.

And the BSF people think they are kings. See if I go somewhere in a van and we happen to pass any BSF person on the way, the driver of the van has to get off and walk while crossing them. As a mark of his submission he cannot sit and ride the van. Why? Are they kings? They will stop the men, even though they know the men are from this village, but still they will ask them what they do, where they are going and why. Just some months ago a young girl died. I don't know what really happened. I hear that there was a 'thrower' and the BSF people were chasing him, and the girl happened to be in the way and got shot. But what does it matter, who is right or wrong? The young girl paid with her life. We are not Bangladeshis, so we can never ever forget to take our Ids. Anywhere we go, we are so scared of being called Bangladeshis and put in prison. There is no peace, no peace, this is torture. The only way we can escape all this is by buying a house on that side, but it's too expensive. The moment they erected the fence, the price of land on that side shot up and on this side it went down. So who will buy our house? And where will we get the money to buy a house on that side? No, we have to live here and suffer here; that is our fate.

Srabanti Karmakar
Constable: Border Security Force
Haridaspur

I am from Bankura district village, Soldah. I went to a government primary school nearby. We are three sisters; I am the eldest. My father's mother also lives with us. My father is a carpenter, and my mother a housewife. I had a kaka who worked in the army, lived in the village, and I loved to see him in his uniform. Since then I had harboured this dream that I too would join the forces one day. I loved history most of all, I completed Madhyamik in 2004 and Higher Secondary in 2007. Then I enrolled in college. High school was 45 metres away from my house; I used to go to school on my cycle. We took classes in a coaching centre for help with all the subjects that we studied in school. The teachers used to come to school, but did not teach us fully. They would show us somethings, for example, some mathematics or come and tell us what we had to study in history. Then we had to do it on our own, so that's why we went to the coaching centre. Boys and girls studied together in the school. College was 45 minutes away. I went to the bus stand by cycle, left the cycle there and took the bus to college. On way back, I came by bus, took the cycle and cycled back home. There was no fear that the cycle would be stolen, and we were in a group, as most girls in our village studied. Most of the people in the village were farmers and some were not, like my father was a carpenter. Others had small businesses, like a ration shop, or a small shop selling knick-knacks. In college, I did NCC, and did not choose honours. I knew from Class IX that I would join the forces. I used to read the employment newspaper that my father usually brought for me. It is in this newspaper that I found the advertisement for my job. Actually I wished to join the air force, but that's a very advanced field. However, I knew that I would join the forces, perhaps the West Bengal police. So I knew I had to have some higher education for it, so I studied history and Bengali and Sanskrit. I am not married, and I never thought of marriage. I studied in the pass course and 45 per cent was the minimum needed to pass. I studied for two years and then took the first year exam for my college degree. Before the second year I got recruited. I went back and took the second year exam; however, I got the appointment for here. So, I have not yet completed my graduation. In my village, people appreciated me. Some would tell my parents to get me married off. My mother was under tremendous pressure, but my father stood by me. He always told people, my daughter has ambitions; she is not doing anything illegal. I would run in the field each day and people would see me work hard on my form and physical fitness. My second sister is now doing a diploma in computers and my youngest sister is in school but she too runs and wants to join the forces.

Initially my parents did not like the idea of me joining the forces because it is really tough work, difficult and painful. And BSF work is even more difficult. The training is so hard, and if I failed to pass the training it would have been so humiliating. I had to fill in my height and weight details too. Then I had to go to Kalyani to the BSF outpost there for physical test. I had to run for 800 metres, do 3-feet high jump and 9-feet long jump. Then we had a written test, viva and medical tests. My father accompanied me to Kalyani. We rented a hotel room; but it was a little expensive for us, since we had to pay for the accommodation out of our own pockets. My father would accompany me and wait outside. In the test I wrote that I wanted to do something for my country and also that I had dreamed of being in the forces since childhood. I was very tense and nervous. There were some 420 applicants, and only 32 were selected. We had all the tests over a period of six days. The commanding officer of Kalyani was there. This was in 2008. I was so tensed up that I would not eat anything. I would eat something in the morning and only after I returned to the hotel in the night. The snacks I would take with me to the test each day would remain in my bag. Then on 2 September I got the appointment call. We joined in September in Kalyani and then we were sent to Punjab in November for training. There were many officers there; we got training in drill, in shooting, rifle training, training in light machine gun, pistol, training in physical fitness and agility. We had training for nine months and learnt how to adjust with each other. There were Punjabi girls too and I learnt how to live with non-Bengalis. The first border I was in Wagah. I was very scared the first time I saw it. Especially because there the border is with Pakistan and Pakistan is always causing some trouble or the other for India. So I used to be nervous and wondered if I ever had to serve on such a border, would I be up to it? My father likes to read newspapers and discuss politics, so since childhood I knew about Pakistan's harmful intentions. Then I came to know about Taliban, that everyday there is some blast, some infiltration. Every day one of our jawans is killed on some place in the border or the other. Regarding Bangladesh it's a little different. See wherever there is no fencing they try to take stuff out, so we have to be extremely attentive during our vigils. And where there is fencing we have to be more careful alert, because if any part of the fence is cut or damaged then we have to pay for it. A month's weapon is taken away from us, we have to work 28 days extra over the period which we sign for in the contract. We have been inducted in the forces because so much of smuggling across the borders was being engaged in by women. They were not checked by the other male constables, so they continued. That is why we have been recruited. Regarding Bangladesh, I just feel angry with them. Do you know how much they harass our jawans? They cut the fence and our jawans have to bear the penalty. They take cattle from here, jewellery, clothes, Indian currency, and sometimes weapons too. I really dislike that. I feel no familiarity with them. I really like this place and my work in the BSF. I had many hopes. I came with much hopes and expectations in my heart and I really like this job. It's a lot of responsibility. I am really doing something worthwhile; no woman from my family has worked before. It's peaceful here, though my village is even better;

but I like this work. All the sirs, all the people in the force are really nice, and treat us with a lot of respect. We do miss home, but here all have become like a big family. In fact when we go home on holidays now, we wait eagerly to get back here and exchange all the news. We women constables miss each other when we go away. However, we are told not to be too friendly with the local people here. We are not encouraged to mix with the people here. The moment we become friendly with them, they will take advantage and ask us to help them move goods across the border. You see Bangladeshis can take things from here precisely because they are helped by people here, so we are not encouraged to interact with the people here much. We keep aloof and maintain our distance. So you see, our work is tough and it's really something for the country. I am so proud of doing this work and of doing something for my country. Honestly, I never thought I would be up to it and reach this place and achieve this. The people in my village today look up to me. My mother now says how was I to know that you would become such a big person?

We don't have any night duty till now but sometimes if they suspect anyone of carrying anything, then they call us in the night, based on the case. Then in Jayantipur there is a gate, so if they find some woman without an ID there, or suspect that some woman is carrying something on her person, we are called. I don't have any feelings for Bangladesh. For me they are strangers. It's a different country. Its makes no difference whether the people are Hindu or Muslim; if they are doing something illegal, it is my duty and work to stop them. Just a few days ago I caught an old woman, almost my grandmother's age, who was trying to sneak into India from Bangladesh. She was a Hindu, but she was lying, so much, I was ashamed of her and also embarrassed that an elderly person could lie in such a way. But we caught her and made sure that she was sent back to Bangladesh. I don't allow myself to feel sorry for them; they have seriously endangered the life of people in our country. Indians are also people and we are responsible for keeping the country and our people safe. I do not allow myself to think that the people we catch are poor or doing all these illegal activities out of poverty and squalor. I also grew up in a not well to do family, but I have never tried to engage in any illegal activity. I thank god and I pray to god every day. Sometimes I carry flowers if I find some. My parents are proud of me and I am happy to have set this trend. We are the very first women in the BSF and already my younger sister and some girls in my village tell me that they want to be like me. They too want to join the forces and are working towards that.

Firoza Bibi
Village: Jayantipur

Life for me became hell after the birth of my second daughter. I was brought up to believe that home and family are all that matters. But what bad luck visited me. I studied till Class IV. I have three brothers and three sisters. I was born and grew up in this village of Jayantipur; my natal house is further down. My father worked on the fields for the rich people and my husband too worked on a rich man's farm. It is on the other side, inside Indian Territory and it is fenced in. I got married when I was 15 years old. I have two daughters—the elder one is about 13 years, she began menstruating recently. The younger is about six years old. Life was hard, but alright for us; my husband worked on the farm and we raised some poultry too. When I was pregnant for the second time, I noticed that my husband began craving sex in a way he never had. He would demand sex like an animal, that's when I began to feel that something was changing. But I was pregnant, and he began visiting other women. I did not immediately understand what was going on. I know now that when you begin smoking heroin, you become sex crazy initially, and then gradually you become like a small boy, unable to perform at all. But I did notice that he began to lose his looks. He became dark. Also, things and money began to mysteriously go missing from the house. We are poor people, and money became short more and more. Then one day I saw him try to steal some of our chicken and I threw a row. He began losing his appetite. It is then that I came to know that he was addicted.

He lost the ability to work; all he wanted was money, money and money. Life became hell. I had two daughters to look after; I was not too strong myself physically. Then I learnt that there were others in the village who were afflicted like him. I felt strangely consoled that he was not the only one. I came to know that you can never be addicted by yourself; you need company, a group. I tell you that I even followed him a couple of times to see where he went. Once I followed him pretty far, but it became dark and it was almost 5 p.m. That's when curfew begins here. I got scared and turned back. Another time I saw him sit with some others and put some things on a piece of paper, light a matchstick over it and lick it. I was horrified, but he was in a group and I came back. I want all the peddlers to be punished. Those like my husband are fools. They are being ruined, but the main culprits are the ones like Yaar Nabi. They are the rich ones who sell the stuff, and those like my husband get addicted. Even the sons of rich get addicted, I know my rich neighbour, who takes pity on me and often lets me take her ration rice, and she lost her son too to this madness. Her son committed suicide. I am lucky that my husband is still alive and trying to improve. But it is difficult.

Initially I cried over his addiction, but then I began to hit him. I turned him out of the house. But all that was of no use. I could not stop him. I told my parents and my brothers and they spoke to him but it was useless. I had to start working in the homes of others to sustain myself and my children. Then I filed an FIR with the police who refused to take it, so I went to Bongaon court and signed papers and paid ₹200 and got my husband imprisoned for three months. During this time they gave him treatment. Then after three months, I paid ₹300 and got him released. He had become so ugly. He had withdrawal symptoms and it was hell to watch him like that. He used to shiver, get fits and go into spells. It was like when he was addicted too. He would demand money and if I did not give him any, he would take a knife and start slashing his wrists, threatening to commit suicide. How much I have cried over this only I know. Sometimes I think about how much I have had to cry in this life. But I am just continuing because I want my daughters to lead a proper life. I pay for my husband too. He is out of work now. We just have some chickens and we sell those eggs, and I work in people's houses here in Jayantipur. He seems to be okay now, but twice before he seemed to have given up his addiction and then went back again. So I am not sure how long this will last this time. I feel sorry for him sometimes. He was persuaded into addiction. He is not the real criminal. Criminals are the people who trade in the drugs. May they find no place in hell for ruining people's lives like this? I think the police and a lot of big people are involved in this drug trafficking business. Otherwise, how is it that they cannot stop it? I know this dealer, but no one can lay their hands on him. How? All the people know that it is this person who is the main drug lord in these parts, but are we to pretend that the police do not know?

Now sometimes the Dadas from the BSF come and talk to my husband. They threaten him not to go back to his life of addiction. They urge him to lead a normal life, which gives me some relief that he will not go back to addiction out of fear. I hope the BSF people can keep a watch and can find out the culprits and prevent other innocent people from getting caught in this nightmare. There are one or two of them (the BSF personnel) who are like my brothers. I trust them and I think they will deal with this sternly. I have heard worse things happen in places like Jamtala where people cut themselves up on the streets to feed their addiction. I have two daughters to bring up. Life is so hard, as we have no land and have to work for others. But I love my husband. I can never think of leaving him. Leaving him? Where would I go? And what would he do by himself? He would die in a day. I just hope the culprits will be exposed and punished. I hope my husband will be back to normal and will lead a normal life like before. That is my greatest hope. Otherwise, living in this border village, there is not much significance or anything of particular concern in my life. I have lived here my whole life and I am used to it. Yes, sometimes, there may be some problems from the BDR people on that side. Problems between BDR and the forces on this side can happened as they run around chasing each other, but they know me and my husband and we have no problems. Like last year, when there was problem between the BDR and the BSF. The BSF people told us, that if anyone from that side comes here, we should let them come and offer them shelter, but we were to also eventually bring them to the BSF. No one has ever robbed me; we are too poor to take anything from us. If we are fenced out, I do not know what will happen. I have not thought of it. I work in the house and then in other people's houses and then raise some poultry for income. I am too busy the whole day and then I have to return home to look after a recovering addict as a husband. We have security for now. I will think of other things when they happen.

Rita
Village: Shutiya

My name is Rita and I am 24 years old. I am a widow. My husband died of HIV/AIDS. I was born and grew up in Shutiya where my father is a farmer. I have a younger brother and sister. My husband was from the village right next to us. There are no jobs in the village, so most people are migrating. A lot of boys are leaving the village and going to other towns in search of jobs. Our farm is too small, and since I have only one brother he will inherit my father's farm. But when there is more than one son in the family, the land is too small to be shared. My father grows mustard, rice (dhaan), and path. Ours is a mixed village of Hindus and Muslims. Most families in our village have relatives across the border. Previously, men also used to send cattle across the border, but now I think it is becoming difficult. We have never sent cattle across. I went to school and studied till Madhyamik and then was married off. My husband is one of those who migrated out from the village. He went to Mumbai where he worked as a driver for a babu. A lot of boys from my village went to Mumbai. I lived in his house, with his mother who was considerably old. He visited me and his mother for a few months, during which I fell pregnant. Right after I got pregnant my husband again left for Mumbai. Six months into my pregnancy, I had a miscarriage. My blood tests revealed that all was not well with me. The doctors asked me what my husband did. The hospital in Habra referred me to R.G. Kar Hospital, where the nurses behaved very badly with me. When they came to know of my HIV status, they told it to everyone and I was shunned by all.

I was 19 years old when I first heard of my HIV status. I wanted to commit suicide, especially when I came to know how we were perceived. People were disgusted with me. They hated me, but worst of all they were frightened of me. But it is only now that I know that it is not so easily contagious. Anyway, my husband came down from Mumbai after I was diagnosed with HIV and this time and he underwent a blood test. It was revealed that he was HIV+ too. That's how I contracted it, because my husband is the only man I have been intimate with in my life. I had never heard about this disease in my village. I do not know if anyone else has it, but I have not heard of it. We moved to Gobordanga, where my husband found work as a driver. Initially he did not accept the diagnosis. My sister-in-law and her husband first blamed me. But they knew well that the only way I could have contracted it was from my husband. Initially I was angry and hurt with my husband. I went away to my mother's place, but he begged me for forgiveness. Moreover, how long could I live in my mother's place? My father had three more mouths to feed with the income from his tiny piece of land. When my parents came to know about our HIV status they simply did not believe it. They could not understand what it was all about.

Meanwhile my husband was becoming weaker; he explained to me that his unprotected sexual encounters had taken place before our marriage. He was lonely and alone in Mumbai. He needed some warmth and so he visited some women from whom he contracted the disease. But he told me that he did not visit any woman after our marriage and I believed him. Anyway, now he is no more, so it makes no difference. However, I like to believe that he did not visit any woman after we got married. My husband lived in Gobordanga for nine months and worked as a driver, but the income was not good. Eventually he went back to Mumbai, where he earned more and would send money home. But he kept falling sick, his condition deteriorated and he came back to Gobordanga. It was during this time that I conceived again. This baby was an accident. When I found out that I was pregnant again, I wanted to abort the foetus. I took some pills for terminating the pregnancy, but nothing happened. After this, I just wanted to keep the baby even though I knew its future was already doomed. For my second baby I visited Barasat government hospital. The attitude there to an HIV+ patient was also extremely bad. Often the doctors tried to avoid treating me. But the counsellor there was really good. She got me admitted, made me stay there and got doctors to treat me. It was she who told me about NN+, about people living with HIV/AIDs. It was during this time that my husband passed away. While he was alive, anti-retrovial therapy (ART) was still not available to us. This was two years ago. Then my baby was still born. Life lost much of its meaning for me. It was the counsellor didi who helped me through it. I used to cry and tell her about my life and she put me in touch with a positive network. I joined it more than a year ago. We have a meeting once a month in Bongaon and I simply love the meetings. It is difficult for me to come. It's a long way off Shutiya, where I stay now. After my husband's death, I moved back into my parents' home. Where else can I go? My husband left very little money for me. I do not have any skills. I do not know, maybe I will find some work through this group.

Right now it's enough for me to know that I am not alone in the world, there are others like me. We are normal human beings. It's not that anyone talking to me or sitting next to me would contract the disease. I meet others like me at the network meetings, and I have been benefited through the network. I had to have a gall bladder operation some months ago and the network helped me to have the operation in the Calcutta Medical College. Doctors initially were cold, but gradually attitudes got changed. I see much more patience in the doctors and also greater publicity about HIV+ patients.

Medicines for HIV+ began soon after my husband died. For more than a year now, I have been taking ART and I feel much better. Soon after my second baby was still born I used to feel very weak. Now for the last two months the medicines are available at Barasat which is more convenient for me to access rather than go all the way to Calcutta. People in Shutiya spread rumours about me and gossiped a lot. They would talk to me, but also avoided me. Thank god that my sister got married before my positive status was discovered, otherwise it would have been difficult for us to find a match for her. But I am glad they are advertising about HIV on TV now. My advice to all other girls would be to get a blood test done, if you are getting married and do not know their husband well. This is especially true if the prospective groom is living away in another city or town.

Firoza Begum Halsana
Village: Hatkhola

I grew up in Chapda and studied till Class V. And then at age 15, I got married. My husband was a widower and had a daughter from his first wife. We are farmers, my husband has land and we hire people to work on it. He is a Congress member and was the panchayat samiti member. Now he is the ex-Pradhan of Gongda. So, when the next elections were held and a seat was reserved for a woman, he asked me to stand for elections. I have two daughters and a son. My eldest daughter is 12 years old. I had absolutely no idea what to do. They said all will be taken care of. Of course people respected me because of my husband, and my husband is well respected in the village and in all of the villages of our panchayat. We have seven villages under our panchayat. Now Habibur Rahman Khan is Panchayat pradhan. I was busy with my housework and the responsibilities of bringing up my children, so I did not campaign. My husband campaigned for me, and his friends. Also people liked me as they respected my husband. This area of ours is a Congress stronghold—they listened to him and I won by 154 votes and became a panchayat member. Our Panchayat has 17 members out of which 5 are women. Now I have to go out two to three times a month for meetings in Hatkhola Gram Panchayat. Initially, my husband accompanied to the meetings, now I can go alone. I know the people, and I have the support of the women in the village, as they are all like sisters to me. I have to sign papers from time to time, but I do not deal with money matters. My 'shachiv' fixes up everything and I simply sign. However, I do have to go to the anganwadis and inspect the food from time to time see if the children are being looked after properly. Also, I got toilet steps/feet installed in the houses in this village. I have to sign papers and meeting minutes, even if I am not in the meetings; however, I try to be there. I sign job cards for the NREGS. I don't know who the cards are for, but I trust the people handling it.

The women and girls here respect me. They come to me with their problems. When they bring me their domestic problems I give them advice. I tell them how to handle their husbands and look after their children. When couples have problems they come to me and I counsel them on how to live amicably with each other. Of course, the men will have their ways and will sometimes beat up the women, but women should be patient. Women should be able to sometimes go out and the husband should look after them. Young girls like me and tell me they want to be like me. Actually, I like to look after my home, which is the most important thing for me. My husband and home is my priority, but since my husband's work is mixed up with the panchayat, I have to help out also. Yes, it is nice to be a panchayat member. I did not ever think of it, but now it is here and I am part of it. I will try to make life a little better for my sisters.

We have no problems with the BSF people. If sometimes people complain, then they should know that the BSF are here for our own safety and security. Maybe it is people from beyond the fence who sometimes have some problems with ID cards, etc., but we do not. If you are good with people then they will also be good with you. But there are people who want to send out some things to those on the other side. You know the 'throwers' sometimes like grains and food and of course then they will have problems with the security people. After all the security people are here for us, for our safety and we have to have good relations with them. There is no use in antagonizing them. We should understand how to behave. Why go out after 5 p.m.? What need is there for women to go anywhere after that? Why should she return home late and alone? In our village everyone must return home by 5 p.m. for security and there is no problem if you do. If the people ask you for ID, then you should not create any problems. Of course she must work and study—my daughters also study and I encourage parents to send their daughters to school. All girls in our village go to the school nearby. The older ones take vocational training too. But family and home is important.

Tanya Sharif
Bangladeshi
Charged and convicted under the **Foreigner's Registration Act 1946**
Presidency Correctional Home for Women

My name is Tanya Sharif. I was born and grew up in Panigati village in Khulna district. I had three elder sisters and a younger brother. I studied till Class V in the village school. We were extremely poor and suffered much poverty. Often there was nothing to eat. I came to India when I was about 13 years old, with my mother and elder sister. We used to see and hear people going to and coming from India. My elder sister got married to a man from the village of Pedoli, who lived and worked in Mumbai kabarkhana. On a visit to Bangladesh he married my sister, who is four years older than me. He stayed on till sometime, then after my sister had a child he went back to Mumbai. Soon he made arrangements for my mother, my sister and me to go to Mumbai with a dalal. Since were very poor, we felt it would be a good option for us to go and work in Mumbai.

We heard that some others had done that and were living well. A lot of people from my jamai babu's village were also coming to Mumbai and his brother fixed a dalal who charged us ₹2,000 to help the three of us get to Mumbai.

We left our village early in the morning, and travelled by bus to a place near the border. I do not remember much about it. I just went blindly holding on to my mother. There we waited below some trees. I remember for it to be dark and I fell asleep. I did not know we were crossing a border, and that too an illegal one. Along the way our dalal spoke to different people at different places. Later on I came to know, on my subsequent trips to Mumbai and back that some of the people the dalal spoke to were BDR and BSF people, but none stopped us from crossing over. I don't remember about the first journey, where we stopped and where we crossed into. It was a long journey and we travelled by bus, then sometimes we walked, and at other times we crossed a shallow stream with knee-high water. The dalal took us into a house where there were other women and children. A day later we were taken to Howrah station; I had never seen a place like it before. There we boarded a train and were taken to VT in Mumbai. At VT my jamai babu came to receive us and took us to his house in Meera Road. We lived in a basti, with other Bengalis. I missed my father and brother, who were in Bangladesh.

I found a job in an apartment nearby, working for a family of 7–8 people. I cleaned, washed the dishes, wiped and swept the floors and dusted. I was paid ₹500 per month for the work. I lived for about two years in Mumbai thus. Once I got the hang of the work, I took up work in two more houses and was earning ₹2,000 per month, plus I got food and clothes from the houses that I worked in. In the meantime I got married, because the young men in the basti used to harass me. My mother used to worry for my safety, and soon a friend of my brother-in-law intervened and proposed to me. He was a construction worker by the name of Raju Seth, also a Bangladeshi Muslim. He lived far away from our basti. Initially after marriage I lived with my mother, as I was scared of living away from her; but, after a while I joined my husband. I was about 13 then.

It was then that I made my first trip back to Bangladesh with my mother and didi. My jamai babu got in touch with the broker, from Mumbai we came to Howrah and one man came and met us. I do not remember his name or what he did. He took the three of us to a village. We spent a day there in someone's house and the next night a group of us—about 15–20 people, also my jamai babu's brother and his wife, who were working in Mumbai—crossed the border at night at Bhomia. This time I saw some armed men, but they did not do anything to us, or stop us. Our guide went and spoke to them. I do not remember which year this was, but that by then I had been living in Mumbai for almost two years. My mother wanted to visit home and see my father and brother and so did I. Again we had to swim, and I remember that our hands got cut. We stayed for almost two months in Bangladesh and then crossed the border back once again at Bhomia into India. This time my mother stayed back in Bangladesh with my father. From there we went to Howrah and back to Mumbai. Again none of the guards, neither on the Bangladesh side nor on the Indian side stopped us. At one time, I remember the guide (dalal) made us stand aside, went and negotiated with a guard on the Indian side for a while, and then we were allowed to cross over.

We returned to Mumbai and I joined work again. I did not join the same houses that I had worked for in the past, as they had hired other help in my absence. I found employment in other apartments near about. Few months after I came back from Bangladesh, I became pregnant. This time my husband also wanted to visit Bangladesh, as he wanted to meet my family who too wanted to see him. A few of my husband's friends also wanted to visit desh and so a group of us again got together, paid the dalal, came to Howrah and crossed the border near Bashirhat. The cost had already gone up, as we paid ₹1,000 per person to the dalal, who lived near the border and helped us to cross over. This time I carried saris for my mother, children's clothes and stayed home for two months. After my return to Mumbai after this second trip back to Bangladesh, I had the baby at a government hospital. After the birth of my daughter, my husband's relationship with me deteriorated. He went out with other women, beat me up, and humiliated me. So, I decided to go away to Bangladesh again. I got together with two girls from Jessore who worked in the same building as I and together with their families we returned to Bangladesh. This time I paid the dalal ₹2,000. We went from Mumbai to Kolkata, crossed the border at Benapole, at about 8:30 p.m. Again neither the BSF nor the BDR guards said anything to us. I stayed home for a month or so, and showed off my baby to others. When I was out of money I had to return to India. I left my baby with my mother. Again I returned with a group, entered India and went to Mumbai.

In Mumbai my husband treated me worse than he had done before. One day he thrashed me mercilessly. It was then that I decided to leave him. I thought of returning to Bangladesh, together with another Bangladeshi man called Prince

who lived near my house in Mumbai. He helped paint people's homes and I
called him 'brother'. He promised to accompany me to Bangladesh, as I did not
dare travel alone. He went to Howrah first and I followed a few days later. He
picked me up from the station and took me to a place near Bashirhat. There
the dalal gave him a sack of ₹5,000 of ₹500 notes. It was while we were in
the bus stand that we were caught by the police. The ₹500 notes all turned
out to be fakes. When interrogated by the police I was very scared and said that
this man was my husband. This happened 17 months ago. We were produced
in Barasat court. Then I was brought here to Presidency Jail and my so-called
'brother' was taken to Dumdum. My didi from Mumbai came to visit me once.
She has a ration card, her children were all born in India, and they have papers.
I have filed a petition to employ a public prosecutor for me. I am now waiting
for my case to continue and for justice to be done. I am innocent and I simply
got caught because of a dalal's cunning and avarice. I do not remember the
name of the dalal.

Moyna Sardar
Bangladeshi
Charged and convicted under the **Foreigner's Registration Act**
Presidency Correctional Home for Women

I have been here for two years. I was convicted, and ordered to serve a two-
and-a-half year sentence. So far, I have served 19 months and 11 months are
left. But I don't think that when we are set free we can go home immediately.
I have seen many women freed but they cannot go home. I do not know why.
I hope I do not have to wait long to get home. This is the first time that I came
to India, and here I am, in a correctional facility. I was 17 years old when I
came here. I am originally from Rangpur, but my mother moved to Dhaka to
work, and I stayed with her and grew up in Dhaka. I was married at 14 years,
but have no children. I came here three years after my marriage. My husband
works in Bangladesh, in Dhaka. He has a shop, where all kinds of broken goods
are sold. We had a love marriage. I used to work too. I can stitch and do some
embroidery. I can make kurtas. My mother used to work as a domestic help
with a family. My husband and I had a fight once. Actually, his mother used to
cause a lot of problems for us. I had a friend also from Rangpur who had also
moved to Dhaka with her mother. We grew up together. She got married to a
man and worked as a domestic help in Dhaka. Her husband also worked as a
domestic helper. He was from Jessore. Once I had a bad fight with my husband,
his mother beat me up. So, I went off in a huff to my friends. She advised me to

live apart from my husband for some time, so that he would miss me and would come to get me. We wanted to teach him a lesson so he would behave better. My friend informed me that to help me survive during that period of separation she arranged for a job for me in Jessore. Also, she told me that I could stay with her husband's parents in Jessore.

I believed my friend, and so I left the next day with her husband, who she said would take me to Jessore. I had never been out of Dhaka so had no idea where Jessore was and how I could reach it. I followed her husband blindly. We would take a bus to Jessore, that's all my friend's husband told me. In reality we crossed a river in a boat and then took a van. It was already night by then. I did not know then that we were crossing into India. We crossed over sometime around 8 p.m. I understood later that he wanted to sell me off at Pune. We took a van to the station, and from there he took me to Howrah. It was there that he began talking over phone to someone and I overheard him telling the person on the other end of the phone that I was with him and that he was taking me to Pune. I understood that I had been duped. I walked away from him, looked around, then spotted a policeman and went up to him. I told him that I had been brought from Bangladesh by a man who pretended to be a friend and was going to be taken to Pune to be sold. The police called me to the police station, and took down the details. I was caught wearing this kurta and jeans that I am wearing now. Then the lady police took me over for some medical tests. The next day I was produced in Bankshall court. Therein began what seems like my endless sentence even before I was formally sentenced. My cases continued and sometimes I was produced in court once in 15 days and sometimes once a month. I have served much of my sentence, but am scared that once my term is over I will have to wait a long time to get back home. I want to go back to Bangladesh. The food here is horrible, we get three meals a day, but often they have insects in it. So how can we eat it? We are 21 women in my cell. Sometimes I am called to sweep the fields or the floors. I am waiting for my time to be over and to get back home. I don't want to come here ever again.

Radha Rani Das
Bangladeshi
Bashirhat

I came here about 4–5 years ago from Khulna, Daulatpur. I am Hindu. One of my daughters, my mother and my brother are still in Bangladesh. I am about 45 years old. I got married when I was about 12 years old. My husband died five years ago. He had a damaged liver. I have three daughters; one is 22, another is 18 years and the younger is 15 years old. The elder two are married, but the younger one is still with me. I have one son. The elder daughter is still in Bangladesh but the others are here. I went to school till Class IV and then got married. My father had sweet shop. My in-laws place was in Jessore. My husband used to be a dhobi. We had both Muslim and Hindu neighbours. But Muslims were the majority in numbers and that's why I had to come away. I could not continue to live there with my daughter. I had not seen disturbances in my childhood, as we lived amicably, but later a lot of persecution began. This began about 10 years ago. There has been a lot of harassment. I do not know why the problems began, but if leaders (neta) start messing up things then we can no longer survive there. I suppose there the people are ok, all living amicably, buts it's on the Hindus that the persecution is carried out more.

Say, they tortured my daughter. I know that if any girl looks nice they are abducted, there were two goons after my daughter. They are Muslims ... we are Hindus. If they harass a girl then all our pride and respect is gone. Isn't it? Unable to bear the torture we came away here. They harassed the men too, but they would harass the women more. And of course there would be attacks on homes, and land. We could not sell and bring anything. We had to leave everything behind. They said, leave and go, everything yours is in that country (India). They said that in that country you have everything. What luck .... Now I have to work to survive. In that country, no woman, no (house)wife ever went to work outside. In this country I am working. I run my household myself. I am working in another's house and surviving. I don't have any respect. I am surviving. But in Bangladesh I could not do it, I never went outside the house (to work). After marriage also (we) never stepped out. If ever there was any problem of survival in the village, the menfolk would go outside. We women would not. We housewives never went out. Maybe, if my husband had been alive, I might not have come here. My husband never wanted to come here. So, it is because there was no male member in my family that I came away. My son was still small, now he is growing up but he does nothing. And I had adolescent daughters; I was scared that they would take my daughter away, that's why I came here. What ill luck, in this age. Otherwise does one leave one's country? It was so painful. But what to do, soon after the death of my children's father, the brothers-in-law started telling us to go away with the adolescent girls.

It was good when Hasina was there. But it was politics of course. BNP–Awami League, like that. Yes you have heard of Hasina, Kalida Zia. Hasina is for the Hindus. She used to help us a lot but when she stepped down and that other one came to power it was all over. So now they want us to leave the country. We are poor people; we had to face much trouble. But the ones causing all the problems are rich ruffians; they survive by hitting others on the head. They are educated, they know everything. Now again I hear Hasina has come back, but we are here. We had to leave everything behind. I had some land, they took it away. They did not do it because we were women, but because we were Hindus. So when my brother-in-law decided that we should come here, we agreed to his proposal. They (brothers-in-law) helped me to come here. Brokers were known to us, so they brought us. The girls have all grown up, so they took care of us while bringing us (here). We were four of us when we came here—two daughters, me and my son. We had to pay ₹400 each and we spent a total of ₹1,600. We did not have to face any problem as such but we had to spend a night at the border, and crossed over in the morning, at dawn. We do not know if the police or security guards created any problems. They may have, but that was not our responsibility. It was the broker's responsibility; of course, there would be problems on the way.

The journey was painful, extremely painful. We were on the road for a long time and it was terrible leaving behind my mother, brother and other relatives. One day we did not eat for a whole day. We fasted an entire day, of course it was difficult. After crossing the border, we were put up at someone's place for the night. It was the broker who had arranged to put us up. Next day we came here to Bashirhat. It was the first time that we had come to this country. Before coming, I did not think a lot about India, but people there (in Bangladesh) used to say that it was good in India. I could live in peace with my children. People used to recommend that I go to India, so that I could live in relative safety and security with my children. That is why we came away. After coming here I found it was true.

Well, in any case if people here are good then it's good and if they are bad then it's all right. Now it's all the same, as I won't get the same people I had left behind back home any more. Am I not right? It took time for us to get a house to rent. We have not yet built a house, yet. I have to work, so I work in people's houses. It took me six months to find this work. They pay ₹300 each. I get ₹900 from three houses. From that I pay ₹300 as rent and with the rest (₹600) I manage to run my family somehow. There are problems at work. After doing everything for an entire family I get only ₹300. I survive with difficulty. My brothers-in-law helped me run the family.

No, I have not received any ration card and neither have my daughters. No,
I have not submitted money. They said it will take time. So, why to submit
money? If I don't get a ration card, there's no point in submitting money. But
I feel safe and secure here, better here than back home. Here no one harasses
us. We are free here. No one tries to take advantage of us. I can depend on my
neighbours if I need any help. But no political leader has done anything for us.
We are just struggling. Back home (Bangladesh) there would have been relatives,
but now we are all here, working and feeding ourselves, struggling. Some of the
people that I work for are nice. They give me money when I fall sick and tell
me to go to the doctor. I do not have fixed holidays, but can take leave when
I require any.

However, I always miss Bangladesh. Some times I cry for it. But I cannot
return to it. How will I go back home? My children are my family and I don't
have a husband. I don't have a family; I am like a bird flying around here and
there. But this is not home (desh). Back home, I could celebrate religious festivals
and rituals. But here, I have to work all the time. It becomes difficult as I always
wonder should I work in another's house to survive, or should I keep up the prac-
tices, fasts and all? But during festivals like Durga Puja there is no trouble here,
as opposed to all the troubles one had to face in Bangladesh. So, I think I did the
right thing to come here. But my mother is there. I cannot bring her here, as she
is too old and moreover the roads are terrible. So if she died, I'm just thinking
aloud, then I would have to go there one last time.

8

Voices of Women in a Border Town Called Moreh

Chitra Ahanthem

INTRODUCTION

The available studies on borderlands reveal interesting linkages between transnational capitalism and relationship between modern nation states. While the 'economic' borders continue to shrink under well-administered and well-engineered economic policies and new trade routes are carved out, still the global world feels the need to securitize and control the resources to ensure territorial sovereignty as far as geopolitical 'borders' are concerned. The state management of 'borders' as William Van Schendel[1] argues reflects 'state's pursuit of territoriality—its strategy to exert complete authority and control over social life in its territory—produces borders and makes them into crucial markers of the success and limitations of that strategy'. In this context, it is important to understand 'borders' not from the perspective of state management of the geopolitical space where 'borders' are joining what is different but also dividing what is similar. Thus, in the study on borders it is not only important to trace how states manage borders and the relationship between border and state but also realizing as Van Schendel would argue reconfiguring the spatial politics of border through social relations.

In this section, which is on the narratives of women living in the border town of Moreh, on the Indo-Myanmar border, I would like to examine the contradiction, paradox, difference and conflict of power and domination in contemporary global capitalism and the nation state, especially as manifested in local level practices. The everyday life stories of these women reflect not only their identity as women but how these realities are shaped by their location near a porous international border town Moreh. Here the border not only divides the lives of women but also plays a crucial role in joining them in their labouring lives as women continue to cross borders and take on multiple roles as traders/sex workers, service givers and clients. The lives of women in Moreh indicate the multiple realities faced by women living at a border area with a history of protracted conflict.

The Indo-Myanmar border town of Moreh is located in Chandel district (formerly known as Tengnoupal district) and lies in the south eastern part of Manipur. It is the border district of the state with Myanmar (erstwhile Burma) on the south, Ukhrul district on the east, Churachandpur district on the south and west and Thoubal district on north. It is about 64 km away from Imphal (see Map 8.1). The National Highway No 39 passes through this district. The Moreh town, the international trade centre of the state, lies on the southernmost part of the district. When the Trans-Asian Super Highway comes into existence, Chandel district will be one of the gateways to the Asian countries. It is a hill district with an area of 3,313 sq. km. As per Census 2001, the population of the district is 134,462 (males 67,965 and females 66,497) and, the literacy rate is 42.73 per cent (male 48.77 per cent and females 36.56 per cent). The density of population per sq. km. is 41.

The district is inhabited by several communities. It is sparsely inhabited by about 20 different tribes. They are scattered all over the district. Prominent tribes in the district are Anal, Lamkang, Kuki, Moyon, Monsang, Chothe, Thadou, Paite, Maring, Zou, etc. There are also other communities like Meiteis and Muslims in small numbers as compared to the tribes. Non-Manipuris like the Tamils, Bengalis, Punjabis and Biharis are also settled in this town.[2] This first segment of the population is traced to the British era when timber traders and loggers were brought in by the British, who settled down over the years and either married into the existing communities along the border or have family extensions coming over. India and Myanmar share a total of 160 km border, which is not fenced properly.

Map 8.1 District Map of Chandel, Manipur

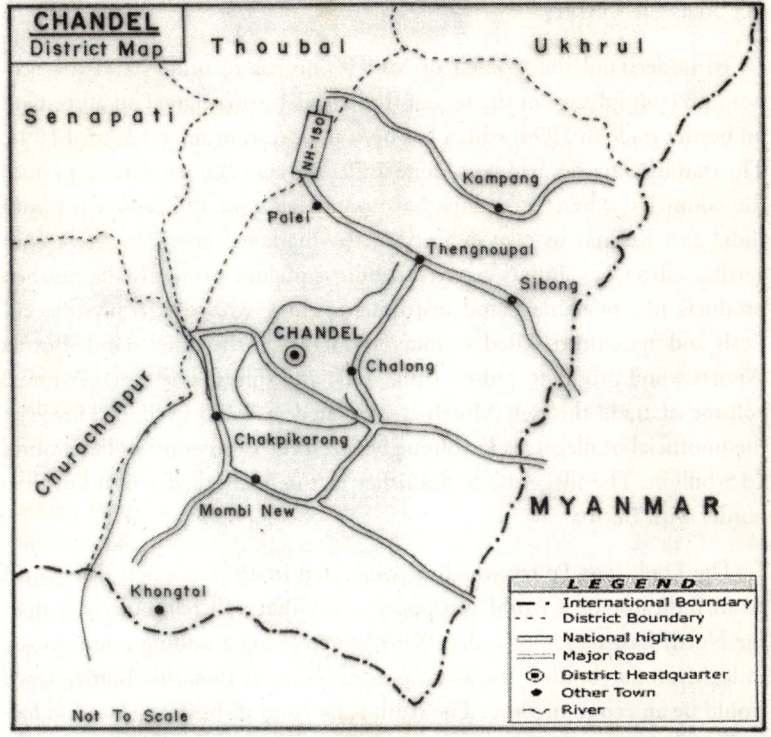

Source: Map drawn by Falguni Biswas.

India shares a porous boundary with a country that is recognized for its military regime and its physical proximity to the famed Golden Triangle comprising an area of around 350,000 sq. km., which overlaps the mountain regions of Myanmar, Laos, Thailand, Vietnam and Yunnan Province of China. Moreh also has a link to the conflict between the Kuki and the Naga tribes that had huge social and political impacts besides leading to hundreds of people belonging to both communities being killed in the early 1990s. The demographic profile of the small border town changed following the Kuki–Naga clashes which had its origin from this place.[3]

The study is based on personal interviews to understand and capture the background and circumstances of women in Moreh, including women who stay in the town during daytime, crossing over from the Myanmar border as traders/sex workers.

To understand the women of Moreh one has to understand the economical compulsions of the region. India and Burma signed an agreement on border trade in 1994, which has been in operation since 12 April 1995. The trading activities had been done under the laws and regulations of both the countries, where provisions have been made for the buyers (of both India and Burma) to take delivery of the marketed goods in freely convertible currencies. India's exports to Burma include primarily the finished products like machinery and instruments along with drugs, pharmaceuticals and agriculture-based various products. On the other hand, Burma exports wood products, pulses, fruits, nuts and spices. The average annual volume of trade through Moreh is estimated at ₹250 million. However, the unofficial or illegal trade volume between the two countries lies around ₹15 billion. The illegal trade flourishes in the unchecked 1,640 km long border with Burma.

The Look East Policy which was initiated in 1991 is often flagged off as an indicator of a world of opportunities that will particularly benefit the North East region of India. With Moreh being a trading point on the Indo-Myanmar border, the natural assumption is that this border town would be an economic hub. The truth is far from it. Both legal and 'informal' trade is carried on between Manipur and Myanmar, especially in the border town of Moreh on the Indian side and Tamu on the Myanmar side. Moreh is famous for all kinds of illegal arms and drug consignment deals meant to enter the India's North east region, destined for various part of the country. Since the Indo-Myanmar border area is unfenced, porous with thick forests and unmanned, drugs coming from the old Golden Triangle of South east Asia have their easy entrance. Contraband drugs are brought in by Burmese smugglers and transshipped to the inner parts of Manipur by various militant groups after deducting their share of percentage. However, they allow the purchaser to resell outside the state only. Proliferation of small arms in the area is an open secret and there is no lack of contacts at the Moreh market for illegal deals, though problem lies with further transshipment. The positioning of Assam Rifle (AR) troops along the Indo-Myanmar border does not make much difference and illegal trans-movement of men and goods even takes place at a few metres from the observatory RP-post of the AR camp positioned at a distance of 1 km east of Indo-Myanmar border gate number two. Four major ethnic groups, namely, Kuki, Naga, Meitei and Tamils controlled the trade along the Indo-Myanmar border, though a large number of Muslims and other communities were also engaged in this border trade. There is now a growing competition among these different communities living in the border areas for acquiring control over trade.[4]

VOICES OF WOMEN

Meira Peibis

Universally, and in the course of history, the impact of armed conflict on women is telling and needs no further mention here. But in places like Manipur and within the state, given the complexities and the interweaving of various strands like ethnic tensions, social norms and practices, women continue to be affected by the course and interplay of armed and ethnic conflict. Contrary to the portrayal of women in this part of the country as 'empowered', women instead continue to be dogged by ties of ethnicity and issues of loyalty.

My first meeting is with a 62-year-old Meira Peibis in Ward no. 5. She recounts her story to me sitting in the courtyard of another Meira Peibis since her own house has a security person garrisoned at her gate.

Sanahanbi Devi (62 years old, name changed), a Meitei, says:

I have lived here for more than 50 years. Moreh is very near to the International border with Myanmar where there are various armed groups having their training camps etc but once the ethnic grouping came about, even Meitei armed groups entered the picture to make their presence felt. I cannot understand who is getting any good out of this but in the long run, it is the women of this town that has paid the price of this situation.

About 8 years back, some Meitei Under Ground (UG) cadres came to her house seeking shelter and food.

They stayed for over 3 days: I was mindful of what would happen in case security forces came to know about that but what could one do? All I hoped was that they would go away soon. What I did not know was that my daughter would get into their notice: she ended up leaving home to live with one of the men. She never had a proper marriage: she still goes back and forth across the border to meet him or he comes escaping notice from security forces to be with her. They have two children now but how can I be happy about the situation? I have a younger daughter left with me and now I tell them that they can ask me to help them in any sphere: I will because they have the gun power but never ever to stay at my home.[5]

Sanahanbi is like many other women who are deeply scarred by existing situations in manifold ways. In 1997, her younger brother who went fishing in the outskirts of Moreh disappeared; we never saw him again and till date have no idea what happened to him. The irony is that she holds a position in a women's group of the Meiteis and takes the lead when there are crisis points with security forces, while remaining unable to influence any of the actors in conflict in any substantial way.

On 3 June 2007 Yumnam Shanti's 22-year-old son Roshan, an auto-rickshaw driver was shot dead by suspected Kuki armed cadres at the Community Variety Market Auto stand. This incident would spark off a series of violence among the Meiteis and the Kukis. Within a week, a total of 11 people got killed out of which 6 were Meiteis and 5 Kukis.[6]

Three years on, it is the families of the young men who got killed that are struggling to live with one another in the same locality with their resigned grief. 42-year-old Yumnam Shanti's voice breaks down as she says:

> My son's life did not matter to those who wielded arms in their hand. Instead his death led to other retaliatory deaths and on both sides, it was us women who had to bear the loss of our children in the prime of their lives.
> She adds that unable to bear the loss of their son, her husband passed away within a year. A similar feeling of loss is echoed by Tongkholun's mother who does not want to give her name. Tongkholun was just 16 years when he was killed by alleged Meitei insurgents, right after Roshan was killed. Both were civilians and yet, got killed in the dynamics of power and control between two armed groups belonging to two different ethnic groups.[7]

Meitei Pangals

Displacement fuelled by poverty is often at the root of the majority of the population flows into Moreh. The irony of course is the fact that Chandel district under which Moreh lies has the highest poverty ratio in the state of Manipur, which is at 64.07 per cent.[8] As in all other hill districts of Manipur (except Senapati) there is higher proportion of the population living in abject poverty here in comparison to the valley districts.[9] The Muslim community (also known as Meitei Pangals) living in Moreh now are mostly migrants from the adjoining district of Thoubal and live as a minority group in the ethnic cauldron.

Trying to normalize my meeting with the women of the community is difficult: various questions are asked on why a Meitei woman would want to talk with them and then, write. As I sit down with Noor-Jehan and Mehr-an on the mud caked verandah, there is a curious crowd of onlookers, especially men who hover around, while the women look to them before they answer any of my questions. This makes me realize how much of an intruder I am to their world, but the borders of doubt break off when I say I have been talking to other women in the area. They open up to me as I tell them that I had met women representatives of the Meitei community. Both women weave in their narratives together for me.

Noor-jehan, Secretary and Mehr-an, President of the Minority Women Development Society claimed that:

Our organization was established in the year 2004 for we felt that as a minority group/community in this place, our issues were getting lost. Also, the sense of ownership is never there unless you have your own group. So we got together. Having your own group means that there is a rallying point for responding to the issues that we face. Belonging to a small minority group is not easy: we end up as the last persons to be taken into account. We felt that coming together as a group would be the only way to stand up for our selves. Now, anytime there is a social issue or a matter of unrest, we are called upon to take part in deliberations and give our viewpoint. Earlier, we were never represented.[10]

The designations of Noor-jehan and Mehr-an can be misleading for the group they are heading does not have even an office. Noor-jehan and Mehr share living quarters in one house along with another family. The space is so cramped that they cook in the verandah of the house where 28 people live together:

Both of us are second generation migrants whose parents came to the town of Moreh for better avenues of earning a living. Both of us like many others have been born in the town to parents who came to the town after hearing about small time trade activities happening at the border. Our families hail from Wangjing, (Thoubal district) a predominantly Muslim area where most people do not own agricultural land. The poverty and the lack of any avenues for earning for livelihoods forced our parents to set out for Moreh, which at that point of time was sparsely populated, added Mehr-an.[11]

Labouring Lives

It was evident that Moreh was a mere trading point which in turn meant that only those with money or power or both prospered there. The expanse of shops at Namphalong just across the boundary gate from the Indian side is where traders and businessmen come from other parts of Manipur to buy an array of goods in bulk. Depending on economic power, one can go into the business of gems, gold and even drugs and guns. At Moreh itself, the Tamil population had settled in the town after they came in as lumbers during the erstwhile East India Company continuing to exert a hold over the trade in the town but the majority of people make their living as daily wage earners, working as porters and carriers. The abject poverty and the lack of avenues for people to earn a living, compounded by the lack of quality infrastructures like schools, hospitals, etc., only add to the cycle of vulnerability which has manifested in cases of trafficking of children by agents and even religious leaders who tell unsuspecting parents that their children are being taken away to be given free education:

> 35 year old Shakila is a daily wage earner. On a good day, she earns about ₹70 after a full day of carrying goods for traders across the border gates. I meet her sitting in her courtyard and she tells me that if it wasn't for the highway bandh, she would have been carrying loads for the day.
>
> I don't know the number of times I go back and forth over the border gate. For me, every time I cross the gate, it means more money to take home and run the family.
>
> Shakila's husband was also a daily porter. 16 years ago he was arrested by the Myanmarese Army on the charges that the load he was carrying contained heroin.
>
> His job was to ferry goods back and forth across the border gate and not to query. We heard that he had been picked up but no action was taken on the man whose good he had been carrying. He was imprisoned for a whole 16 years and there was nothing that we could do. We had no idea if he was

dead or alive but three years back he completed his prison term and came home. I had to fend for myself and my daughter on my own. When my husband came back, he said he had been tortured and after 9 months, he just collapsed one day while ferrying goods at the border gate.

Shakila had in the meanwhile got pregnant with her second child, a son who is now 3 yrs old. She barely makes ends meet but takes on any amount of labour to be able to send her elder daughter to school, collecting fodder for people (in which one month of work amounts to Rs. 1500) or doing quarry work by breaking boulders into smaller pieces. The latter is a back breaking exercise that often leaves her exhausted and with minimum wages that is hardly enough to run her family.

I get Rs. 7 per bin but the maximum number of bins I can manage in a day is about 4 or 5.[12]

A bit further in the tribal inhabited section of the town, 26-year-old Yaosenlien Zou runs a local alcohol vending joint in a small unventilated boxed-in room that she has been renting. Last year, Yaosenlein handed her two children and son to a local pastor who told her that her children would be given free education in Chennai:

Since he was a man of religion, I believed him. In any case, I did not have the means to support the costs of my children's education. A few months I came to know through the newspaper that my children along with 20 other children from here were being kept in deplorable situations in a Children's home in Chennai. They called it trafficking but I had no idea that sending my children for their education with someone needed rules and regulations. I am just happy that they are back.

Her daughter Nengjengdin (12 yrs) recounts how she and the other children were made to clean floors, wash utensils and sent to just a few hours of class. 'We got even less than the food that we had at home', she says happily showing off the report card of her latest examinations where she was ranked first. After she and her brother were rescued along with the rest of the 20 trafficked children by the Child Welfare Committee (Chandel), she has been staying in a shelter run by an NGO under central funding from the Ministry of Women and Child Welfare. The costs of education are being borne by the NGO.[13]

Ibemhal (name changed) is an office bearer of a Meira Paibi group in Moreh. And though Meira Paibis in Manipur are generally known for their stand against alcoholism, she brews rice beer to make a living. In every locality, there is a Meira Paibi (torch bearer) association that takes up the responsibility of shutting down alcohol vending units, punishing vendors and those

who indulge in intoxicants. An uprising led by Meira Paibis began around
the mid-1970s against the sale and consumption of liquor and intoxicants.
In the year 1991–92, their efforts finally paid off. A prohibition order on
sale and consumption of liquor was passed and Manipur was declared a dry
state and is still in vogue.[14] Yet, in Moreh women holding posts within the
Meira Paibi associations brew rice beer at their own homes:

> What other options are there? Sometimes, we work as porters but that
> does not bring in the money. The choices are either to open a small
> paan shop, depend on the men who come to Moreh for trade or to carry
> arms or drugs across the border. In any given situation, we are the ones
> who are left to fend for our selves. We also get labels from the rest of the
> society—says Ibemhal.[15]

WOMEN AND HIV/AIDS

The day I am in Moreh, a daily newspaper has a headline story that
declared 'Moreh: a sex worker's paradise'. This is a popular concept held
by most people—that women in the town are 'immoral' and are there to
make 'easy money'. Ironically though, women in Moreh who work as sex
workers explain their circumstance as one out of a lack of choice but are
disapproving of women who come in from other districts or who cross over
from the border to take up sex as work. The marking of Moreh as a high
HIV prevalence area on the other hand has meant access to HIV/AIDS,
STI and drug use treatment options for people from across the border
who live under a military regime that is highly critical of a HIV positive
status. But for the residents of Moreh, there are genuine needs for regular doctor attendance and setting up infrastructural support systems like
testing centres, etc.

The National AIDS Control Organisation (NACO) reveals that 0.75 per
cent of pregnant women in the state are infected by HIV (according to 2007
estimates), more than twice the national average of 0.36 per cent:

> For people like K T Shangrein, secretary of the Chandel Network
> of Positive People, the irregular attendance of doctors at the district
> hospital means that when she goes to get her monthly stock of anti-
> retroviral (ART) medicines, she cannot always get a health check-up at
> the same time.

'I always end up coming to Imphal to go to the main hospitals or have my check-up done by the doctors who give time to the Manipur Network of Positive People', she says. 'The doctors posted at the district hospital are from other districts and do not turn up regularly'. This is true for most departments but for people living with HIV/AIDS who have opportunistic infections that need to be treated immediately, it means that we have to take out time and spend money to go to Imphal.[16]

Sanatombi (about 45 years, name changed) is one of the many women who 'depend on the men' who come to the town to trade: drivers, security personnel, traders etc. Every day or every night, she runs a small paan shop at the Moreh main market where I sit as she points to me the security personnel who 'go to the immoral women who come to Moreh'.

I have a husband who drinks all day and four children to bring up. Do I have any other choice? Those who can manage by carrying loads do that but I cannot make do on the Rs. 70 odd that you get from that work. I run this paan shop every night and when things work out, I settle the time and charge with the men who come who come here: they are mostly people from outside Moreh and are decent people. It is so easy to level us as immoral women at one go but do we want this life? Would we be doing this if we could have another means of earning a livelihood? I do not do sex work daily and with a series of men unlike the women who come from other districts and the women from Tamu in Myanmar.[17]

BORDERING LIVES

Apart from the interplay of conflict, power play and ethnic tensions that tell on the lives and circumstances of women living in Moreh, there are also intimate nuances on what the 'border' has come to denote. In my own experience while writing this chapter, I had great difficulty demarcating the borders of each section since all strands wove in as one whole. My dilemma was in separating one narrative from the other, not in terms of lived experiences but in how one aspect led to the other: gender, social status, marital status, impact of conflict and ethnicity. What was clear though was that the crisis of living in perpetual poverty, conflict, poor infrastructure and development, compounded with a ready association for drug use and its associated HIV/AIDS companion has only served to marginalize and isolate the women of Moreh in terms of social standing, access to basic services and from the 'mainstream society'. Many women drug users would not allow their narratives to be included in the study despite recounting their experiences on the grounds that they would be more stigmatized and singled out in terms of being the 'other', responsible for the 'bad name' given to the town. Women, who worked at poppy plantation along the porous boundary refused to share their narratives and took affront that they 'would be involved in such activities'.

Asked what the border means to her, Shakila who lost her husband twice: once when he was imprisoned for 16 years in a jail in Myanmar and then his death after a homecoming of 9 months says:

> It (the gate) has come to mean many different things: my source of livelihood, a force that took away my husband and a barrier that comes in the way of a better manner of life. You know, I have a childhood friend who moved away from Moreh to Churachandpur district after her marriage. She does not have to worry about where her next meal is coming from: when we do meet about once a year on her trips to her family here, I see the difference between us in the way we dress, in the way we look and the way we cope with life. Compared to her, I am like a small bird that flutters half heartedly in the vast sky looking for crumbs on the ground, unsure whether I can get that crumb.
>
> Physical boundaries of state and nation borders do not make sense for Sanathoi who crossed the border from Myanmar 16 years ago to marry a Meitei man. Sanathoi has another legal Burmese name and still possesses a Burmese ID card.
>
> But I have my name entered in the electoral rolls here and so I am a legal Indian as well. I have voted since the last three general elections—she says.
>
> Yet, Sanathoi considers herself first as a Meitei since her ancestors crossed over to Myanmar during the late 16th century following the then King of Manipur's edict that his subjects convert to Hinduism from the earlier Meitei formless way of worship. Those who refused to convert were persecuted and killed and many fled to neighbouring kingdoms. Sanathoi's forefathers ran to Yangon inside Myanmar where over the years they assimilated themselves to a different nationhood but kept their earlier/original cultural identity intact. The name she is known by now 'Sanathoi' that is entered as her official Indian name is of Meitei origin, meaning the most precious one and is a common Meitei pet name for the youngest daughter of a family.[18]

Sanathoi's story only mirrors that of many other women to whom the idea of citizenship is a blurred line. Her living testimonial of her cultural affinity and her own name in itself is in direct contrast to the political, social and economic subtext of borders. From across the Myanmar border, crossing over to the Indian side ironically means an opportunity to better health care and improved finances. For the people living with HIV/AIDS in Myanmar, the dictatorial regime in the country coupled with a high level of stigma and discrimination means a clamour for the HIV-related services that are available on the Indian side of the border. To them, crossing the border means hope and better health.

At the Angel's Care Center run by an NGO called the Meitei Leimarol Sinnai Shang (MLSS), 33-year-old Ching Toi Kim from Myanmar and her infant son have been staying for a week now:

> My husband was an alcoholic but what I did not know was that he was a drug user as well. He died about two years back after he was diagnosed with HIV/AIDS. They tested us for HIV/AIDS free of cost but did not have any other avenues of help for us. I came to know about this Center from my friends and came here.[19]

Besides Ching, there are other Myanmarese nationals staying at the Care Center who get to receive free anti-retroviral therapy (ART), most of which are women.

As far as the position of women in the context of conflict (political, ethnic, identity positioning), N. Vijaylakshmi Brara[20] questions whether questions of identities and nationhood in light of Meitei–Naga identity politics and conflict would be met with emotional zest had the youths of both the communities had employment opportunities, other avenues and a developed infrastructure. Would there be assertions of such non-compromising stands if there were no excesses by the security forces. In her own words:

> Women in Manipur have understood such problems. Among the Meities we have the 'Meira Paibis' (the torch bearing women). They hold Mashaals and roam in the locality to keep a watch on drunkenness and drug-abuse. They make a human wall in cases where innocent local youths are forcibly being taken away by the Armed Forces in the name of insurgents. They are the only one who can dare to warn and scold the people in under-ground movement for their accesses. Everybody is cautious of them. They dare to get lathicharged, to sit for hunger strikes and even go

to jail for a right cause. So are the women's groups in the hills. The Naga Mother's Association and the Kuki women's association are the guardians of their respective tribe. They played a pivotal role during Naga–Kuki clashes, where barbarism got unleashed in its naked proportions in the name of ethnic cleansing. It was at that moment that NMA and Kuki women went long stretches in the hills (sometimes walking 3–4 days continuously) to meet their respective underground outfits to tell them to stop killing each other. The voices of these mothers are heard. If they shed their ethnic loyalties and come together only as Mothers, not a Naga mother or a Kuki mother or a Meitei mother peace and development will not be far. Unless there is peace, Human Rights and Civil Liberties are neither safe nor possible. We should call the mothers. They should be targeted and focussed by the social planners and activists who are interested in this region.[21]

One common thread that ran through all the women who gave their narratives and experiences was the leitmotif of having to eke out one more day of survival, one more day of fending for their children, home and lastly for their own self. For the women whose lives are interlinked with Moreh, the border is a mere geographical footnote that enhances their vulnerabilities further but also gives opportunities, though it is little and too far in between. These would be universal of people living in border areas and women especially. But for the women of Moreh, the nature of conflict in terms of power equations and the armed conflict add various other nuances that blur for them the political context of borders and boundaries.

NOTES

1. Van Schendel (2005).
2. http://www.chandel.nic.in (accessed on 15 February 2010).
3. The killing of 21-year-old Onkholet Haokip on 3 June 1992 at Bongjang village under Moreh Police Station by suspected armed Nagas in the backdrop of Naga insurgents collecting 'house taxes' from four Kuki inhabited hill districts of Manipur which included Chandel. This killing provoked Kuki youths who, supported by their leaders, got together in various groups demanding a Kukiland homeland that would carve out Naga settled areas. This sowed the seeds of conflict that escalated into the violent Kuki–Naga clashes in 1993–94 leaving many brutally killed, maimed and rendered homeless. See Phanjoubam (1996: 215–16).
4. Shivananda (2010).
5. Sanahanbi Devi was interviewed on December 2009.
6. http://www.indianexpress.com/news/clashes-leave-11-dead-in-manipur-border-town/33270/0 (accessed on 15 February 2010).

7. Yumnam Shanti was interviewed on 15 December 2009.
8. Singh (2007).
9. Ibid.
10. Noor-jehan, Secretary and Mehr-an President of the Minority Women Development Society were interviewed on 12 January 2010.
11. Ibid.
12. Shakila was interviewed on 15 December 2009.
13. Yaosenlien Zou was interviewed on 16 December 2009.
14. Lanky (2010).
15. Ibemhal was interviewed on 27 December 2009.
16. Ahanthem (2010).
17. K.T. Shangrein, secretary of the Chandel Network of Positive action was interviewed on 10 January 2010.
18. Shakila was interviewed on 15 December 2009.
19. Ching Toi Kim was interviewed on 15 January 2010.
20. Brara (2002).
21. Ibid.

Consolidated Bibliography

PRIMARY DOCUMENTS

Banerjee, Amiya Kumar. 1972. *Hooghly District Gazetteer*. Calcutta: Government of West Bengal.

Choudhury, R.D. 2009. 'Floodlights to Aid BSF Night Patrol', *The Assam Tribune*, 3 December.

Census Organisation. 1951. *Census of Pakistan, 1951*, Vol. III: East Bengal, Report and Tables. Karachi: Government of Pakistan.

Government of India. 1951. *District Census*. Malda. Table 1.24, p. 79.

———. 1965. *West Bengal District Gazetteers*. Nadia, Gazetteers of India, Government Documents, National Library.

———. 2001. *Census of India*. New Delhi. Available online at http://www.censusindia. gov.in (accessed in January 2010).

———. 2006–07. *Annual Report 2006–07*. 'National Domestic Worker's Movements— North Eastern Region', New Delhi.

———. 2008. *Annual Report 2007–08*. Ministry of Home Affairs, New Delhi.

Government of West Bengal. 1932. *List of Active Decoit Gangs in Bengal 1930*, pp. 186–204. Bengal Police, Calcutta. Procured from Hogolberia Police Station, Shikarpur, Nadia.

———. 1951. *Census Handbook*. Malda: Government of West Bengal.

———. 1971. *District Census Handbook, Nadia*. Directorate of Census Operations: Government of West Bengal.

———. 2007a. *District Statistical Handbook*. Malda: Government of West Bengal.

———. 2007b. *District Statistical Handbook*. Murshidabad: Government of West Bengal.

———. 2009. *District Statistical Handbook, Hooghly: 2007*. Kolkata: Bureau of Applied Economics and Statistics.

———. 2004. *West Bengal Human Development Report*. Development and Planning Department, Government of West Bengal.

Government of Mizoram. 2003. 'Guidelines for Regulating Entry of Myanmarese Tribals into Mizoram', Notification No. D.32030/146/2003-HMP(BMC), dated 5 November 2003, *Mizoram Gazette*, 32 (347): 1–14.

Human Rights Documentation Unit, National Coalition Government of the Union of Burma. 2008. *Burma Human Rights Year Book*, pp. 946–71. Available online at http://www.burmalibrary.org/docs08/HRDU_YB-2008/pdf/refugees.pdf (last accessed in January 2010).

Human Rights Law Network. 2006. *Trafficking and the Law*. New Delhi: HRLN.

IB File No. 1238 A/47 (Nadia), 'Extract from the weekly report of the Superintendent of Police, Nadia, for the week ending 1.12.50', WB State Archives, 43 Shakespeare Sarani (hereafter WBSAIB).

IB File No. 1238 A/47 (Nadia), Memo No. 7491 (5) / 23:50 (Tehatta), 'To the WB Police, DIG Central Range', DIGIB, DM 24 Parganas, WBSAIB.

———. 1238 A/47, Memo no. 1908, 2/1238 A-47 / For date 7.5.1951, pp. 809–41, 'Fortnightly report on Border incidents in West Bengal during 2nd Half of April 1951', WBSAIB.

———. 1238 A/47, Untitled Memo No. 25522 / 1238 A-47 / For date 20.6.1951, p. 867, WBSAIB.

———. 1355-28, Serial No. NSP XLVI, 'Sushil Kr. Chatterjee s/o Upendranath of Basantapur PO Haringhata and Gaori, Krishnanagar, Nadia', No. 55, WBSAIB.

District Minority Board Proceedings, File No. XIX, Serial No. 19, 'From Manager of Hooghly Imambarah to Chaiman of the District Magistrate Board, 1949–50' (unpublished primary source collected from the Imambarah strong room).

Mitra, A. 1953. 'Census 1951', *District Handbook Nadia*, p. XXXVII. Calcutta: Bureau of Applied Economics and Statistics, Government of West Bengal.

Planning Commission. 2003. 'Demography', *Jammu and Kashmir Development Report*, p. 26, State Plan Division, Government of India. Available online at http://planningcommission.nic.in/plans/stateplan/sdr_jandk/sdr_jkch2.pdf (accessed on 15 January 2010).

O'Malley, L.S.N. 1912. *Bengal District Gazetteer: Hooghly*. Calcutta: Bengal Secretariat Book Depot.

The Gazette of India. 1905. 'Government of India Notifications', Saturday, 22 July. Simla: Government of India.

'Young Mizo Association: A Profile' (pamphlet) (undated) Mizoram: Central YMA.

BOOKS/ARTICLES

Addha, Akhay Kumar. 2007. *Hooghly Chuchurar Nana Kotha* (in Bengali) (Many Stories of Hooghly and Chinsura). Hooghly: Hooghly Sangbad.

Afsana, Rashid. 2008 'Violence touches each family in Kashmir', *The WIP*. Available online at http://thewip.net/contributors/2008/08/violence_touches_each_family_l.html (last accessed on 5 January 2010).

Agamben, Giorgio. n.d. 'We Refugees', European Graduate School website. Available online at http://www.egs.edu/faculty/giorgio-agamben/articles/we-refugees (last accessed on 1 June 2010).

Agarwal, Ravina. 2004. *Performance and Politics on the Disputed Borders of Ladakh, India*. North Carolina: Duke University Press.

Ahanthem, Chitra. 2010. Available online at: http://www.hivaidsonline.in/index.php/
Vulnerable-Groups/insurgency-makes-health-care-dangerous.html (last accessed on
15 February 2010).

Akbar, M.J. 2003. Kashmir *Behind the Vale*. New Delhi: Viking.

Alvarez, Jr. Robert. 1995. 'The Mexican–US Border: The Making of an Anthropology of
Borderlands', *Annual Review of Anthropology*, 24: 447–70.

Ashima Kaul. 2007. Rigorous Road to Rehabilitation,' *Women's Features Service*. Available online at www.indiatogether.org/2007/oct/wom-roadrehab.htm (last accessed
on 5 January 2010).

Bagchi, Jasodhara, Subhoranjan Dasgupta and Subhasri Ghosh (ed.). 2009. *The Trauma
and the Triumph: Gender and Partition in Eastern India, Part 2*. Kolkata: Stree.

Balraj, Puri. 1983. *Simmering Volcano: Study of Jammu's Relations with Kashmir*.
New Delhi: Sterling.

Bandyopadhyay, Gobindalal. 2007. 'Syed Keramat Ali: The Great Architect of Hooghly
Imambarah', in Ranjit Kumar De (ed.), *Hooghly Imambarah*, pp. 13–20. Hooghly:
Bhraman Barta Paribar.

Banerjee, Kishna and Purna Banerjee. 2003. 'Lives Delimited by Barbed Wires', *Refugee
Watch*, 13 (18): 6–8.

Banerjee, Paula. 2003. 'News from the Indo-Bangladesh Border', *Refugee Watch*, 19
(August): 2.

———. 2009. 'Women, Trafficking and Statelessness in South Asia', in Roohi Sanam and
Ranabir Samaddar (eds), *Key Texts on Social Justice in India, Volume IV*, pp. 343–443.
New Delhi: SAGE Publications.

Banerjee, Paula, Sabyasachi Basu Ray Chaudhury, and Samir Kumar Das (eds). 2005.
Internal Displacement in South Asia. New Delhi: SAGE Publications.

Banerjee, Upala Devi. 1999. 'Sexual Exploitation and Trafficking of the Girl Child:
The Indian Scenario', *Migrant Labour and Trafficking of Women: Workshop Report*,
pp. 32–36. Nepal: National Network against Girl Trafficking.

Berg, Eiki, and Piret Ethin. 2008. 'What Kind of Border Regime Is in the Making?
Towards a Differentiated and Uneven Border Strategy', *Cooperation and Conflict*,
March, 41 (1): 53–71. Available online at http://www.csa.com/ids70/gateway.php?
mode=pdf&doi=10.1177%2F0010836706060935&db=polsci-set-c&s1=2a
8ce637cd352c8de3c93418fca12d33&s2=878f07eac4de2168b5e51583e473e21d
(last accessed on 3 December 2009).

Betts, Alexander. 2010. 'Towards a "Soft Law" Framework for the Protection of Vulnerable Migrants', Research Paper No. 162, *New Issues in Refugee Research, UNHCR*, May.
Availale online at http://unhcr.org/48b7f9642.html (last accessed on 6 June 2010).

Bhargava, R. and H. Reifeld (eds), 2005. *Civil Society, Public Sphere and Citizenship:
Dialogues and Perceptions*, p. 290. New Delhi: SAGE Publications.

Bhattacharjee, Ajit. 1994. *Kashmir the Wounded Valley*. New Delhi: UBSPD.

Bhaumik, Subir. 2003. 'The Returnees and the Refugees: Migration from Burma', in
Ranabir Samaddar (ed.), *Refugees and the State: Practices of Asylum and Care in India,
1947–2000*, pp. 182–210. New Delhi: Sage Publications.

Blank, Yishai. 2007. 'Spheres of Citizenship', *Theoretical Inquiries in Law*, 8 (2): 114–49.

Bose, Nirmal Kumar. 1968. *Calcutta: A Social Survey*. Bombay: Lakshmi Publishing House.

Bose, Sumantra. 1997. *The Challenge in Kashmir: Democracy, Self Determination and a
Just Peace*. New Delhi: SAGE Publications.

Bose, Sumantra. 2003. *Kashmir: Roots of Conflict, Paths to Peace*. Massachusetts: Harvard University Press.

Bosniak, Linda S. 2008. 'Ethical Territoriality and the Rights of Immigrants', *Amsterdam Law Forum*, 1 (1): 1. Available online at http://ojs.ubvu.vu.nl/alf/article/viewArticle/54/73 (last accessed January 2010).

Brara, N. Vijaylakshmi. 2002. 'Women's Role in Human Rights and Peace in the Northeast', *PUCL Bulletin*. Delhi: PUCL.

Busia, Abena P.A. 1995. 'Liberation', in Stella and Frank Chipasula (eds), *The Heinemann Book of African Women's Poetry*, p. 53. Oxford: Heinemann's Educational Publishers.

Butalia, Urvashi. 2008. *Speaking Peace: Women's Voices from Kashmir*. New Delhi: Kali for Women.

Bukhari, Shujaat. 2007.'Living in Hope,' *Hindu Sunday Magazine*. Available online at http://www.hinduonnet.com/mag/2007/02/18/stories/2007021800030500.htm (last accessed on 5 August 2010).

Chakrabatti, Monmohan (ed.). 1918. *A Summary of the Changes in the Jurisdiction of Districts in Bengal 1757–1916*, Kumud Ranjan Biswas (revised and updated). Kolkata: West Bengal District Gazetteers.

Chatterji, Joya. 1999. 'The Fashioning of a Frontier: The Radcliffe Line and Bengal's Border Landscape: 1947–1952', *Modern Asian Studies*, 33 (1): 185–242.

———. 2002. *Bengal Divided: Hindu Communalism and Partition 1932–1947 (Cambridge South Asian Studies)*. Cambridge: Cambridge University Press.

———. 2007. *Spoils of Partition: Bengal and India 1947–67*. UK: Cambridge University Press.

Chattopadhyay, Basudeb (ed.). 2007. *Bengal Partitioned* (West Bengal State Archives, Higher Education Department). Calcutta: Government of West Bengal.

Chaturvedi, Sanjay. 2007. 'The Excess of Geopolitics: Partition of 'British India', in Stefano Bianchin, Sanjay Chaturvedi, Rada Ivekovic and Ranabir Samaddar (eds), *Partitions: Reshaping States and Minds*, pp. 125–60. USA: Frank Cass.

Chimni, B.S. (ed.). 2002. *International Refugee Law: A Reader*. New Delhi: SAGE Publications.

Choudhury, Kalyan. 2001. 'Disturbed Border', *The Frontline*, 28 April–11 May, 18 (9). Available online at http://www.hinduonnet.com/fline/fl1809/18090220.htm (last accessed on 3 December 2010).

Chowdhary, Rekha. 2008. 'Gender is Just a Political Tool', *Women's Feature Services*. New Delhi: Women's Feature Service.

Chowdhury, Zafar. 2008. 'Being Muslim in Jammu', *Economic and Political Weekly*, 23–29 August, 43 (34): 11–14.

Chugtai, Ismat. 2001. 'Communal Violence and Literature', trans. Tahira Naqvi, *My Friend, My Enemy: Essays, Reminiscences, Portraits*. New Delhi: Kali for Women.

Cockburn, Cynthia. 2004. *The Line: Women. Partition and the Gender Order in Cyprus*. UK: Zed Books.

Crisp, Jeff. 2008. 'Beyond the Nexus: UNHCR's Evolving Perspective on Refugee Protection and International Migration', *New Issues in Refugee Research, UNHCR*, Research Paper No. 155, April 2008. Available online at http://www.unhcr.org/4818749a2.html (last accessed on 6 June 2010).

Das Vina. 2006. *Life and Words: Violence and the Descent into the Ordinary*. New Delhi: Oxford University Press.

DasGupta, Sumona. 2008. 'Time and a Place; Survivorhood in Dardpora', *Himal Southasian*, January. Available online at http://www.himalmag.com/component/content/article/949-Survivorhood-in-Dardpora.html (last accessed on 31 March 2011).

———. 2001. *Breaking the Silence: Women and Kashmir*. New Delhi: WISCOMP.

DasGupta, Sumona and Arvinder Singh. 2006. 'Athwaas Exploring New Paradigms of Engagement', Working Paper, Stakeholders in Dialogue IV. New Delhi: WISCOMP.

DasGupta, Sumona and Navanita Sinha. 2008. *Gender, Violence and Rights: Exploring Responses from Jammu and Kashmir, Building Constituencies of Peace: Stakeholders in Dialogue XII*. New Delhi: WISCOMP.

de Beauvoir, Simone. 1953. *The Second Sex*. New York: Alfred. A. Knopf.

Doty, Roxanne Lynn. Undated. 'Democracy and the Undocumented'. Available online at http://www.re-public.gr/en/?p=62 (last accessed in January 2010).

de Jong, Kaz, Saskia Van de Kam, Nathan Ford, Kamalini Lokuge, Silke Fromm, Renate van Galen, Brigg Reilley and Rolf Kleber. 2008. 'Conflict in the Kashmir Valley II : Psychological Impact,' *Conflict and Health*. Available online at http://www.conflictandhealth.com/content/2/1/11 (last accessed on 5 January 2010).

De, Ranjit Kumar. 2007. 'The Call of the Hooghly Imambarah', in Ranjit Kumar De (ed.), *Hooghly Imambarah*, 6–12. Hooghly: Bhraman Barta Paribar.

Devadas, Vijay and Jane Mummery. 2008. 'Protean Borders and Unsettled Interstices', *Borderland e-journals*, 7 (1). Available online at http://www.borderlands.net.au/vol7no1_2008/editors_protean.htm (last accessed on 20 January 2010).

Dey, Shumbhoo Chunder. 1906. *Hooghly: Past and Present*. Calcutta: M.M. Fey & Co.

Dutta, Mondira. 2006. 'Status of Women and Areas of Concern in Jammu and Kashmir', p. 4–5. Workshop on Population Sponsored by United Nations Population Fund. Available online at www.isca.org.in/reports/29.pdf (last accessed on 5 January 2010).

Foucault Michel. 2003. *'Society Must Be Defended', Lectures at the Collège de France, 1975–1976*, trans. David Macey. New York: Picador.

Geddes, Arthur. 1937. 'The Population of Bengal, Its Distribution and Changes: A Contribution to Geographical Method', *The Geographical Journal*, April, 89 (9): 344–61.

Goodwin-Gill, Guy S. 1996. *The Refugee in International Law*, 2nd Ed. Oxford: Clarendon Press.

Guhathakurta, Meghna and Suraiya Begum. 2005. 'Bangladesh: Displaced and Dispossessed', in Paula Banerjee, Sabyasachi Basu Ray Chaudhury and Samir Das (eds), *Internal Displacement in South Asia*, pp. 344–61. New Delhi: SAGE Publications.

Gupta, Prakriti. 2003. 'Divorce as the Price of Displacement,' *Women's Feature Service, The Tribune Online*, 7 December.

Harris, Nigel. 2010. 'Immigration and State Power', *Economic and Political Weekly*, 30 January, XLV (5): 8–11.

Hasan, Mushirul. 1997. *Legacy of a Divided Nation: India's Muslims since Independence*. Delhi: C. Hurst & Co. (publishers) Ltd.

Hathaway, James. 1991. *The Law of Refugee Status*. Toronto: Butterworths.

Herman, Judith Lewis. 1994. *Trauma and Recovery: From Domestic Violence to Political Terror*. London: River Oram Press.

Honneth, Axel. 2007. *Disrespect: The Normative Foundations of Critical Theory*. UK: Polity Press.

Human Rights Watch. 2009.'We Are Like Forgotten People: The Chin People of Burma: Unsafe in Burma, Unprotected in India, Human Rights Watch 2009', p. 65.

Available online at http://www.hrw.org/en/reports/2009/01/27/we-are-forgotten-people (accessed in December 2009).

Hunter, William Wilson. 1876. *A Statistical Account of Bengal*. London: Trübner.

IANS. 2010. 'Indo–Bangla Border to be Fenced by March 2010: BSF chief (Lead). Available at http://www.thaindian.com/newsportal/uncategorized/indo–bangla-border-to-be-fenced-by-march-2010-bsf-chief-lead_!00279489.html#ixzzlGdizckql (last accessed on 25 December 2010).

Ishaque, Rubina. Unpublished. 'Migrations across Line of Control in Azad Jammu Kashmir'. Islamabad: Quaid-i-Azam University.

Joshi, Manoj. 1999. *The Lost Rebellion*. New Delhi: Penguin.

Kaul, Shridhar and H.N. Kaul. 1992. *Ladakh through the Ages: Towards a New Identity*. New Delhi: Indus Publishing Company.

Kapur, Ratna. 2007. 'The Citizen and the Migrant: Post Colonial Anxieties, Law and Politics of Inclusion/Exclusion', Article 8, *Theoretical Inquiries in Law*, July, 8 (2): 544.

Robin K., (ed.). 2009. *Chin: History, Culture and Identity*. Delhi: Dominant Publishers and Distributors.

Kazi, Seema. 2009. *Between Democracy and Nation: Gender and Militarisation in Kashmir*. New Delhi: Women Unlimited.

Khonumthung News. 2009. 'Four Burmese Arrested in Arms Case in Mizoram', *Khonumthung News*, Aizawl, Mizoram, 24 March.

———. 2009. 'Mizoram police arrest Burmese nationals', *Khonumthung News*, Aizawl, Mizoram, 15 June.

———. 2009. 'Mizoram to Deport Burmese into Criminal Activity: Home Minister', *Khonumthung News*, Aizawl, Mizoram, 2 March.

Kishore, Alpana. 2009. *Nationality and Identity Shifts in Jammu and Kashmir's Armed Conflict*. New Delhi: WISCOMP.

Kundu, Jagabondhu (ed.). 2003. *Hooghly Jelar Sahitya O Sanaskriti* (in Bengali) (Literature and Culture of Hooghly District). Kolkata: Sahitya Setu Prakashani.

Lalneihzovi. 2006. *District Administration in Mizoram*. New Delhi: Mittal Publications.

Lamb, Alistair. 1993. *Kashmir a Disputed Legacy*. Karachi: Oxford University Press.

Lanky, Robert. 2010. 'Tigress–Don't Chicken Out'. Available online at http://www.e-pao.net/epSubPageExtractor.asp?src=leisure.Essays.Tigress_dont_chicken_out (last accessed on 15 February 2010).

Levesque, Julien and Mirza Zulfiqar Rehman. 2008. 'Tension in the Rolling Hills: Burmese Population and Border Trade in Mizoram', *Institute of Peace and Conflict Studies*, April. Available online at www.ipcs.org (last accessed on July 2009).

Leydet, Dominique. 2006. 'Citizenship', *Stanford Encyclopedia of Philosophy*. Available online at http://plato.stanford.edu/entries/citizenship/ (last accessed on January 2010).

Manchanda, Rita. 2001. 'Guns and Burqa: Women in the Kashmir Conflict' in *Women, War and Peace in South Asia: Beyond Victimhood to Agency*, pp. 42–101. New Delhi: SAGE Publications.

Medina-Revera, Antonio and Diana Orendi. 2007. *Crossing Over: Redefining the Scope of Border Studies*. Newcastle: Cambridge Scholars Publishing.

Menon, Ritu and Kamla Bhasin. 1998. *Borders and Boundaries: Women in India and Pakistan*. New Delhi: Kali for Women.

Mitra, Ashok (ed.). 1956. *District Census Handbook: Hooghly*. Calcutta: Government of India.

Mitra, Sudhir Kumar. 1992. *Hooghly Jelar Itihash O Somaj* (in Bengali) (History of Hooghly District and Its Society). Calcutta: Dey's Publication.

Mukherjee, Ashit Baran. 2002. *Shara Chuchura* (in Bengali) (Chinsura: A Town). Kolkata: Nabarun Press.

Murayama, Mayumi. 2006. 'Borders, Migration and Sub-Regional Co-operation in Eastern South Asia', *Economic and Political Weekly*, April 8, 41 (14): 1351–58.

Panmanabhan, Chitra. 2010. 'Viewing Politics through a New Frame', *The Hindu Magazine*, 30 January 2010.

Pargal, Sanjeev. 2009. 'Entire Jammu under Siege but Rallies Unabated', *Daily Excelsior*, Jammu, 9 August.

Patnaik, K. Jagdish (ed.). 2008. *Peace and Development in Mizoram: Role of the State and Civil Society*, pp. 72–83. Mizoram: Department of Political Science, Mizoram University.

Pattanaik, Bandana. 2002. 'Where Do We Go from Here?', in Susanne Thorbek and Bandana Pattanaik (eds), *Transnational Prostitution: Changing Global Patterns*, pp. 217–30. London/New York: Zed Books.

Phanjoubam, Pradip. 2009. 'Population Displacement in Manipur in Last 100 Years', in Monirul Hussain and Pradip Phanjoubam (eds), *A Status Report on Displacement in Assam and Manipur, Policies and Practices No. 12*, pp. 22–41. Kolkata: Calcutta Research Group.

Phanjoubam, Tarapot. 1996. *Insurgency Movement in North Eastern India*, p. 212. New Delhi: Vikas Publishing.

Ramachandran, Sudha, Meenakshi Gopinath and Sumona DasGupta. 2003. 'They have a different view', *The Hindu*, 7 October 2003.

Raza, Maroof. 1995. *Low Intensity Conflicts: The New Dimension to India's Military Commitments*. Meerut, UP: Kartikeya Publications.

Rediff News. 2009. 'Pact Hurdle in Fencing India–Bangladesh Border'. Available online at http://news.rediff.com/report/2009/jun/30/indo–bangladesh-border-fencing-pact-hurdle.html (last accessed on 20 December 2009).

———. 2010. 'Curfew clamped on Mahendraganj'. Available online at http://www.rediff.com/news/oct/13curfew.htm (last accessed on 1 January 2010).

Ricoeur, Paul. 2006. *Memory, History, Forgetting*, trans. Kathleen Blamey and David Pellauer. Chicago: University of Chicago Press (paperback edition).

Roohi, Sanam and Ranabir Samaddar. 2009. *Key Texts in Social Justice in India*. New Delhi: SAGE Publications.

Roy, Arundhati. 2008. 'Land and Freedom,' *The Guardian*, August.

Sakhong, H. Lian. 2003. *In Search of Chin Identity: A Study in Religion, Politics and Ethnic Identity in Burma*. Copenhagen: NIAS Press.

Samaddar, Ranabir. 2000. 'The Last Hurrah That Continues', *Transeuropeennes*, 19–22: 31–47.

———. 1999. *The Marginal Nation: Transborder Migration from Bangladesh to West Bengal*. New Delhi: SAGE Publications.

——— (ed.). 2003. *Refugees and the State: Practices of Asylum and Care in India: 1947–2000*. New Delhi: SAGE Publications.

Sambanis, Nicholas and Jonah Schulhofer-Wohl. 2009. 'What's in a Line? Is Partition a Solution to Civil War', *International Security*, 34 (2): 82–118.

Sameer, Arshad. 2009. 'In the Valley of Despair, Women Look for a High,' *http://times ofindia.indiatimes.com/home/sunday-toi/view-from-venus/In-the-Valley-of-despair-women-look-for-a-high/articleshow/4923661.cms* (last accessed on 5 August 2010).

Sanlaap. Unpublished. A Sanlaap Initiative Report on 'Project: Linkage, A Situational Analysis on Trafficking and Prostitution in Dinbazaar (Jalpaiguri) and Changrabandha (Cooch Behar)', supported by Gana Unnayan Parshad and Human Development Centre.

Sangma, Milton S. 2010. 'Dadengiri, People and Their Socio-economic Life and Culture'. Available online at http://dadengiri.gov.in/essay.pdf (last accessed on 1 January 2010).

Sarkar Jadunath. 1948. *The History of Bengal*, Vol. 2. Dacca: B.R. Publishing Corporation.

Sassen, Saskia. 2006. *Territory, Authority, Rights: From Medieval to Global Assemblages*. Princeton: Princeton University Press.

Schendel, Van Willem. 2005. *The Bengal Borderland: Beyond State and Nation in South Asia*. London: Anthem South Asian Studies.

Schofield, Victoria. 1997. *Kashmir in the Crossfire*. New Delhi: Viva Books.

Shamshad, Razwana. 2008. 'Politics and Origin of the India–Bangladesh Border Fence', paper presented to the 17th Biennial Conference of the Asian Studies Association of Australia in Melbourne 1–3 July 2008. Available online at http://arts.monash.edu. au/mai/asaa/rizwanashamshad.pdf (last accessed on 1 January 2010).

Shillong Times. 2004a. 'Assam, Siliguri Main Trafficking Routes in NE', *Shillong Times*, Shillong, Meghalaya, 5 June.

———. 2004b. 'Human Trafficking Cases in Meghalaya Draw US Attention', *Shillong Times*, Shillong, Meghalaya, 16 June.

———. 2009. 'Border Haats of Meghalaya', *Shillong Times*, 23 October.

Shivananda, C.J. 2010. 'Look East Policy: An Opportunity or Uncertainty'. Available online at http://www.merinews.com/article/look-east-policy-an-opportunity-orun certainty/15797260.shtml (accessed on 10 February 2010).

Singh Thiyam, Bharat. 2007. 'Poverty in Manipur', *Economic and Political Weekly*, 20–26 January, 42 (3): 251–54.

Sinha-Kerkhoff, Kothinka. 2001. 'Partition Memories, "Minoritisation" and Discourses of Rootedness in Jharkhand: A Comparison of Cross-border Displaced and "Invisible Refugees" in Jharkhand', paper Presented at the Indo-Dutch Conference on 'Displaced People in South Asia', Chennai, March.

Sinlung. 2009. 'Cattle Smuggling to Bangladesh Poses a Challenge for the BSF'. Available online at http://about Meghalaya.blogspot.com/2009/02/cattle-smuggling-to-bangladesh-poses.html (last accessed on 15 December).

Stacy, Lee. 2003. *Mexico and the United States*. New York: Marshall Cavendish.

Thanhranga, H.C. 2007. *District Council in Mizo Hills* (updated). Aizawl: Lengchhawn Press.

The Foundation for Social Transformation and Department of Social Work. 2008. *Report of the Consultative Meeting with Local Civil Society Organizations in Mizoram*. Guwuhati, Assam. Available online at http://fstindia.org/download/What% 20we%20do/Mizoram%20Consultation%Report.pdf (accessed in January 2010).

Tickner, Ann. 2001. *Gendering World Politics: Issues and Approaches in the Post Cold War Era*. New York: Columbia University Press.

Virilio, Paul. 1997. *The Open Sky*. London: Verso.

Waber, Rachel. 2003. 'Re (Creating) the Home: Women's Role in the Development of Refugee Colonies in South Calcutta', in Jasodhara Bagchi and Subhoranjan Dasgupta (eds), *The Trauma and the Triumph: Gender and Partition in Eastern India*, Vol. 1, pp. 61–79. Kolkata: Stree.

Wali Khanna, Charu. 2008. *Women Silent Victims in Armed Conflict.*, New Delhi: Serials Publications.

WLB and Centre for Refugee Research. 2007. *Looking Forward: A Report from Community Consultations*. University of New South Wales, India. Available online at http://www.crr.unsw.edu.au/news-and-events/new-report-on-burmese-refugees-in-delhi-103.html, (last accessed in November 2009).

NEWSPAPERS/MAGAZINES

Jugantar, 28 February 1950.

The Assam Tribune. 1998. 'Union Home Secretary Chairs a High Level Empowered Committee' Embassy of India, Washington, 10 December 1998. Available online at http://www.indianembassy.org/policy/Foreign_Policy/FP_1998/bangladesh_fp1998.html (last accessed on 10 December 2010).

The Shillong Times, 23 October 2009.

The Assam Tribune, 10–12 January 2010.

Assam Tribune, 17 February 2009.

Anandabazar Patrika, 5 March 1950.

The Statesman, 8 March 1950.

The Statesman, 9 March 1950.

The Statesman, 31 March 1950.

The Statesman, 23 March 1950.

Meghalaya Timeline, 2009. South Asia Terrorism Patrol (SATP). Available online at www.satp.org (last accessed on 15 March 2009).

The Tribune Online, 7 December 2009.

The Guardian, August 2008.

The Hindu, 7 October 2003.

The Hindu Magazine, 30 January 2010.

Shillong Times, 16 June 2004.

Anandabazar Patrika, 14 January 2003.

WEBSITES

www.swadhinata.org.uk/document/chatterjeeEastBengal%20refugee.pdf
http://www.amazon.co.uk/gp/reader/1862300577/ref=sib_dp_pt#reader-page
http://ibnlive.in.com/printpage.php?id=105884 & section id=3
http://news.rediff.com/report/2009/jun/30/indo-bangladesh-border-fencing-pact-hurdle.htm
http://news.rediff.com/report/2009/jun/30/indo-bangladesh-border-fencing-pact-hurdle.htm
http://www.sentinelassam.com/northeast.php?sec=2&subsec=9&ppr=1&dtP=2009-10-06

http://www.csa.com/ids70/gateway.php?mode=pdf&doi=10.1177%2F0010836706060935
&db=polsci-setc&s1=2a8ce637cd352c8de3c93418fca12d33&s2=878f07eac4de2168b
5e51583e473e21d

http://westGarohills.gov.in/history.htm

http://argueindia.org/wallace.pdf

http://www.india-server.com/news/479-infiltrator-captured-along-the-18401.html

http://aboutmeghalaya.blogspot.com/2009/02/cattle-smuggling-to-bangladesh-poses.html
www.westgarohills.nic.in

http://dadenggiri.gov.in/essay.pdf

http://www.rediff.com/news/oct/13curfew.htm

http://www.chandel.nic.in/

http://burmadigest.wordpress.com/2006/07/31/trouble-at-indo-burma-border/

http://www.merinews.com/article/look-east-policy-an-opportunity-or-uncertainty/15797260.
shtml

http://www.indianexpress.com/news/clashes-leave-11-dead-in-manipur-border-
town/33270/0

http://www.e-pao.net/epSubPageExtractor.asp?src=leisure.Essays.Tigress_dont_chicken_out

http://www.hivaidsonline.in/index.php/Vulnerable-Groups/insurgency-makes-health-care-
dangerous.html

http://www.e-pao.net/GP.asp?src=20..130210.feb10

http://www.hrw.org/en/reports/2009/01/27/we-are-forgotten-people

http://www.crr.unsw.edu.au/news-and-events/new-report-on-burmese-refugees-in-delhi-103.
html

http://www.hrw.org/en/node/79892/section/4

http://www.censusindia.gov.in

http://centralyma.org.in

http://www.fstindia.org/sites/default/files/mizoram_consultation_report.pdfwww.ipcs.org

http://unhcr.org/48b7f9642.html

http://plato.stanford.edu/entries/citizenship/

http://www.re-public.gr/en/?p=62

http://timesofindia.indiatimes.com/home/sunday-toi/view-from-venus/In-the-Valley-of-
despair
women-look-for-a-high/articleshow/4923661.cms

http://thewip.net/contributors/2008/08/violence_touches_each_family_l.html

http://www.conflictandhealth.com/content/2/1/11

http://www.mospi.gov.in/research_studies_problen_women_in_kashmir.htm

www.isca.org.in/reports/29.pdf

www.indiatogether.org/2007/oct/wom-roadrehab.htm

http://www.hinduonnet.com/mag/2007/02/18/stories/2007021800030500.htm

About the Editors and Contributors

THE EDITORS

Paula Banerjee specializes in issues of border and borderlands in South Asia. She has published extensively on issues of gender, forced migration and peace politics. Her recent publications include a volume entitled *Borders, Histories, Existences: Gender and Beyond* (2010). She has edited a volume entitled *Women in Peace Politics* (2008) and co-edited books on *Internal Displacement in South Asia* (2005), *Autonomy beyond Kant and Hermeneutics* (2007) and *Marginalities and Justice* (2009). She has been working on themes related to women, borders and democracy in South Asia, and has published extensively in journals such as *International Studies* and *Canadian Women's Studies* on issues such as histories of borders and women in conflict situations. She was the former Head of the Department in the Department of South and Southeast Asian Studies, University of Calcutta, and is currently Associate Professor in the same Department. She is also the Vice President of International Association for Study of Forced Migration.

Anasua Basu Ray Chaudhury is a Research Associate in the Mahanirban Calcutta Research Group (CRG) and a Guest Lecturer in the Department of South and Southeast Asian Studies, University of Calcutta. She specializes in issues of violence and displacement, partition refugees and energy diplomacy in South Asia. She has authored a book entitled *SAARC at Crossroads: The Fate of Regional Cooperation in South Asia* (2006) including three monographs and journal articles. She has received the Public Service Broadcasting Trust (PSBT) Senior Media Fellowship (2007–2008) and the Kodikara Award (1998–99).

THE CONTRIBUTORS

Chitra Ahanthem is an eminent journalist working for *Imphal Free Press*. Her areas of interests include issues related to drug use, HIV/AIDS, conflict and gender. She has won media fellowships for writing on HIV/AIDS in Manipur.

Sahana Basavapatna is a lawyer practising in Delhi. Prior to working full time as a litigating lawyer, she worked for three years as a Program Coordinator in a Delhi-based non-governmental organization (NGO) called The Other Media, where she coordinated their refugee programme focusing on Burmese, Afghan and Somali refugees.

Anjuman Ara Begum is currently pursuing her PhD in Department of Law, Gauhati University, Assam, India. She has been working in Northeast India on the issues of human rights, women's rights, right to information and budget analysis since 2003. She has worked with human rights organizations like South Asia Forum for Human Rights and North East Network. For the last three years, she is actively engaged in documentation of human rights violations in Northeast India. Her main areas of interest are human rights in armed conflict situation and gender rights.

Aditi Bhaduri is an independent journalist and researcher based in India who writes for the Indian and international print and electronic media. With a background in international relations, she began her writing career by covering the Middle East. Currently her work focuses on conflict, peace, displacement and gender. Women's issues form an important part of her work and she acts as a gender and media consultant to various NGOs. Aditi is also a member of several civil society initiatives in India.

Sumona DasGupta is an independent researcher and consultant based in New Delhi. She has written and published on issues related to militarization, gender, conflict and security, democracy, dialogue and peacebuilding. In March 2010, she was guest editor for an issue of *Peace Prints,* a South Asian journal of peacebuilding published by WISCOMP, New Delhi, on gender, conflict and peace. She has authored a book titled *Citizen Initiatives and Democratic Engagements: Experiences from India* (2010).

Anuradha Bhasin Jamwal is a peace activist and executive editor of *Kashmir Times*.

Suchismita is a journalist and works for *Kashmir Times*.

Index